D1126906

La Celestina Studies:
A Thematic Survey and Bibliography
1824-1970

by

Adrienne Schizzano Mandel

WITHDRAWN

The Scarecrow Press, Inc.
Metuchen, N.J.   1971

Copyright 1971 by Adrienne Schizzano Mandel

ISBN 0-8108-0442-5

Library of Congress Catalog Card No. 78-171929

Z
8756.1
.M35

For Concetta Schizzano:

"Mater, dulcissima.... Ma ora ti ringrazio,
questo voglio, dell'ironia che hai messo
sui mio labbro mite come la tua.
Quel sorriso m'ha salvato da pianti e da dolori.
E non importa se ora ho qualche lacrima per te,
per tutti quelli che come te aspettano,
e non sanno che cosa...."

WITHDRAWN
YOUNGSTOWN STATE UNIVERSITY
LIBRARY
266158

Acknowledgments

I wish to express my appreciation to Professor Joseph
H. Silverman for his guidance over the years; to Professor
Edward Dudley for his advice and encouragement in the prep-
aration of this manuscript; to Professor Julio Rodríguez-
Puértolas for offering valuable comments; and as well to
Professors Paul C. Smith and Harvey Sharrer. I also wish
to thank my husband for his invaluable advice and understand-
ing.

Table of Contents

Foreword

The present work consists of two parts: a Survey (comprising the seven chapters) of the abundant scholarly and critical literature which surrounds Rojas' masterwork, and a Bibliography of <u>Celestina</u> studies. The Survey abstracts most of the important items listed in the Bibliography. Since the majority of researchers are likely to be working at any given time on a single aspect of the <u>Celestina</u>, the scholarly and critical contributions are abstracted under seven headings:

1. Author, authorship, and date of composition.
2. Editions.
3. Sources and tradition.
4. The influence of <u>La Celestina</u> in Spain and elsewhere.
5. <u>La Celestina</u> as a work of art.
6. Ethical values.
7. The historic moment of <u>La Celestina</u>.

Under each heading, the arrangement is chronological. Thus the investigator should be able to obtain an historical perspective of the work done by his predecessors in each scholarly or critical area.

When an article or a book makes a contribution to more than one of the seven topics, it is parceled out accordingly in two or more chapters. The student who wishes to obtain a comprehensive picture of this particular article or book is then invited to turn to the Bibliography; here the chapters in which a contribution is distributed are indicated in brackets after each listing.

The Survey is generously cross-referenced not only within each chapter but also, in cases where a certain overlapping of interest takes place, across different chapters.

Not all the items listed in the Bibliography are abstracted in the Survey; I have omitted from the latter distinctly minor contributions, unpublished doctoral dissertations, and most review articles. The decision to omit certain items from the Survey is, however, the only editorial interference I have allowed myself to make. Basing my procedure on the premise that the researcher will want to evaluate on his own

YOUNGSTOWN STATE UNIVERSITY

266158

the work done in his field of interest without having to cope
with (or dispose of) the bibliographer's judgments, I have ex-
cluded all comments and valuations from my summaries.

The Bibliography is as exhaustive a compilation as is
currently available, though it would be hazardous to claim
that nothing has escaped me. Omitted from the Bibliography
are minor editions and reprints of the Celestina, modern
translations, accounts of stage productions, and occasional
review articles which make no significant addition of their
own to the subject they cover.

Items in the Bibliography which are abstracted in the
Survey and a few items which I have not been able to examine
are appropriately marked. Details are given in a headnote
in the Bibliography.

* * * *

It goes without saying that the Survey is not meant as
a substitute for a thorough study of the articles or books
themselves. My goal will have been achieved if this guide
can lead the researcher rapidly past the work he does not
need to look up, and to the work he does need to examine in
detail. So much has been written about the Celestina,
especially since World War II, that the time for a labor-
saving survey has clearly arrived. [Two earlier surveys of
scholarship are useful but limited in scope: Margot Kruse
(1956) and D.W. McPheeters (1958).]

Labor-saving is the main purpose of this volume.
Another purpose, however, is to assist future researchers in
locating areas which have not been covered at all by previous workers. Again, I have not obtruded suggestions regarding future contributions in my text, but at this point it
seems useful to offer three possibilities, two for scholarship, the other for criticism. Most scholars agree that an
acceptable critical edition of the Celestina has yet to appear.
The most dependable edition has been that brought out by
Julio Cejador y Frauca in 1913, which is based on the text
of the 1499 Burgos Comedia and the 1514 Valencia Tragicomedia. In spite of its inaccuracies, Cejador's edition has
been preferred over the critical edition brought out by M.
Criado de Val and G.D. Trotter in 1958. The latter editors
used as a basic text the least reliable of the six editions
bearing the 1502 date, namely the 1502 Sevilla. The principal obstacle to a reliable critical edition is the absence of a
princeps edition. The problem is further complicated by the
fact that two different versions of the Celestina exist: the
sixteen-act Comedia and the twenty-one act Tragicomedia. It
still remains uncertain whether the 1499 Burgos Comedia and

the more recently discovered 1507 Zaragoza Tragicomedia reproduce the text of the princeps edition. At this point, no extant text can be regarded as authoritative, since all editions require emendations. Homer J. Herriott is the only scholar who has undertaken the formidable task of reconstructing the text of the princeps edition of the Tragicomedia, with the express purpose of arriving at a precise knowledge of Rojas' own words. It is to be hoped that his textual investigations will lead to a definitive critical edition.

On the question of the authorship of Act I much has been made of the stylistic and syntactical disparities between this opening episode and the rest of the Celestina. But it has not been shown that such a disparity proves the existence of two authors. What is needed is a series of linguistic tests imposed on works of clearly identified young authors--preferably but not necessarily of Rojas' own time--which would determine whether sharp changes can occur in a growing writer over a period of, say, five or ten years. A negative result would not be decisive, but a positive one would pose a strong challenge to the method hitherto followed to ascertain dual authorship.

On the critical side, a study might well be made of the tension set up in a text between its overt declarations and its actual effect. Is there a possible contradiction between the ostensible moral argument proposed in the prolegomenous material, or even a passage like Pleberio's lament, and the actual lusciousness of the love scenes? What does Rojas actually and genuinely achieve--a sense of condign punishment for guilty lovers, a far different sense of a world well lost for such unparalleled pleasure (and here one would have to consider that in the five interpolated acts this intoxication is deliberately prolonged and intensified), an oppressive sense of universal chaos, a combination of effects, or something still different? It is probably fair to say that no one has as yet provided an unclouded reading of the Celestina.

These are suggestions, and they are perhaps debatable, which is all to the good. The present work will have accomplished an important task if it opens other doors into other rooms. The metaphor is apposite, for the Celestina is like a palace second only in beauty, by general consent, to the Quijote itself.

The Celestina achieved instant fame and popularity, as is shown by the large number of editions in Spain, the wave of imitations, and the interest it sparked abroad. As early as 1535 the Celestina engaged the attention of scholars, notably that of Juan de Valdés, who, in his Diálogo de la lengua, finds insufficient motivation for Melibea's loss of virginal modesty and an overabundance of rhetorical elements in Rojas' language. And in 1587, in Bernardo Gómez de Bobadilla's Primera parte de las Ninfas y Pastores de Henares, we find the first indication of the controversy still surrounding the geographical setting of the Celestina. The Celestina had enjoyed more than a century of unabashed vitality when the Index of 1640 imposed its first excisions of the text. A few expurgations were ordered in the Index of 1667 and the whole work was forbidden by the Holy Office in 1793. The interest in the Celestina underwent a general decline during the seventeenth and eighteenth centuries. A new wave of interest arose during the Romantic Age; and the man who initiated it was the expatriate scholar José María Blanco White. Accordingly I have begun this thematic survey with Blanco White's contribution of 1824.

Note. The abbreviation LC is used throughout the text to refer to La Celestina. The 16-act version is referred to as the Comedia and the 21-act version as the Tragicomedia.

The entries under any given year are placed in alphabetical order.

The cross-references within each chapter and across different chapters are indicated in brackets.

Chapter 1

AUTHOR, AUTHORSHIP, AND DATE OF COMPOSITION

1824

Blanco White, José María (José María Blanco Crespo), "Revisión de obras: La Celestina, Tragicomedia de Calisto y Melibea," Variedades o Mensajero de Londres, I (April 1, 1824), 224-246.
Blanco White examines the structure of LC and concludes that the work is a "paño de la misma tela." According to him, it is absurd to suppose that the numerous threads thrown out in the first act could be taken up and woven so skillfully by anyone except the inventor of the entire plot. Since it was by no means unusual for writers of Rojas' time to disclaim authorship, there is no valid reason for crediting Rojas' own disclaimers.

Many scholars have used Sempronio's statement "ganada es Granada" in Act II to determine the composition date of at least the beginning of the Comedia. For Blanco White, the fall of Granada reference belongs to a series of improbable future spectacular events. Consequently, he sets the date of composition of the work before 1492. In order to arrive at the terminus a quo, Blanco White draws on the allusions to the autos da fé in Acts IV and VII. Since the Inquisition was established in Castille in 1480, this represents the terminus a quo of composition.

Blanco White supposes that Rojas was reluctant to assume responsibility for writing LC for fear of losing his reputation as a jurist. Moreover, Blanco White states that Proaza, a contemporary of Rojas, did not believe the story of the two authors.

1838

Moratín, Leandro Fernández de, "Orígines del teatro español," Tesoro del teatro español, Vol. I. Paris, 1938.
For Moratín, too, LC is to be considered the work of a single author. Moratín maintains that if Rojas had not disclaimed paternity of Act I, succeeding generations of

11

scholars would never have found any difference in style in reading the work as a whole. It was Rojas himself, says Moratín, who led critics to dwell on the question of authorship.

1841

Lavigne, Germond de, ed. La Célestine. Paris, 1841.
Lavigne in his Introduction to LC takes the opposite view of Blanco White with regard to the Granada reference. He sees it as an example of a spectacular past event, thus setting the date of composition after the fall of Granada.

1849

Ticknor, George, History of Spanish Literature. London, 1849, pp. 239-248.
Ticknor takes Cota as the author of Act I, asserting that "what we have of Cota falls in quite well with the conjecture that he wrote it." Ticknor accepts the prefatory remarks of Alonso de Villegas to his Selvagia (1554) in which the beginning of LC is attributed to Cota. He suggests that LC was written around 1480.

1894

González Aguejas, Lorenzo, "La Celestina, " La España Moderna, VI, No. 67 (1894), 78-103.
Unlike Ticknor, González Aguejas is content to assign Act I to Rojas, along with the rest of the Comedia. But he also differs from Blanco White and Moratín in taking the view that the additional five acts break the integrity of the work and are therefore by another hand.

1895

Soravilla, Javier, La Celestina. Madrid, 1895.
Following Ticknor, Soravilla attributes Act I to Cota and suggests that Rojas wrote the rest of LC as a tribute to the author of Act I.

Wolf, Ferdinand, "Sobre el drama español - La Celestina y sus traducciones, " La España Moderna, VII, No. 80 (1895), 99-123.
Wolf agrees with Moratín that Rojas is the sole author of LC. Wolf questions Rojas' sincerity in his prefatory statements, and argues that his claim to have found an

old manuscript and written the work in 15 days while taking
a leave from his studies is a literary hoax. Wolf finds it
impossible to believe that a second person could so fully
have entered into the spirit of the work.

1897

Eggert, C.A., "Zur Frage der Urheberschaft der Celestina,"
Zeitschrift für Romanische Philologie, XXI (1897), 32-42.
     Eggert sees in the Historia de Talavera de la Reina*
a valid indication of Rojas' existence as a man but not a solution to the problem of authorship. Although most scholars
echoed Moratín's acceptance of Rojas' authorship of LC, Eggert remains skeptical on the question. His skepticism will
be surpassed only by that of Foulché-Delbosc. While the
latter believes that Rojas was the invention of a clever editor,
Eggert merely argues that Rojas was the editor and not the
creator of the work. In a further departure from other
critics, Eggert names Juan del Encina as the probable author
of at least the first act. He feels that Rojas mentions Mena
and Cota in a later edition to cloud the issue of authorship
and to protect Encina.
     As to the fall of Granada, Eggert reads it as a refer-
ence to an improbable future event. However, he placed only the first three acts before 1492, stating that the work as
a whole was probably written between 1491 and 1500.
     *[The Historia was discussed by Manuel Cañete in
Farsas y églogas al modo y estilo pastoril y castellano
fechas por Lucas Fernández. Biblioteca Selecta de Autores
Clásicos Castellanos. Madrid, 1867, pp. viii-ix.]

Michaëlis de Vasconcellos, Carolina, "Zwei Worte zur
Celestina-Frage," Zeitschrift für Romanische Philologie,
XXI (1897), 405-409.
     Miss Michaëlis de Vasconcellos finds little of value
in Eggert's line of argumentation. She returns to the hypothesis that LC, including Act I, is to be attributed to a
single author.
     In the phrase "ganada es Granada" she sees a refer-
ence to the kind of event which creates a furor but is soon
forgotten. Accordingly, she sets the date of composition
after 1492.

1899

Menéndez Pelayo, Marcelino, ed. La Celestina (E. Krapf).
Vigo, 1899-1900.

The pro-Rojas faction received impressive support
from Menéndez Pelayo. After rejecting Rojas' disclaimer
of paternity and disallowing the candidacies of Cota and Mena
(he does not mention Encina), Menéndez Pelayo introduces a
new argument, to the effect that Rojas called Cota or Mena
the authors of Act I because he was reluctant to accept responsibility for its moral laxity. Like many previous critics,
Menéndez Pelayo bases his argument on internal evidence:
unity of thought, tightness of the intrigue, unity of intent
from beginning to end, stylistic unity, and the clear control
of a single master. In Menéndez Pelayo's view, Rojas himself saw the need to strengthen the moral character of his
work and therefore added the moral reflections and the Prologue of the 1501 edition.

1900

Foulché-Delbosc, R., "Observations sur La Célestine,"
Revue Hispanique, VII (1900), 28-80.
        Even after scholars were able to consult the manu-
script of the Historia de Talavera de la Reina (MS V - 184,
Biblioteca Nacional, folios 256-7), Foulché-Delbosc maintained that Rojas is a "personnage inventé de toutes pièces
par l'auteur de la lettre et des vers acrostiques." According to the French critic, the contradictions found in the
prefatory material invalidate all evidence of authorship presented in it, including the reference to Mena and to Cota.
The "éditeur malicieux" has succeeded with his "supercherie
littéraire" and the author of LC remains unknown to posterity.

1901

Michaëlis de Vasconcellos, Carolina, "Foulché-Delbosc:
'Observations sur La Célestine'" (rev. art.), Literaturblatt
für germanische und romanische Philologie, XXII (1901), 19-
32.
        Miss Michaëlis de Vasconcellos expands her original
argument of 1897, where she accepts Rojas' authorship of
the Comedia, to include a discussion of the additions of the
1502 edition. Her position is that Rojas, wishing to be drawn
into the stream of taste of his time, probably commissioned
another writer to compose the additions in an effort to add
naturalistic Renaissance colors to the original version.

1902

Foulché-Delbosc, R. , "Observations sur La Célestine," Revue Hispanique, IX (1902), 171-199.
          The evidence presented by the publication of the In-
quisitorial records [1902, Serrano y Sanz] did not alter
Foulché-Delbosc's position. After examining at first-hand
the Heber edition [Chapter 2, 1902, Haebler] of 1499, Foulché-Delbosc reaffirms the superiority of the 16-act version.
Since it is inconceivable to him that an author would have
disfigured his own masterpiece, Foulché-Delbosc vigorously
reasserts his dual-authorship theory.

Haebler, Konrad, "Bemerkungen zur Celestina," Revue Hispanique, IX (1902), 139-170.
          Further disagreement with Foulché-Delbosc is ex-
pressed by Haebler. The statements in the Letter and the
acrostic disputed by Foulché-Delbosc are to be considered as
part of the literary convention of the time and not as unresolvable mystification. Haebler's conjecture is that Rojas
became fascinated by a manuscript and decided to continue it.
A long time elapsed before he actually undertook the task,
but once the work was begun he quickly completed it, possibly in 15 days. The Letter is Rojas' way of coming out of
anonymity and the acrostic his way of revealing his authorship.
          A picturesque biographical approach to the question of
the five additional acts is presented by Haebler. He conjectures that since the first editions of the Comedia were successful, Rojas was urged by his friends to expand the work.
Unfortunately, Haebler adds, the intercalated acts show that
Rojas was not a great poet and was incapable of creating an
equally great work in a second attempt. Fully aware of his
own limitations, Rojas abandons authorship and relegates the
editorial responsibilities to his friends and to Proaza.

Martinenche, E. , "Quelques notes sur La Célestine," Bulletin Hispanique, IV (1902), 95-103.
          Martinenche accepts the hypothesis of a single author
for the Comedia, dismissing the contradictions found in the
prefatory material as "coquetteries d'auteurs" and as proof
of Rojas' playfulness. He echoes the opinion of Menéndez
Pelayo [1899] that the changes made in the 1501 and 1502
editions indicate the author's desire to underline the moral
intent of his work by use of maxims, proverbs and sentences. Again like the Spanish scholar, Martinenche asserts
that it was Rojas' desire to dissociate himself from the ques-

tionable morality of Act I which led him to ascribe it to another author.   In order to support his contention that Rojas
wrote Act I himself, Martinenche resorts to an eccentric argument: accepting the judgment that Act I does differ in
style from the rest of the Comedia, he sees this fact as evidence for, rather than against, single authorship.   Had Act
I been written by someone else, he argues, Rojas would not
have deviated stylistically from it; he would have patterned
his own style after his model.

It appears to Martinenche that Act I at first stood by
itself, as is evidenced by its length, and that Rojas continued it at a later date.   Moreover, the changes made suc-
cessively in the three stages of LC are all by the same
hand.   In spite of the stylistic differences between Act I and
the rest of the work, the essential unity of LC shows that it
stemmed from a single author.

In a clear presentation of the problem of the Tragicomedia Martinenche compares his own views with those of
Foulché-Delbosc.   In Martinenche's view, the display of erudition does not necessarily point to an authorship other than
Rojas' and he is willing to ascribe the learned additions to
Rojas himself.   Moreover, he finds the question of dramatic
unity irrelevant in this case.   While the dramatic impact of
Calisto's sudden death after the first garden scene might
have been important on stage, it is not of primary importance in a work which was meant to be read.   Besides, Martinenche holds that the additions have not destroyed the beauty
of the original version.

Serrano y Sanz, M. , "Noticias biográficas de Fernando de
Rojas, autor de La Celestina y del impresor Juan de Lucena,"
Revista de Archivos, Bibliotecas y Museos, VI (1902), 245-
299.
The publication of the Inquisitorial documents by M.
Serrano y Sanz furnished scholars with historical evidence
for the existence of Rojas and his authorship of LC.   These
documents also gave historical validity to the much-disputed
Historia de Talavera.   Serrano y Sanz reprints facsimilies
of the trial records of the Inquisition of Toledo, before which
Rojas appeared in 1517 and again in 1525.   During his trial
in 1525, Alvaro de Montalbán--Rojas' father-in-law--referred
to Rojas as the author of LC and named him his counsel.
But Rojas was rejected as counsel for the defense by the Inquisitors because he was a converso.   Serrano y Sanz also
furnishes documents pertaining to Catalina de Rojas, the
daughter of Fernando de Rojas.   He further establishes that
Rojas was Alcalde Mayor of Talavera from February 15 to

March 21 of 1538. In Serrano y Sanz's view, these documents offer sufficient evidence to conclude that the whole of
LC belongs to Rojas.

1904

Bonilla y San Martín, Adolfo, "Algunas consideraciones
acerca de la Tragicomedia de Calisto y Melibea y sus autores," Anales de la Literatura Española, I (1904), 7-24.
After reviewing the recent scholarship, Bonilla y San
Martín finds no sound basis for refuting the statements found
in the prefatory material of LC. He fully accepts Rojas' af-
firmation that he completed a play he discovered in manuscript form. Thus it is significant that the 1502 edition
shows fewer alterations for Act I than for any other portion
of the previous work. This would seem to indicate respect
for the work of another author. On the other hand, Bonilla
y San Martín believes that Rojas reworked the entire play
many times and that every stage we possess is to be regarded as a discrete and authentic work.
      Similarly, Bonilla y San Martín rejects Foulché-Del-
bosc's hypothesis of an "adicionador." However, he agrees
with the French scholar that the shorter version is aesthetically superior to the 21-act work.

Desdevises du Dezert, M. G., "La comédie de Caliste et
Melibée," Revue des Cours et Conférences, XII (1904), 739-
756.
      For Desdevises du Dezert, a review of the different
approaches to the question of authorship results in a conclusion similar to that of Foulché-Delbosc, namely that Rojas
was only the editor of LC. Since the real author was unknown even in Rojas' time, the latter attributed the work to
himself.

1910

Menéndez Pelayo, Marcelino, Orígenes de la novela, Vol.
III. Madrid, 1905-1910.
      Of great interest in this period is Menéndez Pelayo's
scholarship on LC. In his Orígenes de la novela, he concludes that Rojas is the sole and original author of the entire
Tragicomedia. In writing the additional five acts, according
to Menéndez Pelayo, Rojas yielded to the public's desire to
have the love episodes drawn out. Menéndez Pelayo's basic
argument is that, in spite of the modifications, a "unidad e
identidad de estilo" pervades the whole work.

Menéndez Pelayo reviews the questions raised by
Foulché-Delbosc. While agreeing with other critics that these
additions are not always an improvement on the original Comedia, he believes that they are the work of Rojas.

1913

Cejador y Frauca, Julio, ed. La Celestina. Madrid, 1913.
Menéndez Pelayo's statements in support of Rojas' authorship of the entire work did not end the controversy, as
can be seen from Cejador y Frauca's introduction to his edition of LC. For Cejador y Frauca, Rojas is the author of
the original 16-act version. But in discussing the 1502 version, Cejador maintains that Alonso de Proaza is responsible
for the additions, basing himself on the contradictory nature
of the prefatory material and the lapses in style and tone of
the new version. He discards one by one the elements added
by the "corrector" Proaza, who, striving for a more refined
and rare erudition, succeeded only in coarsening the character portrayal and making an indiscriminate use of refranes.
Furthermore, the additional acts destroy the most admirable
element of the Comedia, namely the sudden change from
comedy to tragedy. He rejects the additional episodes as
useless, supporting the general view that the Comedia is aesthetically superior to the Tragicomedia.

1914

Azorín (Martínez Ruiz, José), "La Celestina," Valores literarios. Obras completas, Vol. II. Madrid, 1959.
Azorín, too, disputes Menéndez Pelayo's contention
[1910] of the "unidad e identidad de estilo" which sustains
the hypothesis of single authorship. Azorín maintains that
the new elements and the burdensome classical references
in the 1502 edition furnish evidence of dual authorship. In
his view, the additions are the work of an officious corrector who destroyed the spontaneity and simplicity of Rojas'
original version.

1916

Cejador [y Frauca], Julio, "El bachiller Fernando de Rojas,
verdadero autor de La Celestina," Revista Crítica Hispano-
Americana, II (1916), 85-86.
Cejador reconstructs from documents the genealogical
tree of Rojas' family. His intention is to prove that Rojas
was not of Jewish blood. He points to Rojas' family crest,

a golden star in a blue field found in a chapel of Valladolid, as further proof that he was of "pura sangre" and not a "converso" as the Inquisition had made him out to be.

Valero Martín, Alberto, "El barrio de Calisto y Melibea," Castilla madre Salamanca. Madrid, 1916, pp. 193-203.
_____Valero Martín believes that Rodrigo de Cota wrote all 21 acts of LC. A reading of Cota's "Diálogo entre el amor y el viejo," and the "Coplas del Mingo Revulgo" suffices to justify this hypothesis.

1923

Allen, Warner H. , ed. Celestina, trans. by James Mabbe. London, 1923.
        A rebuttal to Foulché-Delbosc's chief argument [1900], namely the denial of Rojas' authorship on the ground that the Letter is a deliberate mystification, is presented in Allen's Appendix II to his edition of Mabbe's translation of LC. Further, Allen does not believe that Rojas fraudulently attributed the authorship to himself, as is believed in some quarters, but that he is the author of the original version and of the 1502 edition.

House, Ralph E. , "The Present Status of the Problem of Authorship of the Celestina," Philological Quarterly, II (1923), 38-47.
        Opinions concerning the authorship of LC remained "impressionistic" until House called for a statistical examination of grammatical, lexicographical and stylistic details. It was House's expectation that a scientific analysis of the text would settle issues which had hitherto been discussed on the basis of feelings and literary taste. To begin with, however, House suggested that Menéndez Pelayo's assertion of identity of style for the entire LC be rejected.

1924

Castro Guisasola, F. , Observaciones sobre les fuentes literrarias de 'La Celestina.' Madrid, 1924.
        On the ground that the literary sources of a text can give evidence of authorship, Castro Guisasola examines the Petrarchan sources of LC [1961, Deyermond]. He discovers no identifiable reminiscences of Petrarch in Act I, though they are present in the rest of the work. Turning to the borrowings from Juan de Mena, Guisasola notes that only one borrowing from the Laberinto occurs in Act I, whereas the

borrowings from both the Laberinto and Los pecados mortales
are numerous in the other acts.   It is also significant that
only in Act I are the sources actually named in the text.   The
conclusion, according to Guisasola, is that Act I is by another
author.
      Once again using his study of sources from Petrarch,
Castro Guisasola states that Acts II-XVI were not written before 1496.   He finds that in all probability Rojas drew his
material from the 1496 Basel edition of the Alphabetical Index to Petrarch's Latin works.   As for Act I, he adds, its
linguistic and stylistic archaisms point to a different author
and a much earlier date of composition.

Herrero García, M., J. Vallejo, and F. Castro Guisasola,
"Notas sobre La Celestina: ¿Uno o dos autores?," Revista
de Filología Española, XI (1924), 410-412.
      Herrero García points out a contradiction between Act
I and Act II.   In the former, Sempronio seems to deny that
Calisto is of noble blood when he refers to "lo de tu abuela
con el jimio ... testigo es el cuchillo de tu abuelo." In
Act II, however, he tells Calisto, "no te estimes en la clari-
dad de tu padre, que tan magnífico fue, sino en la tuya."
For Herrero García this contradiction is evidence enough
that two authors are involved in LC.

House, Ralph E., Margaret Mulroney, and Ilse G. Probst,
"Notes on the Authorship of the Celestina," Philological
Quarterly, III (1924), 81-91.
      House reports on the series of studies made under
his direction on the text of the Tragicomedia, with a view to
testing the authorship of the additions of 1502.   If Acts II-
XVI of the 1499 Comedia show reasonably uniform percent-
ages in the areas tested, he assumes that these give us a
norm to which material of a similar kind from the works of
the same author should correspond.
      He studied eight different categories of inversion of
natural word order:
      1. Verb before its noun subject except in an interrogation.
      2. Verb before the pronoun subject with the same excep-
         tion as above.
      3. Direct or indirect noun object before a finite verb.
      4. Predicate noun before the finite verb.
      5. Predicate adjectives, including past participles used
         predicatively with ser and estar, before a finite verb.
      6. Past participle before haber.
      7. Noun object before the infinitive.
      8. Complementary infinitive before the finite verb on which

it depends.

The frequency with which the verb precedes its noun or pronoun subject (types 1 and 2) for the sake of emphasis or to keep together subject and its modifiers is so great in both the <u>Comedia</u> and the <u>Tragicomedia</u> that this type of inversion <u>cannot be</u> used for evidence. In types 3 to 8, Act I shows the highest proportion of inversion, and the additions the lowest. Acts II-XVI are consistently in the middle. Thus both the first act and the additions stand clearly apart from Acts II-XVI. For example, for the large group including types 3, 4, and 5, which produce the same stylistic effect, there is an average of about 30 per cent of inversion for Act I, slightly above 20 per cent for Acts II-XVI, and under 15 per cent for the main additions of 1502. The cumulative evidence for all types tested proves that a difference of style exists between the first act and Acts II-XVI, and between the additions and either part of the older version.

House's team studied the dialogue to see whether it shows the same characteristics throughout. The most evident trait capable of objective comparison is the length of the speeches. The measurement of these is based on full-type lines as printed in the Cejador edition. The results show that Acts II-XVI differ very little from one another in speech length, while Act I and the additions differ widely from the other acts. Act I is noteworthy for the preponderance of short speeches, nearly one-half of which are under one line in length. Beginning with the second act, the dialogue begins to slow down somewhat. Although less frequent than in Act I, the short speech has a real place in the dialogue of Acts II-XVI, with an average of 20 per cent. In the additions, however, the proportion of speeches of less than a line in length is only 10 per cent, and an examination of the cases shows that they are nearly always used to mark entrances or exits.

The next area of study was the use of pronouns, which reveals interesting material bearing on the question of authorship.

1. Disjunctive and conjunctive pronoun objects.

The point of difference between the various parts of LC is the relative frequency of use of the disjunctive personal pronoun object alone as against the combined conjunctive and disjunctive object. In the first act, only one example is found in which the disjunctive and the conjunctive pronouns are used together, "ni la quiero ver a ella." In Acts II-XVI, both constructions are found with about equal frequency. In the additions, the combined use is favored in a proportion of about three to one.

2. Le and lo as masculine singular accusative referring
   to persons and things.

    In referring to persons, there is no difference between
Act I and Acts II-XVI in the use of lo, but in the additions
lo appears with sufficient frequency to attract attention.   Lo
appears as against le referring to things in a proportion of
one to six in the first act, two to three in Acts II-XVI, and
of more than two to one in the additions.   Results indicate
a strong use of le both for persons and things in Act I.   In
the additions, lo is used one-fourth of the time for persons
and two-thirds for things.

3. Position of conjunctive personal pronoun object with infinitive prepositional phrases and with the future indicative, either the split future of the modern form.

    For both cases, a similar proportion occurs between
the old and the modern construction throughout all the parts
of the 1499 version, namely about one to two in favor of the
latter.   The additions, however, incline toward the modern
construction of the pronoun following the infinitive in a ratio
of one to three in the prepositional phrase, and of one to
five in the future, the modern form of which predominates.

4. Possesive pronoun.

    The short form before the noun is the usual posses-
sive in all parts of LC.   The more archaic el padre tuyo
occurs in greater abundance in the 1499 version than in the
additions.

    In addition, the frequency of archaisms was studied:

1. gelo, gela occurs three times in the first act and not
   at all elsewhere.

2. se lo type found only once in the first act, but common elsewhere.

3. entrambos found once in Acts II-XVI, seven times in
   the additions.   Acts II-XVI have entrambos eight times,
   amos once, and ambos twice.   None of these forms
   occurs in Act I.

4. de nos found once in the first act, not at all elsewhere.

    From the statistical data collected, House concludes
that the additions of 1502 stand apart in all of the eight types
of word order studied.   Avoidance of unusual inversion is
the striking characteristic of the additions.   The form of
dialogue is likewise distinct from that of both parts of the
earlier version.   The pronouns, the only syntactical group
that was studied, yield other striking points of difference.
The greater preference for lo in the 1502 additions as a
masculine singular pronoun in the accusative case is more
favorable to the theory of different authorship than to any
other hypothesis.   Finally, the 1499 edition shows a larger

proportion of obsolescent forms.

The differences between Act I and Acts II-XVI are not so marked, and it is not impossible that Rojas found and worked over an old story. But the differences found between I-XVI and the additions offer the strongest indication of dual authorship. Like Cejador, House concludes that Proaza was the author of the additions of 1502.

Vallejo, J., F. Castro Guisasola, and M. Herrero García, "Notas sobre La Celestina: ¿Uno o dos autores?, Revista de Filología Española, XI (1924), 402-412.

While accepting House's findings with regard to the additions of 1502, Vallejo ventures out on his own statistical investigation of the 1499 edition. He introduces the findings of his own stylistic and grammatical examination of the sixteen-act version, with emphasis on the stylistic peculiarities of Act I.

1. Preposition a with direct object. Less frequent in Act I. Omitted ten times in Act I, against five times in Acts II-XVI.

2. Archaisms. Found only in Act I.

3. Conjunctions: no (sólo) ... más (aún) and no (sólo) ... pero (aún). Both found in the work, but the latter is exclusively found in Acts II-XVI and the Prologue.

4. puesto que expressing concession. This is a cultismo found four times and only in Act I.

5. assi que, to introduce a conlusive phrase. Found 33 times in Acts II-XVI and the Prologue, but only once in Act I.

6. Act I prefers the conjunction mas to pero. Mas is used in Act I 50 per cent of the time, and only one-fourth of the time in Acts II-XVI.

7. Causal use of pues. Found twice as often in Acts II-XVI as in Act I.

8. Other peculiarities noted:
    1) Rarely is the future indicative used instead of the subjunctive. No examples in Act I; two in Acts II-XVI.
    2) Frequent use of expressions like assimesmo, mayormente in Acts II-XVI.
    3) en especial used only in Act I.
    4) como with subjunctive, a cultismo, fits in with the style of Act I, where it appears four times more frequently than in the rest of the work.

While the study made by House's team concerned itself with the characteristics which distinguish the additions of 1502 from both Act I and Acts II-XVI, Vallejo takes up

solely the question of Act I.   He concludes from his collection of data that Act I is the work of a different author.

1928

Davis, Ruth, "New Data on the Authorship of Act I of the
Comedia de Calisto y Melibea," University of Iowa Studies in
Spanish Language and Literature.   Iowa City, 1928.
        Miss Davis studies the differences in syntax, sentence
structure, exactness and variety of expression, word order,
spelling and use of archaisms in Acts II-XVI of the Comedia
to establish the stylistic differences which separate Act I from
Acts II-XVI.   Since Acts II-XVI contain about four and a half
times as much material as Act I, a common construction
should appear between four and five times as often in Acts
II-XVI as in Act I, if the subject matter is similar.   A notable variation from this proportion would constitute a significant stylistic variation.
        The results of Miss Davis' investigation show that Act
I differs from Acts II-XVI in the following respects (I quote
Miss Davis' Summary, p. 56):
  1. In act I, the tendency to substitute other verbs for ser
      and estar with the past participles appears with about
      one-fifth as great relative frequency as in acts II-XVI.
      The same tendency is apparent in constructions other
      than the past participle.
  2. In act I the progressive occurs relatively about one-
      fourth as often as in acts II-XVI.   Estar is the only
      auxiliary found in act I.   In acts II-XVI, ir, venir and
      andar also occur.
  3. In act I the present participle occurs with about one-
      third the relative frequency of acts II-XVI.
  4. The -ra form of the past subjunctive occurs in act I
      only in connection with conditions.   In acts II-XVI, it
      is found in several types of clauses.   The -ra form is
      used in the conclusion of the condition with about four
      times greater relative frequency in acts II-XVI than in
      act I.   Aside from conditions, the ratio between the
      -ra and -se forms, in acts II-XVI is between one-third
      and one-fourth.   There are no -ra forms in act I aside
      from conditions.
  5. The assimilation of the -r of the infinitive to the l- of
      an enclitic object pronoun is not found in act I.   In acts
      XX-XVI it occurs in eighteen out of a possible sixty-five
      cases.
  6. In Act I, the ratio between mas and pero, as simple
      adversative conjunction, is one to two.   In acts II-XVI,

it is almost one to five.
7. De, replacing que after a comparative, does not occur in act I. In acts II-XVI, there are ten cases of this usage.
8. The indefinite pronoun al occurs four times in act I and not elsewhere.
9. Acts II-XVI present nine cases of the union of otro with the demonstrative. This compound form is not found in in act I.

From this data, it is apparent that there are numerous and wide differences between the language of Act I and Acts II-XVI. All indications show that the language of the later acts is closer to modern usage. Miss Davis advances the following conclusions (p. 57):
1. On the evidence, it is scarcely possible that Rojas could have written act I in his youth. The little time that could have elapsed between the writing of the two parts could hardly explain the differences that exist.
2. It hardly seems possible that Rojas deliberately introduced an archaic appearance into the work.

Miss Davis proposes that we accept the statements in the Letter. Rojas may have used something he found without significantly altering its language.

1925

Valle Lersundi, Fernando del, "Documentos referentes a Fernando de Rojas," Revista de Filología Española, XII (1925), 385-396.
Valle Lersundi, a descendant of Rojas, is able to solidify the evidence of Rojas' existence and of his authorship of LC by publishing important documents which had been among his library holdings. Included among his documents is testimony presented in 1582 by Rojas' grandson to prove the hereditary hidalguía of the family.

1926

Espinosa Maeso, Ricardo, "Dos notas para La Celestina," Boletín de la Academia Española, XIII (1926), 178-185.
Expinosa Maseo not only concurs with the scholars who believe that the fall of Granada is a reference to a past event, but he is able to solidify his hypothesis with other references to past events found in Sempronio's speech of Act III, which bring the date of composition to 1498. For example, he points out that "la puente es llevada" refers to the tremendous rains of 1498 which caused a great deal of

damage to Salamanca and which demolished the arches of the
bridge. "Aquel es obispo" refers to the new Bishop, Fray
Diego de Dega, whose entrance in Salamanca in 1497 was
considered an extraordinary event. "El rey entra hoy" could
have alluded to Fernando's coming to Salamanca after the
death of his son don Juan, on October 4, 1497.

1928

Reischmann, Karl, Die stilistische Abwechslung in der span-
ischen Tragikömodie 'La Celestina'. Bonn, 1928.
          In a detailed study of certain elements of Rojas' style
[Chapter 5], Reischmann speaks of an "absolute linguistic
unity" which inclines him to favor the single author theory.
It should be noted, however, that Reischmann is concerned
primarily with stylistic variety rather than the authorship
problem, and that his feeling for the unity of the work is in-
tuitive. He makes no mention of the work of House and Vallejo.

1929

Spitzer, Leo, "Note sur La Celestina," Revista de Filología
Española, XVI (1929), 59-60.
          Spitzer's article is a reply to a study by Herrero
García [1924]. Spitzer rejects the conclusion in that study.
The passage in Act II shows, according to him, that Rojas
was writing with Aristotle's Ethics fresh in his mind. Rojas
was more interested in the erudite display than in a logical
"liaison entre les repliques." Consequently, the contradiction between the two passages cannot be advanced as evidence
of dual authorship.

1929-1930

Valle Lersundi, Fernando del, "Documentos referentes a Fernando de Rojas," Revista de Filología Española, XVI (1929),
366-388; XVII (1930), 183.
          Valle Lersundi reprints the text of Rojas' will, dated
in Talavera, April 3, 1541. It is supposed that Rojas died
between April 3 and April 8 of 1541. Valle Lersundi also
publishes the contents of Rojas' library, giving a description
of the volumes in it.

1932

Küchler, Walther, "Die erste bekannte Ausgabe der Comedia

de Calisto y Melibea," Romanistisches Jahrbuch, VI (1953-
54), 315-323. (This article was actually written in 1932 and
later found among Küchler's papers.)
    Küchler concludes that the additions are in all prob-
ability the work of Alonso de Proaza, since these first appear in an edition prepared by him.

Rauhut, Franz, "Das Dämönische in der Celestina," Festgabe
zum 60. Geburtstag Karl Vosslers. Munich, 1932, pp. 117-
148.
    Rauhut gives the entire Comedia to Rojas, and points
out that even if Rojas did not write Act I originally, he must
have reworked it sufficiently to integrate it with the rest.
The authorship of the five intercalated acts remains doubtful,
however.

Wright, Leavitt O., "The -ra Verb Form in Spain," University of California Publications in Modern Philology, XV
(1932), 1-160.
    Wright's study traces the history of the use of the
Spanish verb form in -ra. Wright examines literary texts
from the twelfth to the twentieth centuries and makes a historical study of the frequency of the forms in -ra, -se, -ría,
and -re. Through a system of ratios between parallel or allied forms, he has attempted to make a tabulation of the relative change in usage of these forms from period to period.
This tabulation offers several possible scales of measurement which might prove helpful in determining the date of
composition and the authorship of a given work. Furthermore, this detailed study of the history of verb forms will
help clarify the interpretation of certain types of obscure
passages in the texts.
    As regards LC, Wright compares the use of the -ra
from in Act I as against Acts II to XVI and reports the results without further comment.

1938

Careaga, Luis, "Investigaciones referentes a Fernando de
Rojas en Talavera de la Reina," Revista Hispánica Moderna,
IV (1938), 193-208.
    Careaga reviews the documents published by Serrano
y Sanz [1902] and by Valle Lersundi [1925 and 1929-30].
Most of the article is devoted to the excavations around Rojas' grave, initiated by Careaga, which culminate in the supposed discovery of Rojas' remains "en actitud meditativa."

1943

Giusti, Roberto F. , "Fernando de Rojas. Su obra de humanidad española y de arte renacentista," Boletín de la Academia Argentina de Letras, XII (1943), 121-142.
        Giusti affirms that LC was conceived by a single au-
thor and executed at two different though not distant times.
It is possibly the creation of a young man, since the text is
replete with references to the humanistic literature of the
period, which appears to be still fresh in his mind.   The
pessimism of the work also points to Rojas' youth, for youth
is naturally inclined to pessimism--consider Werther--when
the events of life do not fit into a neat order.
        Giusti sets the date of composition of the Comedia
after the conquest of Granada, around 1496.   But for the
terminus ad quem he chooses 1498, at which time Rojas was
already familiar with Petrarch's Latin works.

1944

Heller, J. L. , and R. L. Grismer, "Seneca in the Celestinesque Novel," Hispanic Review, XII (1944), 29-48.
        The authors agree with Castro Guisasola [1924], and
find support in the conclusions of House [1924] and Davis
[1928] that there is a striking difference between Act I and
the other acts in the character of the citations from Seneca.
Act I contains seven quotations from the first seven Epistolae.   Seneca is named in one of these but he is named
nowhere else in the "novel."   In Acts II-XVI, quotations from
the Proverbia Senecae abound, whereas quotations from the
genuine Seneca, though not entirely absent, are rare and
much less close to the original than those found in Act I.
This indicates a difference in intellectual level between the
first act and the other acts.

1946

Montesino Samperio, José V. , "Sobre la cuantificación del
estilo literario: Una contribución al estudio de la unidad de
autor en La Celestina de Fernando de Rojas," Revista Nacional de Cultura, LV (1946), 94-115; LVI (1946), 63-68.
        Montesino Samperio sets out to prove that LC lacks
the admirable unity of style proclaimed by Menéndez Pelayo
and other scholars.   His conclusion, based on a statistical
analysis of the work, is that LC exhibits two distinct literary
styles which defy the theory of single authorship.   He proceeds as though nothing more had been said on the subject

after Menéndez Pelayo, thus omitting mention of the linguistic studies undertaken by the House team [1924], J. Vallejo [1924] and Ruth Davis [1928], all of which clearly set Act I apart from the rest of the work.

Using the random sample method, he studies samples from each of the three parts of LC: Act I, Acts II-XIV, and the five additional acts and interpolations:

1. The first 100 paragraphs from Act I, up to Calisto's description of Melibea.
2. The second 100 paragraphs following the above in the same act.
3. The 100 paragraphs from the beginning of Act II into the fourth.
4. The 100 paragraphs from the beginning of Act VI.
5. The 100 paragraphs from the beginning of the interpolated part of Act XIV.

Each paragraph was analysed for the number of sentences it contained, the number of words in each sentence, the number of words in the paragraph, the number of each type of punctuation marks, the number of repetitions, duplications, enumerations, "similicadencias," as well as the frequency of the word Dios.

An analysis of the results obtained from the different samples reveals a significant analogy between the two samples taken from Act I. The samples taken from the third and sixth act are also analogous. They reveal significant discrepancies with respect to the first two samples from Act I, but not with respect to the samples taken from the interpolations.

His results confirm that a difference of style exists between Act I and the rest of the work and that Act I could be attributed to a different author. Sufficient evidence exists to suggest that the additions are by the same author who wrote the original Acts II-XVI. In the first two samples there appears an appreciable preponderance of short paragraphs with short sentences, whereas in the remaining three samples the long paragraphs with long sentences predominate.

Finally, Montesino makes a statistical analysis of the samples to avoid a subjective interpretation of the results. The statistical evidence reaffirms the conclusions given above.

1947

Delpy, G., "Les profanations du texte de La Célestine," Bulletin Hispanique, XLIX (1947), 261-275.

Basing his judgment on the impression of unity gained from the work, Delpy attributes the first 16 acts to the same

author, and suggests that the Letter should not be taken literally.

Delpy considers the additions of 1502 so damaging to
the original that he rejects the suggestion that these are by
the same author. Instead, he believes that the additions betray the hand of a well-intentioned man, namely that of the
zealous Proaza.

1950

Menéndez Pidal, Ramón, "La lengua en tiempos de los Reyes
Católicos," Cuadernos Hispano-Americanos, XIII (1950), 9-
24.

According to Menéndez Pidal, it is "una arbitrariedad
hipercrítica el seguir hoy negando la diversidad de autor para
el primer auto." He reminds us that Rojas declares it in
the Prologue, Juan de Valdés affirms it and modern scholars
have confirmed it through studies of style and literary
sources. Moreover, it is evident that the author of the first
act had other stylistic preoccupations than Rojas. He used
linguistic forms that were becoming obsolete, though still in
use at the beginning of the sixteenth century. Among the
forms which do not appear in the second and successive acts
are the enclitical pronoun gelo for selo, the neuter al for
otra cosa, the conjunction maguera for aunque and the use of
Latin adverbial adjectives. Rojas, on the other hand, offers
linguistic traits which are alien to the first act, especially
the use of the future indicative when the subjunctive would be
expected. Linguistically, Act I belongs to an author of a
"región arcaizante," probably Salmanca, where Rojas found
the manuscript, whereas the rest of the work reflects linguistic characteristics of the region around Toledo.

The unity of artistic conception, the chief argument
favoring single authorship, is possible, because in the first
act we find "como en semilla la obra entera." It is also possible that the first act was accompanied by an "argumento de
la comedia."

1953

Krause, Anna, "Deciphering the Epistle-Preface to the Comedia de Calisto y Melibea," Romanic Review, XLIV
(1953), 89-101.

Miss Krause's opinion is that the details of the Letter
fit into the academic and literary conventions of the time.
By judging the Letter within its medieval rhetorical tradition,
she finds the problem of authorship less contradictory than

heretofore. The informative epistle-preface addressed to a
friend was an accepted convention of the fifteenth century.
If we therefore conceive of Act I as a glorified rhetorical
exercise, a "terenciana" executed with greater brilliance than
ever before, as stated in the acrostic, we can give greater
credence to the words of the Letter.

The Letter, therefore, is an actual letter sent out
with the manuscript of the primitive Comedia to a friend and
conterráneo, in which the author seeks to protect himself
from criticism and purposely mystifies his readers, in a
spirit of both pride and jest.

Miss Krause notes the discrepancy between the first
act and the following ones on the question of where the first
scene takes place. She suggests that since no further mention is made of the garden in Act II, the chance meeting
probably took place in the proximity of a place of worship.
Discrepancies in the setting of the scene and in the reference
to Calisto's nobility [1924, Herrero García] indicate that there
was an interruption of time in the composition of the work.
Furthermore, the archaic tone of the syntax of the beginning
implies an intervening period.

Miss Krause offers the following conclusions:
1. Both the so-called first act and the 15 succeeding acts
   appear to have been the work of one or more escolares,
   probably of the university of Salamanca.
2. Whether Rojas completed the "terenciana" of a fellow
   student who had died or whether he wrote the entire
   work himself, it is obvious that a period of time
   elapsed between the composition of Act I and the con-
   cluding acts of the primitive Comedia, a supposition
   which would explain differences in style, syntax,
   sources, and literary details.
3. If the motive for completing the Comedia was to show
   appreciation to a friend and benefactor, the dedicatory
   epistle and acrostic might actually have been sent out
   with the manuscript of the work.
4. On the other hand, the dedicatory epistle and acrostic
   may have been written at the instigation of Proaza, and
   in conformity with the humanistic models, for the au-
   thorized edition of 1500, if such existed, and for that
   of 1501.
5. LC, as the work of an escolar, perpetuates the medieval tradition and is steeped in the literary and academic atmosphere of pre-Renaissance Spain.

Samoná, Carmelo, Aspetti del retoricismo nella 'Celestina'.
Rome, 1953.

Samoná sees the additions of 1502 Rojas' own critical
and analytical attitude toward his text. Underneath the aesthetic incongruities of some erudite enumerations and sententious digressions, Samoná discovers the same fundamental
stylistic unity which led Croce to state that "l'autore ideal-
mente o poeticamente fu uno solo" [Chapter 5, 1939].

1954

Adinolfi, Giulia, "La Celestina e la sua unità di composizione," Filologia Romanza, I (1954), 12-60.
      Miss Adinolfi sets out to disprove the separate author-
ship of the additions of 1502 and their supposed inferiority.
An examination of the relationship of the additions to the
original text, reveals a deep and inseparable connection with
the original work, supporting the idea of single conception.
By means of reconstructing the creative process, a continuator can adapt himself to another author's work and remain
faithful to an existing form and structure. An author, however, would tend to evolve and change, but even in the diver-
sity of his new spiritual position his own personality is still
recognizable.
      Miss Adinolfi asserts that the problem of authorship
has remained unsolved because excessive attention has been
directed to the preliminary parts for the questions of date
and authorship. Her opinion is that the additions and modifications themselves offer the best field of study for resolving
the problem. A decisive argument favoring the single authorship theory is to be found through a comparison between the
Comedia and the Tragicomedia. Once this is done, it will
appear that preliminary material presents no obstacles to the
single authorship hypothesis.
      An analysis of the additions and interpolations reveals
that these exhibit an intimate connection with the original 16
acts. As for the preliminary material, it is true that the
greatest difficulty is to be found in the Letter and in the
acrostic verses of 1501. Although Menéndez Pidal has noted
some stylistic differences which would tend to give credence
to the statements in the Letter, Miss Adinolfi suggests that
the use of archaic forms is common to all of the Tragicomedia. If they appear more frequently in the first act, this
is due to internal artistic necessity. Furthermore, she considers it unlikely that Rojas wrote the Comedia in 15 days
since its structure is not that of an improvised work.
      Miss Adinolfi attributes to Rojas' condition as a "judío
converso" the equivocal position he assumes before his own
work. The immorality of the work and the satire of the

clerics made him fear public reprisal.   But once the success
of the Comedia is assured, he seems willing to reveal his
identity.   He tries to conciliate his ambition as an author and
his fears as a converso by hiding his name in the acrostics.
The contradictions of the preliminary material are a result
of the interplay of these contrasting sentiments.   Rojas' fears,
however, are not unjustified, since he creates a world avid
for life and earthly pleasures, "mosso unicamente da un'ansia
sfrenata di godere e fondamentalmente privo di scrupoli e di
riserve morali."   Rojas conceived pleasure as an autonomous reality which accepts only its own limitations and its
own laws.

     Rojas wrote the Letter and the acrostics in self-de-
fense.   He organizes his defense around two main points:
on the one hand, he tries to present a moral justification for
the work; on the other, he tries to limit his direct responsibility for it.   He attributes to LC an arbitrary moralizing
function.   He thus speaks of his activity as a writer as a
marginal experience with respect to his more serious involvement as a lawyer.   That is why we have the fictional
15 days.   All of these subtle arguments reveal a desire to
free himself from excessive responsibility.   For further protection, he invents a fictional author for Act I, and proceeds
to throw the major responsibility of the work on this person.
The existence of an original author places him in relative
safety while assuring him of the glory he desires.   Once having recognized the complexity of his motivation, we are able
to resolve these contradictions as normal, coherent manifes-
tations of an individual situated, by historical circumstances,
in a singular human condition.

Penney, Clara L., The Book Called 'Celestina'.   New York,
1954.
     Miss Penney supposes that Fadrique de Basilea may
have considered the manuscript of LC too prolix, involved,
and expensive to publish.   Thereupon he would have decided
to omit the five chapters of the "Tratado de Centurio" as ex-
pendable, joined the edges together and added the arguments.
She senses a ring of truth in the Letter of the Comedia, but
feels that the preliminary parts of the Tragicomedia were
inflicted upon the work by editors and publishers.

     In her opinion, the archaic usages in syntax and sen-
tence structure which have been detected in the first "chapter" bear out the two-authors hypothesis.

     Miss Penney suggests that the additional five chapters
were part of the original but that they were omitted for
practical reasons.   However, emboldened at seeing Fadrique

de Basilea's Comedia reprinted with the accretions, Rojas
and Proaza, or even Proaza alone, converted the text into
the Tragicomedia by restoring the "Tratado de Centurio" within the work.

Ugualde, Louis, "The Celestina of 1502," Boston Public Library Quarterly, VI (1954), 206-222.
        For Ugualde, the homogeneous quality of the style
throughout the play is now so apparent that one wonders how
this unity could have been achieved had LC been the work of
two separate authors.   The first act contains the germ of
the entire work and the other acts are its logical and unified
development.
        According to Ugualde, we must assume the existence
of an edition prior to that of 1499 since the latter bears the
phrase "con sus argumentos nuevamente añadidos."

1955

Criado de Val, M., Indice Verbal de 'La Celestina'.   Madrid, 1955.
        Criado de Val undertakes an analysis of the verbal sys-
tem of LC in order to determine the state of the Spanish verbal system in the fifteenth century and to arrive at an effective analytical method which would help solve the enigma of
one or various authors.   He uses the Sevilla 1502 edition as
a basis for his study, but does not include minor additions
in the first 16 acts, the arguments, prologues, acrostics,
and verses.   One of his chief objectives is to determine
whether the stylistic variants reflect the author's individual
style and to what extent the individual variant can affect the
linguistic norm.   Criado de Val recognizes that House [1924],
together with his team of researchers, was the first scholar
to apply linguistic analysis to determine the authorship of
LC, but he finds that the inaccuracies of House's morphologi-
cal and syntactical investigation render the results invalid.
        Criado de Val divides the areas of investigation into
several subindexes.   These subindexes correspond to the various internal structures of the conjugation and are grouped
around the two main laws that govern a verb: oposición and
concurrencia.   He studies the proportional frequency between
competing forms and contrasting forms.   He summarizes each
area of investigation as follows:
Subindex 1.   Frequency with which usage of auxiliary verbs
in Act I differs from the rest of the work.   Evidence points
to a different author and a different time of composition between Act I of LC and the remaining acts, including the addi-

tions of 1502. With Act II the frequency of estar as well as
tener increases considerably, whereas the use of ser is greatly diminished. There is also a noticeable decrease in the
use of the passive voice with either ser or haber, favoring
the reflexive impersonal passive form, giving a good indication of the development of the Spanish language in the two
distinct parts of LC.
Subindex 2. Frequency of infinitive and gerund in Act I is
limited. As against the simple scheme of Act I, beginning
with Act II we find a complex use of the infinitive, especially the substantivization in its modern use. The modern ger-
und appears almost exclusively in Acts II-XVI and the additions.
Subindex 3. Frequency of preterite in Act I over all other
past tenses. The pattern of Acts II-XVI instead reveals the
full development of the structure and function of the indicative past tenses.
Subindex 4. The concurrencia between the archaic amar he
and the modern amaré reveals a lapse of time between the
composition of Act I and the other acts, thus substantiating
the findings on the use of the auxiliary verbs (Subindex 1).
Also notable is the absence of the expression tener que in
Act I in contrast to the following acts. No example of the
compound future is present in Act I, whereas its modern
form and use appear in the rest of the work.
Subindex 5. Great difference in proportional frequency of
subjunctive and conditional forms between Act I and Acts II-
XVI. Difference in frequency is complemented by analysis
of meaning, combinations, and function of conditional forms.
These differences lead to the conclusion that the simple system of Act I has acquired a superior degree of complexity in
the rest of the work.
Subindex 6. The modal oposición emphasizes the stylistic
variants between Act I, with its rapid dialogue, and the more
ceremonious and rhetorical dialogue of the following acts.
The concurrencia between the forms ame and amad is particularly interesting in this respect. The stylistic use of
amo, ame, amad is noted, but the use of the subjunctive is
peculiar to Acts II-XVI and the additions. Again a distinct
stylistic and modal tendency separates Act I from the rest.
        In conclusion, the abundance of archaic forms in Act
I as contrasted to a more refined verbal system coupled with
an incredible abundance of subordinate combinations and formulas of great complexity in the rest of the work, supports
the thesis of dual authorship. On the other hand, an analysis of the additional acts of the Sevilla 1502 edition reveals
such an extraordinary resemblance to the 15 earlier acts that

it unmistakably establishes a single authorship for Acts II-
XXI.
          Furthermore, the internal structure of the work be-
trays a difference between authors and periods of composition.   The structure of Act I is similar to that of an auto or
paso corto.   It is probably in this form that Rojas found it.
The aim of the first author is anecdotal and descriptive,
lacking the "vuelo trágico" of its continuator.   This process
of transformation is typical of a theme which has been reworked many times, in that it develops from a simple anec-
dote to the great Tragicomedia where Fate rules.
          In an Appendix, Criado de Val reports on the analysis
of the shorter interpolations previously left out.   In spite of
the limited sampling that these additions offer, it can be
safely stated that these interpolations belong to the author of
Acts II-XVI, and that the frequency of verbal forms is notably similar to that of the second part of the work.

                              1956

Gilman, Stephen, The Art of 'La Celestina'.   Madison, 1956.
          On the question of authorship, Gilman bases his dis-
cussion on the studies of six scholars, each of whom represents a distinct point of view: Valdés (1535), Blanco White
[1824], Foulché-Delbosc [1900], Menéndez Pelayo [1910],
House [1924], and Menéndez Pidal [1950].   For him, only
Menéndez Pidal offers the comprehension of the facts on literary terms.   On his own side, Gilman concludes that   the
authorship problem must be set aside "if we hope to discover
the way of Rojas' creation, his particular and personal art."
          As for House, the only scholar in this group who at-
tempts to solve the authorship problem by means of statistical evidence, Gilman states that by ignoring aesthetic criteria, he ends with literary absurdity.   For Gilman, the authorship of Act I is not a matter susceptible of statistical
proof.   It is a literary problem.   Besides, since House's
study failed to yield correct results with respect to the additions, Gilman concludes that House's evidence for Act I is
also unreliable.
          Gilman takes as an absolute fact that the additions of
1502 are by Rojas.   The differences between 1499 and 1502
can only be due to a change of writing habits which occurred
in the intervening years.   Rojas' additions and interpolations
grow out of a need for "creative clarification."   Gilman sees
the additions of 1502 as an invaluable key both to Rojas' conception of LC as a whole and to Rojas' development as an
artist.   The differences which exist between the Comedia and

the Tragicomedia are part of the whole process of "creative
completion on the levels of character, structure, and theme."
    According to Gilman, it is possible that Act I was a
tentative first version by a youthful Rojas, a first version
which was later completed as the Comedia. But though this
possibility exists, Gilman is willing to accept Rojas' own
statements on the matter. He also considers source studies
of the kind Castro Guisasola had performed inconclusive for
purposes of determining authorship. However, while it cannot be established that Rojas wrote Act I, it is probable that
he intervened in it to an appreciable extent. Gilman finds it
believable that Rojas "as a sardonic and harassed converso
should have disguised the extent of his contribution to Act I
with mock apology for one part and mock eulogy for the other." But he finds three errors of composition in Act I which
give the impression of failure to assimilate an earlier version of a different author.
    Gilman proposes 1498 as the terminus ad quem for the
composition of the Comedia. As for the arguments, Gilman
believes that the general argument and the argument preceding each individual act were written by another hand. These
may serve to indicate how LC was read in 1499. It is likely
that the printers used as a guide the arguments and the scholarly apparatus accompanying editions of Terence printed in
the fifteenth century. Gilman's hypothesis is that when Rojas
sent his manuscript to Burgos in 1499, the editors conformed
to the printing tradition which had already come into being for
the comedies of Terence. He believes it unnecessary to postulate a missing first edition without the arguments. It was
probably Fadrique Alemán's decision to print the work in the
same manner as he had seen Terence's work done. As A.
W. Pollard (1907) has remarked, even the woodcuts of the
1499 edition were closely imitated from the Grüninger Terence
(Strasbourg, 1496).
    The arguments of the additions of 1502 are by a new
author--Rojas himself. There appears in these a change in
style and technique, most notably in the new Act XIV, to wit
"a refusal to reduce the work to the bare contours of action,
to limit it to successive happenings." The arguments of 1502
furnish their own evidence of Rojas' increased critical awareness of the nature of his art.

Kruse, Margot, "Stand und Aufgaben der Celestina-Forschung,"
Romanistisches Jahrbuch, VI (1956), 324-341.
    Miss Kruse presents a critical thematic survey of the
studies dealing with LC, and concludes that the fundamental
work is still that of Menéndez Pelayo in Orígenes de la novela,

Vol. III.   The problem of authorship, however, remains unresolved and unresolvable.   She finds   that the biographical
studies are of little value because little substantial material
is available.   She feels that a critical edition is sorely needed
and that stylistic studies are still in their infancy.

McPheeters, D. W., "Alonso de Proaza and the Celestina,"
Hispanic Review, XXIV (1956), 13-25.
        For McPheeters, the discovery of the 1500 Hagenbach
Toledo Comedia raises the problem of the role of the corrector Alonso de Proaza in the elaboration of this version, which
contains the Letter, acrostic, and verses.   This problem re-
quires principally an investigation of the corrector's function
in the publication of works in Spain and in Europe around
1500, and a review of statements made by Proaza on editorial procedures in works edited by him.
        Miss Penney [Chapter 2, 1954] has shown that typo-
graphically the Toledo 1500 printing copied slavishly that of
Burgos, 1499, and was in turn copied by Stanislao Polono for
the Sevilla 1501 edition.   The question raised is why the Comedia of 1500 and 1501 contains new material when it is a
reprinting of Burgos 1499.   McPheeters' interpretation is that
Hagenbach had almost finished the printing of his 1500 Toledo
Comedia when the complete 1500 Salamanca edition of 21 acts,
edited by Proaza some months earlier, reached him.   It was
then too late to insert the five additional acts, but he was
able to add the Letter and acrostic to the beginning.
        McPheeters finds evidence for the existence of a 1500
Salamanca edition of the Tragicomedia in Proaza's own
verses appearing at the end of the Comedia.   Apparently,
Polono, the printer of the 1501 Sevilla Comedia, also heard
of the longer Salamanca edition too late to use its full text,
and waited until the following year to publish the Tragicomedia (Sevilla, 1502).
        As for Proaza's own intervention in the text, Mc-
Pheeters limits that editor's contribution to an interpolation
in the Prologue, where there is a reference to the arguments,
and to the verses.   McPheeters has considered all major additions to the text in the light of contemporary editorial procedures and Proaza's own statements on editing but finds
nothing to indicate an unusual intervention into the text by the
dutiful corrector Proaza.   He also shows that Spanish authors
of the fifteenth century (as well as of the Siglo de Oro) wrote
accompanying pieces.   It appears to McPheeters that Rojas
saw the need for compositions hors de texte for the 1500
Salamanca reprinting.

1957

Bohigas, Pedro, "De la Comedia a la Tragicomedia de
Calisto y Melibea," Estudios dedicados a R. Menéndez
Pidal. Madrid, 1957, pp. 153-175.
        Bohigas reviews the scholarship dealing with the ques-
tion of authorship of Act I.
        According to Bohigas, the linguistic and literary pe-
culiarities of Act I distinguish it from the rest of the work.
But while Acts II to XIV differ from Act I, they do offer
points of contact with the artistic elaboration of the additional five acts.
        The changes in style and the different use made of
source material in Act I do not necessarily indicate separate
authorship, but they may point to a change of interests, and
the development of the author himself. The internal structure of the work reveals that its parts were composed at different times, but the literary devices remained essentially
the same. Rojas develops elements of the Comedia to create
the Tragicomedia, and he probably reworked Act I.

Garrido Pallardó, Fernando, Los problemas de Calisto y
Melibea y el conflicto de su autor. Figueras, 1957.
        Garrido Pallardó sets out to prove that Rojas wrote
all of LC. In his opinion, Proaza was not talented enough to
add to the work. But he does attribute to Proaza the acrostics because these are "indignos de la pluma de Rojas."
Credit, however, should be given to Proaza for something
other than an artistic contribution to LC. He was Rojas' pro-
tector and the only one who knew the secret of Rojas' authorship.

Ríquer, Martín de, "Fernando de Rojas y el primer acto de
La Celestina," Revista de Filología Española, XLI (1957),
373-395.
        After the conclusive linguistic study of Criado de Val
[1955], Ríquer agrees with other scholars that Rojas found
the first act of LC. But from the textual errors which have
been noted by several scholars, it is apparent that at times
the méaning of the text escaped Rojas. Ríquer, however,
favors accepting the first act as Rojas understood it and
edited it, in spite of acknowledged philological errors and inconsistencies. Accordingly, he approves of Criado de Val's
and Trotter's reprinting of "Minerua con el can" in their edition, even though Green [Chapter 5, 1953] has shown that it
should read "Minerua con Vulcán." Ríquer is convinced that
Act I is the work of an unknown author and that Rojas only

edited it and continued it.

In discussing the textual inconsistencies, Riquer states
that the first encounter reveals that Calisto already knew and
loved Melibea, and that it was not a chance meeting. He
points out that the argument of Act I mentions the falcon,
though no mention is made of the bird during the scene. It
seems unlikely that Calisto would be hunting within a city, on
foot, and without servants. Another point is that the walls
of Melibea's house are high and a ladder is needed for the
later visits, while in Act I Calisto is able to run into the
garden unaided. All of these considerations lead Riquer to
the conclusion that the first scene does not take place in
Melibea's garden. Instead, he suspects that the meeting took
place in a church. It is only in the middle of Act II, where
Rojas' text begins, that an effort is made to connect the
events as described in the argument of Act I to the action.

Riquer agrees with Criado de Val that the structure of
Act I is that of an auto or short paso. He goes on to attribute Act I to Mena. On closer examination, he finds a
similarity between the prose of Act I and Mena's Proemio
for El libro de las virtuosas e claras mujeres.

1958

Martin, John H. , "Some Uses of the Old Spanish Past Subjunctives (With Reference to the Authorship of La Celestina),"
Romance Philology, XII (1958), 52-67.

Martin sets out to show the methodological errors of
the scholars who have sought to identify the syntactic subsys-
tem of an individual author to determine the question of authorship. He refers in particular to the studies on LC by
House [1924], Davis [1928], Wright [1932], and Criado de Val
[1955]. Most syntactic studies have focused, among other
things, on the -ra and -se subjunctives on the assumption
that these are equivalents offering freedom of choice. The
above scholars, in the belief that they had identified individual characteristics in the use of these verbal forms, reached
the conclusion that Act I of LC and the remaining 15 acts of
the 1499 edition are by a different author. They used as central proof ratios of occurrence of these subjunctive forms,
assuming the identity of function of -ra and -se at that historical stage of the Spanish language.

Martin's study proves that the choice of one or the
other form in LC is not a matter of personal preference, but
one of grammatical exigency. He points out that throughout
LC -se and -ra forms perform mutually exclusive functions:
-se appears in non-hypothetical and in non-past hypothetical

functions; -ra only in a past hypothetical function. Furthermore, we find in LC two -ra forms: the simple and the
compound--both used for the expression of the hypothetical in
the past. The Spanish of the text differentiates between the
past contrary-to-fact non-anterior and the past contrary-to-
fact anterior. This distinction obtains neither in modern
Spanish nor in English and has consequently been overlooked
by modern scholars. Martin offers ample evidence for his
premise that the verbal structure of LC's language cannot be
approached with criteria derived from modern Spanish. The
results of previous syntactical studies are vitiated by their
disregard for the differences of the verbal system at varying
historical stages of the Spanish language.

   Martin concludes that in the absence of a broader
knowledge of historical syntax, not a single problem of unknown or disputed authorship has yet been solved.

Moreno Báez, Enrique, "Meditación sobre La Celestina,"
Archivum, VIII (1958), 206-214.
   Moreno Báez states that the facts we know about Rojas' life have enabled us to reconstruct his personal drama
which took him from Judaism to skepticism. His loss of
faith determines his concept of man and prevents him from
fully realizing the aim he had set before him--"enseñar a
resistir los fuegos del amor." Fully aware he has failed to
achieve his aim, Rojas rewrites his work and sacrifices its
tragic abruptness and its relative exemplarity to the development of his characters.

                        1960

González Ollé, Fernando, "El problema de la autoría de La
Celestina," Revista de Filología Española, XLIII (1960), 439-
445.
   González Ollé makes a study of the use of the diminu-
tive in LC to resolve the problem of authorship of Act I.
   The results show that in Act I the diminutives are
used four times as often as in the rest of the work. In both
parts, Celestina uses the greatest number of diminutives, her
total corresponding to that of all the characters together. In
Act I, however, Celestina uses as many diminutives in -ico
as in -illo, although -illo was more generally used at the
time. The suffix -ico is characteristic only of Celestina.
   In the following 20 acts, Celestina uses -illo twice as
often as -ico. Moreover, -ico is no longer used exclusively
by Celestina. It is interesting to observe the preponderance
of -ico in the "Tratado de Centurio."

Besides the disproportion in the use of the diminutives between Act I and the others, González Ollé observes
a difference in the choice of the suffix and of concrete di-
minutive formations--loquillo over loquito--in the speeches
belonging to Celestina. The abundance of these forms in her
speeches provides a basis for comparison between the diminutives of the two parts of the work. Analysis of the dimin-
utive points to definite differences between the original act
and the following 20 acts, and therefore suggests separate
authorship.

The results of other stylistic studies--those of House
[1924], Vallejo [1924], Criado de Val [1955]--add substantial
weight to the hypothesis that the first act was written by a
different author, but that it was reworked by the author who
completed the work.

1961

Bataillon, Marcel, 'La Célestine' selon Fernando de Rojas.
Paris, 1961.

Bataillon reviews the principal questions on the authorship problem, weighing both the supposed anonymity of the
first act and the hypothetical reconstruction of Rojas' motivation for disclaiming paternity. Bataillon perceptively discusses the major scholarly contributions to these questions,
as well as the critical studies dealing with the thematic significance of LC.

The obscure passages and archaic tone of Act I lead
him to conclude with Menéndez Pidal [1950] and others that
Rojas did not write it. It is possible that Rojas left the obscure passages untouched in a gesture of humility toward the
work of another author. For if Rojas had merely been con-
tinuing his own work, it seem unlikely that he would have
left the obsolete linguistic forms unchanged for the sole purpose of proving that Act I was written by a different author.
On the other hand, Bataillon finds no reason to reject the
hypothesis that Rojas wrote the first act ten or even 15 years
before the rest.

Bataillon believes that the editors added the arguments
to each act. He agrees with Krause [1953] and Riquer [1957]
that a discrepancy exists between the first act and the following ones on the question of the setting of the first scene.
However, Rojas' "superstructures," the Comedia and the
Tragicomedia, maintain the moral tone of Act I and sustain
its edifying purpose [Chapter 6].

Bataillon asserts that the author's acrostic is not an
auto-retrato but part of a tradition in which the author pre-

sents the difficulties and perils of the task he is undertaking.

In conclusion, Bataillon states that the time has come to recognize that the critics who have accepted Rojas' declarations in the preliminary material at their face value have chosen the safest path.

Deyermond, A. D. , The Petrarchan Sources of 'La Celestina'. Oxford, 1961.

Deyermond states that once Rojas is accepted as the author of Acts II-XVI [1924, Castro Guisasola], the evidence of the Petrarchan borrowings [Chapter 3] indicates beyond any reasonable doubt that he also wrote the material added in 1502. Both parts of the work use the Index to Petrarch's Opera, borrowing both sententiae and exempla, borrowing both individual index entries and groups of entries. In both the Comedia and the Tragicomedia, material is added to some of the Index entries by a reference back to the text, but in both parts independent use of the Index predominates; in both, great attention is paid to Index entries from De Remediia, De Rebus familiaribus, De Rebus memorandis; both parts use the Index more than any other Petrarchan work; both parts use three books by Petrarch, De Remediis, Re Rebus familiaribus, and Bucolicum Carmen; neither uses Petrarch's vernacular poetry. It follows that the hypothesis advanced by Cejador [1913], Delpy [1947], and others of a different author for the 1502 additions is untenable.

As far as Act I is concerned, there can be no proof that Rojas did not write it, but if he wrote it, he did so some time before he wrote the rest of the Comedia.

Differences in the use of Petrarch between Acts II-XVI and the 1502 additions are differences in the work of one man whose working methods have changed. But the differences between Act I and the rest of the work reflects either the work of two separate authors or the work of one man writing at different times, having undergone a powerful new literary influence in the intervening years.

Since Rojas draws on the Index to the 1496 printed edition of Petrarch's Latin works, and since he borrowed as he wrote, Acts II-XVI were probably composed between 1496 and the first edition of LC--whether 1499 or 1500 as Vindel [Chapter 2, 1951] suggests. Deyermond proposes 1497 or 1498 as a terminus a quo.

Gilman, Stephen, "The Spanish Writer, Fernando de Rojas," Yearbook of the American Philosophical Society (1961), 503-505.

Gilman reports that among the Valle Lersundi [1925,

1929, 1930] papers made available to him were the inventory
of the possessions of Rojas' wife containing previously un-
listed books from Rojas' library [Chapter 3, 1961], and a
great deal of information about their six children, including
a personal letter from the daughter to the eldest son. In
other archives, inquisitorial records yielded interesting background material and insight into the stifling atmosphere in
which Rojas lived. From the documents there emerges "a
life under extreme pressure, a life made intensely self-con-
scious by the necessity of eternal vigilance."

Lida de Malkiel, María Rosa, Two Spanish Masterpieces:
The 'Book of Good Love' and 'La Celestina'. Urbana, 1961.
        Note. This work raises and discusses all the critical
questions which are elaborated with voluminous erudition in
La originalidad artística de 'La Celestina' [1962] (q. v.). I
am therefore omitting a summary here. Nevertheless, Two
Spanish Masterpieces can be recommended for students wishing to obtain a clear and succinct account of the same conclusions reached in her definitive work.

McPheeters, D. W., El humanista español Alonso de Proaza.
Valencia, 1961.
        McPheeters sets out to establish, more extensively
here than he did in his article of 1956, the extent of Proaza's
contribution to the text of LC.
        McPheeters believes that in preparing the 1500 Sala-
manca edition of the Tragicomedia Proaza used the 1499
Burgos Comedia with additional material. This edition was
in turn used for the 1514 Valencia version, in which there
are tentative corrections for two of the three odd errors in
the first act. These corrections were probably made by
Proaza. Proaza also edited the Prologue but he did not
write it. That Rojas--who may have been acquainted with
the Spanish version of Enea Silvio Piccolomini's Historia de
duobus amantibus (Historia de dos amantes), printed in Salamanca in 1496, which contains an epistle-preface--was himself the author of the Letter and prefatory material can be
inferred from the fact that it had become a necessity for
Spanish writers in the fifteenth century to include an epistle-
preface and final verses in their works.
        McPheeters also believes that Proaza was not capable
of writing verses of the quality found in LC. The three
strophes, "Concluye el autor," are too passionate to belong
to Proaza. McPheeters suggests that all the additions incorporated in the edition of Burgos 1499 reached Proaza in
manuscript form. There are no other indications that Pro-

aza's intervention ever went beyond that expected of a "corrector concienzudo."

Moreno Báez, E., "La obra y el autor," Nosotros y nuestros clásicos.   Madrid, 1961, pp. 140-150.
           Moreno Báez states that biographical details open the
way to an understanding of the work.   Our knowledge of
Rojas' life has led us to reconstruct the drama that brought
him from Judaism to skepticism.   Thus, in spite of Rojas'
many Petrarchan borrowings, he never adopted Christian
stoicism.   Rojas is one of the many conversos who aban-
doned their faith without fully embracing the new one.   And
that is why he fails at his professed moral intent.   Realizing his failure as a moralist, Rojas reedits the work--Gil-
man and other scholars having shown that the interpolations
are the work of Rojas himself--and develops the psychological aspect of his characters.   Having failed as a moralist,
he nonetheless succeeds as an artist.

1962

Lida de Malkiel, María Rosa, La originalidad artística de
'La Celestina'.   Buenos Aires, 1962.
           With incomparable erudition and eloquence, clarity of
language and thought, fervent admiration for Rojas and his
work, Mrs. Malkiel studies all the literary themes and motifs found in LC, and guides us to a fuller understanding and
appreciation of Rojas' art and originality.
           No attempt can be made here to do justice to the vo-
luminous erudition which supports Mrs. Malkiel's work.
Only a bare summary of her observations and conclusions
will be given.
           On the question of Rojas' authorship, Mrs. Malkiel
points to the basic LC authorship problems, namely Rojas'
statements in the Letter to the effect that he composed the
work as a young student on a two-week holiday.   She cites
certain humanistic comedies of the fifteenth century which offer declarations parallel to those made by Rojas in the Letter.   Basing herself on the evidence provided by these literary parallels, Mrs. Malkiel concludes that the declarations
in the Letter are not a mystification, but rather coincide
with a conventional literary posture designed to modestly
minimize the value of one's work.   Similarly, the fact that
Rojas first conceals his name and later reveals it in the
acrostic, far from constituting an unusual and sinister occurrence, represents a medieval practice designed to identify the work as an adaptation.

As for Act I, the stylistic and linguistic investigations reveal a decisive difference between the work of the antiguo auctor and the other 15 acts of the Comedia. Act I differs from the rest in size, sources, details, and many characteristics. But above all, it differs in the tone, which is more oratorical. Compare, for instance, the formal rhetoric with which Melibea is described in Act I with the emotive depiction in Act VI. The textual evidence corroborates the author's declarations in the Letter to his friend: that Act I antedates the rest of the work and is written by another hand. Having presented textual and historical literary evidence, Mrs. Malkiel concludes that Rojas is not the author of Act I.

In the case of the Tragicomedia, most of the interpolations exhibit a tendency to rhetorical amplification, while others reveal incomprehension or unfamiliarity with the original text. Following a detailed discussion of each inconsistency, Mrs. Malkiel states that all the literary evidence we have on behalf of Rojas--namely, the Letter, the Prologue, the acrostic, and Proaza's verses--would lead us to believe that Rojas worked surrounded by a group of friends. It is also possible to suppose that this circle of friends collaborated with Rojas in the transformation of the Comedia into the Tragicomedia. Mrs. Malkiel reminds her readers of the collective elaboration of the Romancero, a phenomenon which was also common in Italian Renaissance comedy and in Elizabethan drama. The knowledge we have of the active participation of various artists in a work makes us wonder whether the single authorship hypothesis for LC, put forth at the beginning of the last century, is nothing more than an anachronistic perspective which has distorted the issues. No one before Moratín doubted the statements in Rojas' Letter. It can be said that the concern for single authorship begins with neoclassic criticism.

In conclusion, Mrs. Malkiel attributes Act I of LC to the antiguo auctor; Acts II-XVI of the Comedia to Rojas; the "Tractado de Centurio" and the other interpolations which constitute the Tragicomedia to the interpolador, most probably Rojas himself together with collaborators unknown to us but who had intervened to a much smaller extent in the Comedia.

1963

Herriott, Homer J., "The Authorship of Act I of La Celestina," Hispanic Review, XXXI (1963), 153-159.
        This article is mainly a review of Deyermond's The Petrarchan Sources of 'La Celestina' [1961].

Though Deyermond denies that the sinfonía in praise of Celestina has a Petrarchan source because half of the elements in the sinfonía are absent from Petrarch, Herriott states that if we accept the premise that the author of Act I utilized the preface of De remediis, Book II, for the sinfonía, we begin to find more satisfactory and logical solutions both to the problems of the authorship of LC and to the development of the text.

Herriott is inclined to believe that Rojas wrote Act I in his early years at Salamanca, when his religious training was still fresh in his mind, for Act I contains 14 borrowings from Biblical and religious sources, whereas all of the other acts have only nine. Furthermore, there are many splendid passages in Act I which could have been written only by a genius. One of these is the sinfonía. Other passages, too, reveal an effort to elevate the style of Act I.

Whereas Deyermond leaves the door open with respect to the authorship of Act I, Herriott affirms that Rojas wrote Act I before he experienced the powerful literary influence of 1496 when Petrarch's Opera became available--at which time he determined to complete his work.

McPheeters, D. W. , "Newly Discovered Correspondence of Alonso de Proaza, Editor of La Celestina," Symposium, XVII (1963), 225-229.

On the basis of additional evidence furnished by a recently discovered espistolary exchange between Alonso de Proaza and Juan Calvo, dated 1514, McPheeters states that Proaza constantly displays erudite tendencies which reflect his preoccupation with Lullist works and his teaching of rhetoric. Nowhere in LC do we find any evidence of Proaza's stylistic peculiarities. Moreover, there is nothing anywhere in LC to suggest a personal relationship between Rojas and the corrector Proaza.

1964

Mendeloff, Henry, "The Passive Voice in La Celestina. (With a Partial Reappraisal of Criado de Val's Indice Verbal)," Romance Philology, XVIII (1964), 41-46.

Mendeloff's analysis of the passive voice in LC was motivated solely by his concern with historical grammar and conducted independently of Criado de Val's investigations [1955]. Linguistically, the late fifteenth century is a critical period of transition and LC can serve as the basis for a synchronic study of this evolutionary stage. LC serves as one of the literary indices to the syntax of the late fifteenth-century Spanish.

Admittedly, the passive construction in LC is difficult
to isolate and categorize. It performs with a quasi-syste-
matic framework of concurrence and opposition, complicated
by instances of structural identity and functional divergence.
Mendeloff considers the concurrences which characterize the
passive of action and the passive of state, and the basic opposition existing between them. The tabulations produced by
his analysis of frequency of occurrence give a different ratio
of concurrence than Criado de Val's ratios. Mendeloff discovered errors of method and interpretation in Criado de
Val's investigation which are responsible for the different ratios. Paradoxically, Criado de Val's conclusions with regard
to syntactic constructions and to the problem of attributions
proved to be valid despite the fact that his evidence was erroneous: the unmistakable evidence of the significant varia-
tions in the frequency of ser and estar between Act I and
Acts II-XVI.

Mendeloff finds a remarkable coincidence in the ratios
of concurrence and opposition in the Tragicomedia and in Acts
II-XVI.

1965

Ferreccio Podestá, Mario, "La formación del texto de La
Celestina," Anales de la Universidad de Chile, CXXXIII
(1965), 89-122.

Ferreccio Podestá sets out to reconstruct different
stages of the text of the Comedia and of the Tragicomedia.

First of all, the Letter reveals traits which link it to
a manuscript stage. In the original version of the Letter
there are traces of its connection with the Comedia in manuscript form, namely in the reference to the cross at the end
of the first scene. The cross must have been in the manuscript and when Rojas saw the mark omitted in the editions
which included the Letter, he revised the text so that all that
belonged to the original author formed one single act up to
Act II before "Hermanos míos," etc. We find a further
change in the Letter of the Tragicomedia, where the primera
cena becomes Act II. Apparently, in reworking the Comedia,
Rojas also modified the Letter. The confusion between aucto
and cena, however, remains in the Letter, as Rojas states
"lo del antiguo auctor fuesse sin división en un aucto o cena
incluso." The word and concept aucto was actually alien to
Rojas, since it is a later erudite latinism.

As for the arguments, it was customary for Latin
comedies to have a general rubric and Rojas obviously fol-

lowed their example. But it was not common to have an argument for each act. The model for these is probably to be found in the translation from the French of the novel La historia de los nobles caballeros Oliveros de Castilla y Artús Dalgarve. This work is to be considered both the model and the reason for the individual arguments. But in addition, an editor probably requested the arguments and Rojas adopted the format in the re-elaboration of his work.

Ferreccio Podestá finds a unifying spirit behind the preliminary pieces. The message was so well concealed in all the preliminary parts, that Proaza saw the need to reveal the content in his acrostic. Rojas' verses, however, are not of a later composition. In them, he is actually anticipating the criticism to his work.

In the Prologue, which is of a later date, Rojas informs us that his fears did not materialize and that his work was a great success--though he accuses his readers of superficiality.

Ferreccio Podestá concludes that Rojas' manuscript of the Comedia contained not only the Letter and the general argument, but also the acrostic verses which explain the contents of the Letter.

1966

Gilman, Stephen, "Mollejas el ortelano," Estudios dedicados a James Homer Herriott. Madison, 1966, pp. 103-107.
    The reference to the garden of Mollejas gives us a peek at Rojas' boyhood, an experience which Rojas transfers to Sempronio in Act XVI. This detail was revealed in the legal document proving the hidalguía of Rojas' grandchildren.

1968

Gerday, Jacqueline, "Le remaniement formel des actes primitifs dans La Célestine de 1502." Annali dell'Istituto Orientale di Napoli, Sezione Romanza, X (1968), 175-182.
    See Chapter 5.

Chapter 2

EDITIONS

1841

Gorchs, Tomás, ed. La Celestina. Barcelona, 1841.
    In preparing his text, Gorchs selects witnesses from
both Amarita's and the 1507 Zaragoza edition.
    [Amarita, León, ed. La Celestina. Madrid, 1822.
This is considered one of the best editions of the nineteenth
century.]

1895

Soravilla, Javier, La Celestina. Madrid, 1895.
    Javier Soravilla consulted 27 editions of LC. He out-
lines the variants separately for each act. He also gives a
glossary of words that are now obscure and archaic, adding
their modern equivalents or definitions. He praises León
Amarita's edition of LC of Madrid, 1822.

1897

Michaëlis de Vasconcellos, Carolina, "Zwei Worte zur Celestina-Frage," Zeitschrift für Romanische Philologie, XXI
(1897), 32-42.
    Miss Michaëlis de Vasconcellos believes that possibly
more than one edition existed before 1500, for Rojas speaks
in that year about "los impresores" who had already edited
part of the book. It remains unknown whether these original
editions had a prologue and an epilogue, since the 1499 edition has two sheets missing. Miss Michaëlis feels that the
first sheet had enough room to contain the Letter. It seems
to her that the Letter was written shortly after the Comedia
except for the last sentence, "Para desculpa de lo qual todo,
no solo a vos, pero a quantos los leyeren, offrezco los si-
guientes metros," inasmuch as it refers to the verses that
follow. The verses could not have been present in the 1499
edition.

1900

Foulché-Delbosc, R. , Comedia de Calisto y Melibea. Biblioteca Hispánica, Vol. XII. Madrid, 1900.
        Foulché-Delbosc reproduces the 1499 Heber edition in
his Biblioteca Hispánica, Vol. XII. This is the first 16-act
edition in four centuries.

Foulché-Delbosc, R. , "Observations sur La Célestine,"
Revue Hispanique, VII (1900), 28-80.
        Foulché-Delbosc is the first critic who fully describes
the different editions of LC. Critics had known of the existence of the 16-act edition, but it was not until Foulché-Delbosc's discovery and publication of the 1501 Sevilla edition
that the shorter version became available to them. Foulché-
Delbosc claims that the 16-act version went through three
stages of development. The first stage is a hypothetical edition prior to 1499 which has not survived. Foulché-Delbosc,
however, makes an attempt to reconstruct its essential character. The second stage is the Heber 1499* edition which
has the first and last sheet missing. The third stage is the
1501 Sevilla edition of which we have one copy. The 1501
Comedia has the Letter, verses, incipit, the general argument, and argument before each of the 16 acts, and the six
verses by Alonso de Proaza. The 1502 Sevilla edition is the
fourth stage of the work and the first version containing the
21 acts. Four separate editions of the fourth stage, all
printed in 1502, two in Sevilla, one in Toledo, and one in
Salamanca, are known to us. Besides the additional five
acts, the 1502 edition has a Prologue and three new verses
at the end. The fifth stage is in 22 acts, the addition being
the "Auto de Traso." Three editions are known of this stage,
the oldest being that of Toledo 1526, followed by Medina del
Campo 1530, and Toledo, 1538.
        Foulché-Delbosc outlines the material contained in
each stage. He maintains that the statement "con sus argumentos nuevamente añadidos" appearing in the second stage
has a real meaning and that it refers to a previous edition
which ·has not survived. He further states that these arguments were probably added by the printer or the corrector
of the second stage.
        In discussing the additions of the third stage, Foulché-
Delbosc avers that the Letter contains intentional misinfor-
mation [Chapter 1]. He believes that an editor added this
Letter, the contents of which are intended to attract the public's attention to the new edition.
        The first reference to Mena and Cota is found in the

fourth stage, the 1502 Sevilla edition of 21 acts.   Foulché-
Delbosc believes that these famous names were inserted to
gain wider appeal for the book.   In his opinion, the additions
of this version are the work of an "adicionador."   The work
has been lengthened with the "Tratado de Centurio" and an
abuse of proverbs, maxims, sentences, and aphorisms.
      In the fifth stage, the "Auto de Traso" is an addition
without any interest made by an unknown writer.
      For Foulché-Delbosc, the incipit, "síguese la comedia
de Calisto y Melibea, compuesta en reprensión de los locos
enamorados," is the real title of the work and probably the
only title that appeared in the princeps edition.
      Foulché-Delbosc does not believe that the 1500 Sala-
manca edition which is mentioned in 1514 ever existed.
      *[This copy of the Comedia belonged to Richard Heber
at the beginning of the nineteenth century.]

1901

Schiff, Mario, "La Celestina," Studi di Filologia Romanza,
XXIV (1901), 172.
      Schiff states that there is no proof for Foulché-Del-
bosc's hypothesis that the 1499 Heber edition is based on an
earlier version which has not survived.

1902

Haebler, Konrad, "Bemerkungen zur Celestina," Revue Hispanique, IX (1902), 139-170.
      Konrad Haebler is the first critic to determine that
the 1499 Heber edition was brought out by Fadrique Alemán
de Basilea in Burgos.   Haebler supposes that the beginning
missing sheet was empty.   An examination of the 1499 Burgos and 1501 Sevilla editions reveals that the latter is not
based on the former.   It may be assumed that both are based
on a lost earlier version.   Haebler further believes that
there was an actual 1500 Salamanca edition which contained
all 21 acts.

Martinenche, E., "Quelques notes sur La Célestine," Bulletin Hispanique, IV (1902), 95-103.
      Martinenche disagrees with Foulché-Delbosc's state-
ments [1900] concerning the authorship of the different stages,
and with his attributing the new material contained in each
stage to a different editor or "adicionador."   Martinenche
sees the work as having gone through three different stages:
the 1499 Burgos, the 1501 Sevilla, and the 1502 Sevilla.   In

his opinion, the new material contained in each stage was
composed by the same author.

1904

Bonilla y San Martín, Adolfo, "Algunas consideraciones acerca de la Tragicomedia de Calisto y Melibea y sus autores,"
Anales de la Literatura Española, I (1904), 7-24.
    Bonilla y San Martín reviews the scholarship dealing
with the different editions of LC. He agrees with Foulché-
Delbosc [1900] about the existence of a now lost princeps edition. In his opinion this original edition was the basis of
the 1501 edition. Evidence for the existence of the pre-1499
edition is furnished by the reference, in the 1501 edition, to
a cross placed at the end of the first Cena. As all surviving editions are divided into Autos, we may surmise a lost
edition which was divided into Cenas.
    Bonilla y San Martín divides LC into two stages, one
being the Comedia and the other, the Tragicomedia. He believes that the first edition of the Comedia was printed in
Toledo after 1492 but before 1499. It had the Letter without
the last phrase and the general argument. The subsequent
edition of the Comedia was that of 1499 divided into 16 Autos,
each preceded by an individual argument. But Bonilla y San
Martín does not believe that the missing sheets contained the
Letter and the acrostics. Following this, we have the 1501
Sevilla edition published by Stanislao Polono, divided into 16
acts and carrying the acrostic and the six verses by Proaza.
    The 1502 Toledo edition represents the second stage
of LC. Its text is divided into 21 acts and three final verses
are added to it. Bonilla y San Martín does not believe that
the changes of the second stage were made by a different author.

Desdevises du Dezert, M. G., "La comédie de Caliste et
Melibée," Revue des Cours et Conférences, XII (1904), 739-
756.
    Desdevises du Dezert reports on his examination of
the 1499 Heber edition. He discovers some tampering with
the page numbering and with the last sheet. He states that
the numbers on the first three sheets had been recently
scratched out and renumbered and that a new last sheet had
been inserted at least twice. Desdevises agrees with Foulché-
Delbosc [1900] that the 1500 Salamanca edition never existed.

1910

Menéndez Pelayo, Marcelino, Orígenes de la novela, Vol.
III.   Madrid, 1905-1910.
       Menéndez Pelayo disagrees with scholars who believe
that any edition, with or without the arguments, existed prior
to that of 1499, where the arguments are already present.
His hypothesis is that the printer added the arguments on his
own initiative.   The problem of whether the 1500 Salamanca
edition ever existed remains unsolved for the verse in the
1514 Valencia edition, "Fue en Salamanca impresso acabado,"
does not prove that the 1514 edition is based on a lost Salamanca edition.
       In addition, Menéndez Pelayo gives an exhaustive sur-
vey of the Spanish editions of LC in the sixteenth century and
the Italian editions of that same period.   The number of editions decreases in the seventeenth and eighteenth centuries
as interest in LC declines.   A resurgence of interest in the
nineteenth century culminates in the discovery of the 1501
edition by Foulché-Delbosc.

1913

Cejador y Frauca, Julio, ed.   La Celestina.   Madrid, 1913.
       Cejador y Frauca states that the scholarship of
Foulché-Delbosc [1900 and 1902], Menéndez Pelayo [1910] and
Bonilla y San Martín [1904] is basic to the study of LC.   He
reproduces the Burgos 1499 and Valencia 1514 editions of LC.
He believes that a lost first stage of the Comedia contained
an incipit and an explicit.   But since no absolute proof of
the existence of this first stage is available to us, he is for
accepting the 1499 Burgos edition as the princeps even though
it is the second stage of the work.   The third stage is the
1501 Sevilla edition, which in his opinion shows the hand of
Proaza in all the additional material, for the creator of LC
was capable of writing a better Letter and a better Prologue.
Cejador also believes that Proaza was responsible for the
fourth stage, the 1502 edition.   Cejador considers the changes
made by the corrector Proaza to have damaged the original
text.   It appears that the corrector was aware of Rojas'
predilection for the works of Petrarch and that is why he
plagiarized Petrarch in the Prologue.

1923

House, Ralph E. , "The Present Status of the Problem of
Authorship of the Celestina," Philological Quarterly, II

(1923), 38-47.

House discusses the different editions only in terms of their respective literary merit and stylistic differences. His main concern is whether the additions to the different editions conform to the literary purpose of the original work. The differences between the simple plot of the Comedia and the complicated intrigue of the Tragicomedia will be discussed in later chapters.

1924

House, Ralph E., "Notes on the Authorship of the Celestina," Philological Quarterly, III (1924), 81-91.

House reports on his stylistic and grammatical studies of the different stages of LC [Chapter 1]. He is certain that Acts II-VI of the 1499 edition are by one author and were written in the same period. Furthermore, he is of the opinion that Proaza is responsible for the additions of the 1502 edition.

1930

Foulché-Delbosc, R., "Observations sur La Célestine, III," Revue Hispanique, LXXVIII (1930), 545-599.

Foulché-Delbosc reviews the different stages of the Comedia. Again, he discusses the hypothetical lost edition [1900], but he now establishes this lost first stage of the work as the princeps edition. The 1499 Burgos is reconfirmed as the second stage. But now the French scholar puts the 1500 Salamanca edition, the existence of which he had previously denied, in the third stage together with the 1501 Sevilla edition. As for the Tragicomedia, which is the fourth stage of the work, his study tries to determine which of the five different editions available to us is the first one. The fact that the Comedia of 1501 and the Tragicomedia of 1502 are both from the same printer in Sevilla, leads him to conclude that the 1502 Sevilla edition is the princeps edition of the Tragicomedia. Foulché-Delbosc studies the woodcuts used for the illustrations in the several 1502 editions to determine the chronology of the editions. Here too he finds that the 1502 Sevilla Tragicomedia is the authoritative version and that the other four editions of that year are simply reprintings of the 1502 Sevilla edition. He adds that later editions are probably reprintings of the latter.

A further problem which Foulché-Delbosc explores is how to determine the form of the princeps edition of the Tragicomedia. Did the Tragicomedia reach the publisher as

a manuscript in 21 acts or was it an edition of the Comedia
with the additional five acts in manuscript form? Foulché-
Delbosc chooses the latter hypothesis because he discovers
in the Comedia of 1501 and in the Tragicomedia of 1502 certain typographical similarities which do not appear in the Comedia of 1499. It must also be noted that the 1499 and 1502
edition have other typographical similarities. He offers the
hypothesis that the 1502 edition is not based on the 1501 nor
on the 1499 editions, but that the former two editions are
based on a lost earlier version [1902, Haebler]. Foulché-
Delbosc believes that this lost version belonged to the third
stage of development and that it probably contained the prefatory material. He claims that this unknown edition of the
Comedia was used to print the princeps edition of the 1502
Tragicomedia. As far as he is concerned, all of this points
to the existence of the 1500 Salamanca edition of the Comedia,
a supposition further substantiated by the verses, "Mill y
quinientas bueltas en rueda fue en Salamanca impresso acabado" which appear in the 1514 Valencia edition. He has
thus set out to prove what he had firmly ruled out in 1900.
        However, the question of the princeps edition of the
Comedia still remains unanswered. Foulché-Delbosc repeats
his belief that the phrase "con sus argumentos nuevamente
añadidos" proves that the Comedia had previously appeared
in print and that the editor is pointing to what has been added
to the previous edition. This lost previous edition [1900]
without the arguments is the princeps edition of the Comedia.

1932

Küchler, Walther, "Die erste bekannte Ausgabe der Comedia
de Calisto y Melibea," Romanistiches Jahrbuch, VI (1956),
315-323. (This article was actually written in 1932 and later
found among Küchler's papers.)
        The same argument in determining which version is
the princeps edition of the Comedia is followed by Küchler.
Küchler further observes that none of the older editions have
Celestina at the head of the title and that this name appears
for the first time as the title of the work in the Italian translation by Alfonso Ordóñez, published in 1506.

1936

Peeters-Fontainas, J., "Une édition perdue de La Celestina,
Anvers, 1558," Papyrus, I (1936), 28-30.
        Peeters-Fontainas states that there were three known
editions of LC in Antwerp, all printed by the editor Nutius

in 1545, 1545, and 1558. He found the exact reference to
the 1558 edition in the "Catalogus Librorum ex variis Eu-
ropae." This edition was probably printed by the widow of
Nutius, and a copy probably belonged to León Amarita in
1835.

1950

Baldelli, Ignazio, "Girolamo Claricio, editore della Celestina,"
Giornale Storico della Letteratura Italiana, CXXVII (1950),
111-116.
    Baldelli states that the types of variants found in
Claricio's edition of LC printed in Milan in 1514, which in
turn is based on Ordóñez' translation, point to the linguistic
mannerisms of Claricio himself. The "spagnolismi" which
abound in this edition are not attributable solely to Ordóñez,
since in Boccaccio's Amorosa visione by the same editor the
same types of variants are also in evidence.

1951

Vindel, Francisco, El arte tipográfico en Burgos y Guadala-
jara durante el Siglo XV, Vol. VII. Madrid, 1951.
    Vindel believes that the 1500 Toledo edition is the
princeps edition. Vindel reproduces a few pages of the Burgos edition. An examination of the gothic lettering and woodcuts of the Burgos copy leads Vindel to conclude that the latter is actually a sixteenth-century production.

1953

Thomas, Henry, "Antonio (Martínez) de Salamanca, Printer
of La Celestina, Rome, c. 1525," The Library, VIII (1953),
45-50.
    Sir Henry describes a copy of the edition of LC be-
longing to the British Museum which was catalogued as that
of Salamanca, 1502. Instead, he identifies the copy as an
edition printed in Rome by Antonio de Salamanca around 1525.
The text, however, follows the Sevilla and Toledo edition of
1502.

1954

Penney, Clara L., The Book Called 'Celestina'. New York,
1954.
    Miss Penney's book is an illustrated catalogue of the
many editions of LC at the Hispanic Society in New York.

The book also contains a detailed list of copies of editions
to be found elsewhere.

Miss Penney describes the recently discovered Comedia of Toledo, 1500, which, after the editio princeps of Burgos, 1499, is now the second earliest known, displacing that
of Sevilla, 1501.   All three of these versions are entitled
Comedia de Calisto y Melibea and have 16 acts.

As for the Tragicomedia, the Sevilla, 1502, is the
first extant edition in 21 acts, although one earlier edition
may have been published in Salamanca, 1500.

Ugualde, Louis, "The Celestina of 1502," Boston Public Library Quarterly, VI (1954), 206-222.

Ugualde describes the 1502 Sevilla edition acquired by
the Boston Public Library.   He notes that the large woodcut
of the title page is typically Spanish whereas the 23 smaller
ones are similar to those used by Grüniger at Strasbourg,
notably in his Terence and Horace editions.

1958

Criado de Val, M., and G. D. Trotter, eds.   Tragicomedia
de Calixto y Melibea, libro también llamado 'La Celestina'.
Madrid, 1958.

Criado de Val and Trotter present a new critical edition of LC.   Their text is based on the 1502 Sevilla edition
bearing the title Libro de Calixto y Melibea y de la puta
vieja Celestina [1960, Ferreccio Podestá].

1960

Clemens, J. Th. W., "A Curious Celestina Edition," Revue
de Littérature Comparée, XXXIV (1960), 245-250.

Clemens describes the Venetian edition of Gabriel Gio-
lito de Ferrari of January 20, 1553.   The copy is identical
to that described by Miss Penney [1954] except for the dedi-
cation to Juan Micas.   The copy has numerous printer's
errors and corrupt passages, many of which are corrected
by the hand of Mattia Wolzogen.

Apparently, Wolzogen based his corrections on a more
dependable edition.   Although Clemens has not been able to
discover the edition used for the collation, he suggests a
common source for the 1533 Venice and the 1633 Rouen editions.   The 1553 edition has been in the Hispania Institute
of the University of Utrecht since 1958.

Ferreccio Podestá, Mario, "Una edición nueva de La Celestina," Boletín de Filología (Chile), XII (1960), 259-271.
   Ferreccio Podestá reviews the critical edition of LC
by Criado de Val and Trotter published in 1958. The editors
chose as a basic text the Sevilla edition of 1502 bearing the
title Libro de Calixto y Melibea y de la puta vieja Celestina.
Ferreccio Podestá finds this choice unjustifiable since this
edition has a large number of unique variants. He points out
that this edition is farther removed from the original text
than any of the other six editions bearing the 1502 date. It
is apparent to him that Fernando de Rojas had nothing to do
with any of these editions. But the "puta" edition appears to
be one of the latest and most corrupt of the six 1502 editions.

1961

Bataillon, Marcel, 'La Célestine' selon Fernando de Rojas.
Paris, 1961.
   Bataillon believes that the 1499 edition was printed as
an avant-première for a limited public and that the real entry of LC into the world was the edition of 1500. He disagrees with Miss Penney's hypothesis that the preliminary
material had been omitted from the 1499 princeps edition to
economize some pages.

Poyán, Daniel, ed. Comedia de Calisto y Melibea. Zurich,
1961.
   Poyán reprints a facsimile of the 1500 Toledo Comedia
belonging to the Bodmerian Library in Switzerland. This edition was first described by Miss Penney in 1954.
   Poyán believes that this edition printed by Hagenbach
predates the "supposed" 1499 Burgos edition, and that the
latter was probably printed in 1501 [1963, Montero Padilla].
Poyán states that the 1500 Toledo should be considered the
princeps edition of the Comedia. He bases his argument
chiefly on the fact that this edition contains two illustrations
whereas the 1499 Burgos has 18. Miss Penney, on the other
hand, avers that the 1500 Toledo reproduces the text of the
1499 Burgos edition.

Scoles, Emma, "Note sulla prima traduzione italiana della
Celestina," Studi Romanzi, XXXIII (1961), 155-217.
   Miss Scoles' study is directed primarily to the pre-
sentation of a biographical profile of the translator Alfonso
Ordóñez and to a discussion of what his Italian translation
of 1506 can tell us about the possible existence of a lost
Spanish edition in 21 acts.

Miss Scoles tries to reconstruct Ordóñez' cultural background partly through the dedicatory material accompanying his Italian translation of LC of 1506 and partly through an examination of the text itself. Her conclusion is that the sonnet and dedicatory letter offer indications of a personality permeated with humanistic culture, desirous of approaching the Italian cultural world while making an effort to adhere to the language of the original work. Ordóñez takes for granted the moralistic aim of LC and the multiplicity of its authors.

The main point of this study is that the Italian translation of 1506 is based on a Spanish edition which has been lost. Scoles presents the successive stages which mark the evolution of the text before it reached the 21-act version. She lists all the editions which seem to antedate the Italian translation and of which there is a copy in existence. She refers to Miss Penney's precise documentation [1954] of the editions belonging to the Hispanic Society of America, but finds inaccuracies in the second part where Miss Penney gives a general list of editions and exhibits a condescending attitude toward editions belonging to other collections.

Miss Scoles lists the first stage of the Comedia (A) as the presumed editio princeps of Burgos (?), 1499 (?). The second (B) is represented by the 1500 Toledo and the 1501 Sevilla, both of which contain the preliminary material. The third stage (C) is the Tragicomedia, beginning with the 1502 Toledo edition, followed by 1502 Salamanca and the four 1502 Sevilla editions by Jacobo Cromberger. She states that all other editions are hypothetical ones. She emphasizes that a critical edition is still needed in spite of the edition published by Criado de Val and Trotter, which was based primarily on the 1502 Sevilla.

Miss Scoles lists a number of variants which show how Ordóñez' translation differs from the 21-act 1502 Sevilla Cromberger edition, now in the Biblioteca Nacional, Madrid, and how the Italian version in most cases agrees with both stages of the 16-act version. She also includes variants from the 1514 Valencia.

She underscores the fact that in all cases where the meaning of a phrase is modified by the Italian translation, the Italian version agrees with the Spanish editions of 16 acts, rather than with the pre-1506 21-act editions.

This textual comparison allows us to reject as a possible source for the Italian text each one of the Spanish editions in 21 acts appearing before 1506. Miss Scoles discards the hypothesis that the translator collated a text based on the first or second stage with one of the third stage, ob-

serving that in some cases the first two stages agree with
each other but not with the editions of the third, whereas the
translation follows the example of the latter. Finally, the
passages where the first two stages agree with the translation offer in most cases a text which, from the point of
view of comprehension, logic, and coherence, seems to be
"better" than that offered by the editions in 21 acts prior to
1506. The above considerations suggest the hypothesis that
a lost edition in 21 acts reproduced the text of the first and
second stage of the Comedia more faithfully than all of the
editions prior to the Italian version which are known to us.
Furthermore, F. J. Norton's analysis of the typographical
characteristics of the 1502 editions shows that these are in
reality of a later date (their place and date of printing is indicated only in the last verse of the editor), in which case
they could easily have appeared after the Italian translation.
It is also important to note that the 1514 Valencia edition in
most cases follows the example of the Italian translation.

It is safe to postulate at this point that Ordóñez was
in contact with Juan Joffre, that he was familiar with the
direct source for the 1514 Valencia edition, and that he probably used it as a basis for his translation. It is also possible to suppose that Ordóñez furnished Joffre with the complete text of the work and that he was responsible for the
new edition. Accordingly, the following conclusions can be
drawn:

1. The six different editions of 1502 could not have been
   a source for the Italian translation.
2. The first two stages of the Comedia could not have
   been used as a basic text because of the number of
   acts, in spite of their affinities with the translation.
3. The hypothesis is rejected that Ordóñez built his text
   from a source in 16 acts and another in 21 acts.
4. The 1514 Valencia shows the greatest affinity with the
   text of the translation but cannot be considered a direct source because of its date.

Thus Ordóñez' text is not based on any copy available
to us. But it is possible that with further research, the
Italian translation of 1506 could acquire significant importance as the oldest example of the complete text in 21 acts.

1963

Brault, Gérard J., 'Célestine': Critical Edition of the
French Translation (1527). Detroit, 1963.
Brault states that the French translator in 1527 uti-
lized a Spanish edition as his basic text, but that he occa-

sionally made use of Ordóñez' Italian version. He cites instances where the French is closer to the Spanish and others
where it is closer to the Italian. As this translation in 21
acts has long interpolations, it is less reliable than the
anonymous translation of 1633, but it is closer to the original than Jacques de Lavardin's translation of 1577.

Horrent, Julio, "Cavilaciones bibliográficas sobre las primeras ediciones de La Celestina," Annali dell'Istituto Univer-
sitario Orientale di Napoli (Sezione Romanza), V (1963), 301-
309.
          Horrent reviews past scholarship on the editions of
LC. His own view is that an edition existed prior to that
of 1499 without the arguments, and that the editor is empha-
sizing the difference between his text "con sus argumentos nuevamente añadidos" and a previous edition without them. Similarly,
he reasons that when the five additional acts were first
printed, the title included "y nuevamente añadido el tractado
de Centurio." This conjecture is based on the fact that the
title of the 1525 Toledo edition contains the following words:
"nuevamente añadido el tratado de Centurio y el auto de
Traso y sus compañeros nuevamente historiado." It was a
common practice for editors to point to the new material in
their editions in order to enhance the commercial value of
a newly augmented and revised text. Horrent postulates the
existence of a lost edition of the Comedia prior to that of
1499 which followed more closely Rojas' original manuscript.
          Horrent lists all the extant first editions of both the
Comedia and the Tragicomedia.
          For Horrent, the first edition of the Tragicomedia is
probably that of 1500 Salamanca. It is possible that both
versions were simultaneously printed for a short time, until
the great popularity of the Tragicomedia obscured the shorter
version.

Montero Padilla, José, "Una edición, hasta ahora desconocida, de la Comedia de Calisto y Melibea," Arbor, LIV
(1963), 104-107.
          Montero Padilla describes the recently discovered
1500 Toledo edition of the Comedia belonging to the Bodmerian Library in Switzerland. Daniel Poyán published a facsimile in 1961. Poyán identifies both the typography and
the scutcheon as belonging to Hagenbach.
          The importance of this edition is that it probably rep-
resents the princeps edition of the Comedia. A significant
detail is that the Toledo edition contains two illustrations,
whereas the Burgos has eighteen. The Burgos illustrations

were probably added as a result of the commercial success
of the first edition.   Both Montero Padilla and Poyán believe
that the Burgos edition was actually printed in 1501.   The
colophon and the 1499 date which appear in the Burgos edition also appear in works known to have been printed later.
This is probably what happened in the case of the 1499 Burgos edition.

      Montero Padilla outlines the different stages of the
text:
a. Unfinished manuscript of Act I--author and date
   unknown.
b. Manuscript in 16 acts.
c. Editions in 16 acts: Comedia de Calisto y Melibea.
   1. 1500 Toledo by Hagenbach.
   2. 1501 Sevilla by Polono.
   3. 1501 (?) Burgos by Fadrique de Basilea.
d. Editions in 21 acts: Tragicomedia de Calisto y Melibea.
   1. 1502 Toledo.
   2. 1502 Sevilla, etc.

1964

Herriott, Homer J., Toward a Critical Edition of 'La Celestina'.   Madison, 1964.
      Herriott's purpose is to arrive at a precise knowledge
of Rojas' own words; to reconstruct the text of the princeps
edition of the Tragicomedia; and to trace how the text developed through various editions, including the Italian translation of 1506.   Herriott begins with the assumption that Rojas wrote all the additions in the Tragicomedia and that he
published the revised work in Salamanca in 1500 with the
title of Tragicomedia de Calisto y Melibea.
      Herriott provides a series of 253 graphs in which the
most significant variants are shown and the inter-relation-
ships among various editions are established.   Herriott's
main assumption is that the variants of the early editions
fall into four stemmas or families, and that the prototype for
each one has been lost.   These four stemmas are indicated
as *A, *E, *F, *G, and each one is identified as follows:
Stemma I (*A) represents the princeps edition of the Comedia, before 1499; II (*E) represents the princeps edition
of the 1500 Tragicomedia, which appeared in Salamanca; and
III and IV (*F and *G) represent later versions of the Tragicomedia of 1501(?).
      A collation of the 12 selected early Spanish editions
of LC which are extant reveals some ten thousand variants,

which include textual changes as well as orthographic varia-
tions. More than 85 per cent of the words in the text of
these editions proved to have no variants. Certain variants
are peculiar to only two or three editions, others to many
more. Most of the textual changes and the majority of the
orthographic variants follow the pattern of falling into one or
more of the stemmas. Herriott tested the variants on the
premise that an editor utilized two basic texts in preparing
a given edition. The exceptions found are most frequently
instances where the editor based his text on two editions of
different stemmas and chose the variant now of one, now of
the other. It appears that three editors, whose editions are
of great importance for the reconstruction of the lost princeps edition *E, used two basic editions from different stemmas.

     Herriott accepts the hypothesis of a lost princeps edi-
tion of the Comedia. He believes that the Comedia was not
written before 1496.

     His efforts are directed principally to reconstructing
the text of the lost 1500 Salamanca edition which he posits
as the princeps edition of the Tragicomedia for the following reasons.

    1. This edition is the one cited in the colophon of the
       1514 Valencia edition.
    2. Menéndez Pelayo and Krapf [1899] were convinced that
       the Valencia edition closely followed this lost Sala-
       manca edition, and that the latter was probably the
       princeps edition.
    3. Miss Scoles [1961] indicates that the words which Or-
       dóñez' translation and the 1514 Valencia edition have
       in common with the Comedia differ from those of the
       six editions of the Tragicomedia tentatively dated 1502.

     Herriott's hypothesis is that "when Rojas prepared the
Tragicomedia he used a printed copy of the Comedia, making
small changes on the margin, turning to sheets of paper for
long additions." For this reason, we should normally expect the wording of *A and *E to be the same except for
Rojas' or his editor's changes and any typographical errors.

     The Italian translation of 1506 is very important in
the process of reconstructing the princeps edition of the
Tragicomedia (*E) since, like the 1514 Valencia, it uses *E
as a basic text. Thus it represents an early stage in the
development of the text, as opposed to the variants of Stemmas III or IV or both, which represent a later development.
Ordóñez may have had any of the pre-1506 editions before
him.

     Herriott adopts the following procedure in presenting

the variants. He quotes a brief passage from the text of
LC in order to present on the accompanying graph the word
selected from it and the variants in each edition. He summarizes the matter shown on the graph and comments briefly on the pattern of variants illustrated. The 253 graphs
are the core of the study.

Herriott is convinced from the witnesses that Stemmas
I and II reflect the words of the author. He reconstructs
the prototypes of the missing princeps editions by the witness of other editions. The variants enable him to establish
a filiation of texts of the early editions. The editions fall
into two main divisions: he finds a sharp distinction between the witnesses of Stemmas I and II and those of III and
IV. Even the spelling suggests that the text of Stemma II
antedates that of Stemmas III and IV.

The premise that Rojas used the printed text of the
Comedia in composing the Tragicomedia is helpful in reconstructing *E (Stemma II). Another aid in establishing the
original text of the Tragicomedia is the Pelican episode,
which was probably transposed by the printer. But the number of errors appearing in all three stemmas of the Tragicomedia indicates that neither Rojas nor Proaza read proof
for any of them.

To determine a reason for the orthographic variants,
Herriott accumulates data on the characteristics of the various editors. He also compiles a list of non-variant words.
Both procedures are helpful in determining Rojas' probable
spelling. One of the most troublesome problems is the chaotic use of the initial h- and f- because sometimes an editor switches from initial h- to f- at random. But from his
data Herriott concludes that Rojas preferred initial h- to f-.

Herriott analyzes each Stemma separately:
Stemma I. Comedia, 1499 Burgos. The witness from this
edition command great respect since they are closest in
time to the princeps edition.

Comedia, 1501 Sevilla, Stanislao Polono. The editor
may have had available to him in addition to the Comedia at
least one copy of the Tragicomedia.

It is a mistake, however, to give great credence to
the authenticity and reliability of witnesses of the Comedia,
in spite of their being the oldest extant editions.
Stemma II. The text of the princeps edition of the Tragicomedia represented on the graphs by *E. The text of *E
may be supported by the witnesses of the 1502 Toledo and
Sevilla editions, by Ordóñez' translation, by the 1514 Valencia edition and Gorchs' edition of 1841, or by a combination of two or more.

However, the editor of each of these editions at times
prefers the reading of a text other than *E.
Stemma III. The text of *F changes the original text of the
author and creates a new form which is accepted many times
by the editors of all the editions of Stemmas III and IV.
        Herriott states that whatever the words in the text of
*F and *G were, they aid us little in reestablishing the text
that Rojas handed over to the printer of the princeps edition.
Stemma IV. The text of *G presents fewer problems than
any of the other three stemmas. *G must have had available
at least one edition besides *F and perhaps more. It appears
that the editor of *G was an intelligent, methodical man, who
corrected errors or replaced a word with one of his own
choosing, thus creating a new variant.
        Herriott analyzes separately the numerous representa-
tive textual problems which Act XII presents and for which
he suggests solutions. In this act, we continue to observe
the tendency for the variants to fall into four principal stemmas anywhere in the text. The variants once again demonstrate the filiation of the texts and the peculiarities of each
editor. The graphs for Act XII illustrate a division between
Stemmas I and II and between Stemmas III and IV, which is
common to the whole work.
        Herriott reviews the studies of Foulché-Delbosc [1930]
and Miss Scoles [1961]. Foulché-Delbosc's filiation of early
editions corresponds at times with Herriott's. Miss Scoles
suggests three stages of development of the text of LC instead of Herriott's four. Herriott objects to Miss Scoles'
hypothesis that a princeps edition of the Tragicomedia preceded his *E.
        Herriott establishes the interrelationship of 16 early
Spanish editions, including the four which he considers the
prototype of each stemma and which have been lost--*A, *E,
*F and *G. He also uses Amarita's edition (1822) and
Gorchs' edition (1841), and Ordóñez' Italian translation (1506)
to reconstruct the lost princeps edition *E. The 16 editions
fall into four stemmas. Frequently one stemma supports another, but no extant edition on the graph can replace any of
the lost editions.

1965

Ferreccio Podestá, Mario, "La formación del texto de La
Celestina," Anales de la Universidad de Chile, CXXIII (1965),
89-122.
        Ferreccio Podestá conjectures that in 1499 Alemán
edited LC, divided it into acts, caused the individual argu-

ments to be written, left out the Letter and the verses, but used the incipit. But what Alemán had in his hands was a Comedia [Chapter 1] composed of a Letter, 11 verses with the acrostic, the incipit, a general argument, and the text of the comedy divided into 16 apartados. The text was not divided into acts and did not contain the individual arguments. Hence the 1499 Heber edition contained in the missing page the incipit and the general argument. The text begins on the second page.

The subsequent edition, the 1500 Salamanca, contained the material in Alemán's edition plus the parts which, though in the original manuscript, had not been printed. Proaza, who had been retained to prepare the new edition, decided to reveal the secret of authorship with the addition of his six verses.

Finally, Rojas provided a new revised manuscript of his work--the Tragicomedia--for which Proaza composed a new verse. This was published in Salamanca at the end of 1500 or at the beginning of 1501. It is the edition which Ordóñez used for his 1506 translation and which Proaza used for his 1514 Valencia edition, but of which we have no extant copy. A later unidentified edition, however, became the prototype for all subsequent reprintings of the Tragicomedia.

Ferreccio Podestá, Mario, "Hacia una edición crítica de La Celestina," Anuario de Letras, V (1965), 47-76.
Reviewing Herriott's work, Ferreccio complains that little progress has been made toward bringing out a critical edition of LC which would supplant that of Julio Cejador. Regarding Herriott's attempt to discover what Rojas actually wrote, Ferreccio points out that there is a confusion here between the author's original words and the princeps edition. The two do not necessarily correspond. He concludes, however, that Herriott does have the tools at hand to construct a genuine critical edition.

1966

Herriott, Homer J., "The 'Lost' Zaragoza 1507 edition of the Celestina," Homenaje a Rodríguez-Moñino, Vol. I. Madrid, 1966, pp. 253-260.
Herriott examined a copy of the 1507 Zaragoza edition of the Tragicomedia, which had previously been considered lost, in the Real Academia de la Historia. This edition had been used as a basic text in Gorchs' 1841 edition.
Herriott has added the 1507 Zaragoza edition to his collation [1964] of all early texts. He finds that this edition

is closely related to Stemmas I and II as opposed to Stemmas
III and IV in the development of the text of LC. His collation
"reveals that the exact wording and spelling of the 1507 Zaragoza brings us closer to the text of the princeps edition, but
at the same time leads us to revise some of our former tentative decisions." Some of the variants suggest that the editor of the 1507 Zaragoza edition may have had at hand both
an edition of the Comedia and of the Tragicomedia in preparing his text. Though the 1507 Zaragoza presents new problems especially with respect to the source of some of its
variants, still Herriott feels that it is "a boon in aiding scholars to draw nearer to the original text of both the Comedia
and the Tragicomedia."

Trotter, G. D. , "J. Homer Herriott, Towards a Critical Edition of the 'Celestina'" (rev. art.), Bulletin of Hispanic
Studies, XLIII (1966), 61-62.
        While applauding Herriott's massive work, Trotter ex-
presses misgivings on two points: the absence of a clear
definition of the criteria used in the selection of "significant
variants;" and the use of Cejador's unreliable edition as a
source of quotations.

Whinnom, Keith, "The Relationship of the Early Editions of
the Celestina," Zeitschrift für Romanische Philologie,
LXXXII (1966), 22-40.
        In spite of the formidable task undertaken by Herriott
[1964], Whinnom feels obliged to readdress himself to the
whole problem of the relationship of the early editions of LC.
Herriott has concentrated solely on the perpetuation of mis-
prints and has ignored the evidence of the woodcuts and typography.
        From the evidence gathered, Herriott posits that the
princeps edition of the Tragicomedia is the lost 1500 Salamanca edition. But, according to Whinnom, there is no evidence that the 1500 Salamanca was a Tragicomedia. On the
contrary, he suggest that the princeps edition of the Tragicomedia is a genuine 1502 Sevilla edition. The 1500 Salamanca was not a Tragicomedia and Juan Joffre made no use
either of a 1500 Salamanca Comedia or even of a 1502 Sevilla princeps Tragicomedia, but copied his text from a later
edition.
        The Spanish provenance of the 1502 Salamanca edition
was defended by Miss Penney [1954], although Sir Henry
Thomas [1953] had pointed out that the book was published by
Antonio de Salamanca in Rome, around 1525. Norton (1966)
modifies this to around 1520. Hence there remain three

genuine Sevilla editions, but, on Norton's typographical evidence, none of them was printed in 1502 or by Stanislao Polono. Yet all probabilities point to the former existence of
a genuine 1502 Sevilla edition by Stanislao Polono, the princeps of the Tragicomedia.

Whinnom posits a different filiation of texts for the
Tragicomedia, on the assumption that the princeps is a genuine 1502 Sevilla edition. Furthermore, he concludes that the
date of publication of the non-Sevillian Tragicomedias is not
important. What is important, for Whinnom, is the priority
of the editions from which they derive. The 1507 Zaragosa
takes precedence over the Toledo Tragicomedia and the earliest extant Sevilla Tragicomedia. No extant text can be regarded as authoritative. All require emendations, but the
1514 Valencia text would require fewer ones.

1968

Brault, Gérard J., "Textual Filiation of the Early Editions
of the Celestina and the First French Translation (1527),"
Hispanic Review, XXXVI (1968), 95-109.
          Herriott [1964] posited several editions of the Tragi-
comedia (*E, *F, *G) as having more than one base text as
a source, resulting in an intertwining of stemmas. Brault's
answer to Herriott's statements that the textual variants are
due to editorial procedures--the utilization of two basic texts
in preparing a given edition--is that early printers cannot be
called editors and did not work like Gorchs (1841) or Amarita (1822). The corrector or editor was called in only in
exceptional cases. Brault is inclined to accept McPheeters'
definition [Chapter 1, 1956] of a corrector, as one who was
supposed to establish the best text possible by collating various manuscripts of a work. McPheeters [Chapter 1, 1963]
cites several statements of Proaza indicating precisely this
sort of editorial procedure.

Brault examines the Pelican episode of Act IV and
notes, as Herriott did before him, that it was transposed in
all editions belonging in Stemmas II and III. The compositor
of *G, however, noted the error and replaced the passage
where it belonged in all editions of the fourth family. Since
the 1527 French translation also places the Pelican episode
in its proper position, the author probably used a Spanish
text belonging to the Stemma IV. Brault lists instances
which show that the 1527 Paris translation is closer to Stemma IV, strengthening the possibility that the Spanish edition
utilized by the translator may be any one of those belonging
to Stemma IV.

Though the princeps edition of the Tragicomedia may never be found, Brault agrees with Herriott that the 1507 Zaragoza, the 1514 Valencia, and the 1506 Rome translation are the chief witnesses to be used to reconstruct the lost prototype, a view accepted by both Norton (1966) and Whinnom [1966].

Chapter 3

SOURCES AND TRADITION

1899

Menéndez Pelayo, Marcelino, ed. La Celestina (E. Krapf).
2 vols. Vigo, 1899-1900.

Menéndez Pelayo sees the Pamphilus de Amore as the
prototype of LC. The Pamphilus, written by the twelfth-
century monk Pánfilo Mauriliano, deals with the fulfilled
loves of Pánfilo and Galatea, who are aided by an old woman.
The Corbacho (1438) by Alfonso Martínez de Talavera is the
only Spanish literary antecedent that Ménendez Pelayo suggests.

1902

Foulché-Delbosc, R., "Observations sur La Célestine," Revue Hispanique, IX (1902), 171-179.

Foulché-Delbosc finds traces of Juan de Mena's
Laberinto throughout LC.

1905-1906

Farinelli, Arturo, "Note sulla fortuna del Boccaccio in Ispagna nell'Età Media," Archiv für das Studium der Neueren
Sprachen und Literaturen, CXIV (1905), 397-424; CXV (1906),
368-388; CXVI (1906), 67-96; CXVII (1906), 114-141.

In a series of articles, Farinelli gives an historical
presentation of Boccaccio's and Petrarch's influence in Spain.
Both authors were best known for their moral treatises and
Latin works. For example, the treatise against women in
the Corbacho seems to have been lifted from Boccaccio's De
Claris Mulieribus (Bk. I, Chap. 18). Rojas, as a man
steeped in the culture of his time, made wide use of Boccaccio's and Petrarch's Latin works.

1906

Bonilla y San Martín, A., "Antecedentes del tipo celestinesco
en la literatura latina," Revue Hispanique, XV (1906), 372-
386.
        Bonilla y San Martín traces the development of the
Celestinesque type in Spanish literature. He states that the
type was created by Juan Ruiz, the Arcipreste de Hita, and
perfected by the authors of LC. However, the influence of
Latin writers is not to be minimized since the authors of
LC lived at a time when the humanists made the classics
available. Plautus' Celestinesque type, the anus, closely re-
sembles the character of Celestina, including her affection
for wine. Ovid's Dipsa is also the wine-loving anus (Amor-
um, Bk. I, Elegy 8). Bonilla insists, however, that the
character of Celestina is not to be considered an imitation,
for she is a perennial type in the real world.

1910

Menéndez Pelayo, Marcelino, Orígenes de la novela, Vol.
III. Madrid, 1905-1910.
        Menéndez Pelayo presents the most comprehensive
study of sources up to this date. He cites all the passages
in LC which are drawn from the classics and which demonstrate Rojas' humanistic background. Here again we find
emphasized the contribution of Plautus and Terence to LC.
Rojas assimilated many elements of the Latin comedy, especially the figure of the meretrix and the miles gloriosus.
        Menéndez Pelayo states that the Pamphilus, or, as it
is sometimes called, the Comedia de Vetula, is the principal source of both the Arcipreste de Hita's and Rojas' work.
However, the story of Pamphilus plays a secondary role in
the development of LC, while it is of primary importance in
the Arcipreste.
        Elements from the humanistic Latin comedy are also
considered a source for LC. Three humanistic comedies
are singled out: Philogenia by Ugolino Pisani; Poliscena
attributed to Leonardo di Arezzo; and Chrysis by Enea Silvio
Piccolomini.
        The chief point made is that Rojas' sources are of a
literary and not of a popular nature. A clear example is
his knowledge of Petrarch's Latin works, even though these
contributed to the heavy-handed and pedantic treatment of
many passages of LC. The Prologue is pure plagiarism of
Petrarch's De remediis utriusque fortunae (Bk. 4). Other
passages are taken directly from Rerum memorandarum

(Chap. 5), De vaticiniis, and Epistolae de rebus familiaribus
et variae.
          Boccaccio's Latin works are also a significant source.
Boccaccio influenced Spanish letters more as a humanist and
an erudite scholar than as a poet or a novelist, as had already been pointed out by Farinelli [1905-1906]. De casibus
Principum, the favorite reading matter of Spanish moralists,
left a mark on LC. In Menéndez Pelayo's view, Rojas did
not capture the "alegría sensual," the "pagano contentamiento
de la vida" of Boccaccio. He also points out that the Fiammetta gave Rojas the vehement and "ampulosa" manner of his
last scenes.
          Menéndez Pelayo enumerates other borrowings from
Spanish works and writers: El Corbacho, Juan de Mena,
Alonso de Madrigal (el Tostado), Tractado de Amor, and
Cárcel de Amor.

                              1912

Reynier, Gustave, "La Célestine," Les origines du roman
réaliste. Paris, 1912.
          Reynier cites the Pamphilus as the most direct source
for LC. He attributes to Rojas' pedantic naiveté the abundance of classical citations with which he indiscriminately
loads the language of all his characters.

                              1913

Cejador y Frauca, Julio, ed. La Celestina. Madrid, 1913.
          Cejador asserts that the Prologue of LC is plagiar-
ized from Petrarch [1910, Menéndez Pelayo]. However, he
attributes it to Proaza and not to Rojas [Chapter 2], adding
that Proaza probably knew of the author's predilection for
the works of Petrarch.

Schevill, Rudolph, Ovid and the Renascence in Spain.
Berkeley, 1913.
          Schevill states that LC is a linear descendant of Ovid's
erotic writings. He feels that only the influence of the body
of Ovidian literature and the continuity of the tradition
launched by Ovid can account for some of the prominent characteristics of LC.

                              1915

Cejador y Frauca, Julio, "La Celestina," Historia de la
lengua y literatura castellana desde los orígenes hasta Carlos

V̲, Vol. I. Madrid, 1915.

Cejador's essay contains a good presentation of the critical problems of LC, including a study of the literary sources.

1924

Castro Guisasola, F., Observaciones sobre las fuentes literarias de 'La Celestina'. Madrid, 1924.

In his study of the sources, Castro Guisasola makes a distinction between a direct and an indirect source. He distinguishes between the material which Rojas drew from his own reading of the classics and the material which he obtained from the reading of works which had been influenced by the classics. A further point is that a reference or a resemblance does not necessarily denote influence and therefore does not always constitute a source.

Rojas knew Greek literature only through Spanish or Latin translations. However, the only Greek who had a positive and direct influence on LC is Aristotle.

The debt of LC to the work of Terence has been widely accepted, but its debt to Plautus is questioned by Castro Guisasola. Because of the Terentian character of LC, some critics have considered it to belong with the Latin humanistic comedies written at the end of the fourteenth and beginning of the fifteenth century. Though LC offers some analogies with this dramatic development, Castro Guisasola does not feel that it belongs to the genre. His judgment is based on the fact that Rojas uses Spanish rather than Latin, thus breaking with the erudite tradition. However, Rojas has assimilated Terence's dramatic concept, dramatic techniques and situations. Castro Guisasola reminds us that Menéndez Pelayo [1910] has fully treated the different types, characters and elements that Rojas assimilated from the comedies of Terence.

It remains unknown whether Rojas was directly acquainted with the elegiac comedy which flourished in the twelfth and thirteenth centuries, especially Pamphilus and Paulinus et Polla. But since the best elements of this type are found in the Libro de buen amor, we surmise that Rojas was indirectly influenced by the Pamphilus, so that Pamphilus becomes an influence through the Arcipreste's work.

The Italian sources have already been discussed by Farinelli [1905-1906], Menéndez Pelayo [1910], and Cejador y Frauca [1913]. Castro Guisasola cites about 40 instances where Rojas made use of Petrarch's Latin works. He reproduces Petrarch's and Rojas' texts side by side to show

the degree to which the source was utilized. He shows that
it is the philosophical and moralistic character of Petrarch's
works which caused LC to be a moralizing work, since Rojas
turned most frequently to Petrarch for his sentences.

Castro Guisasola disagrees with Cejador's contention
[1913] that the tasteless adaptations of Petrarch in the additions of LC show Proaza's hand. Castro Guisasola is unable
to distinguish two different manners of adaptation within the
work, except for the Prologue where Petrarch is actually
quoted and the Latin text is given with its translation.

Another question has been whether Rojas read Petrarch's works in the original Latin, since the passages he
used had not yet been translated in his time. Castro Guisasola avers that Rojas took the quotations from the De remediis utriusque fortunae, Epistolae de rebus familiaribus, and
Rerum memorandarum directly from the works, but that the
quotations from the other Latin works were taken from the
Index of Petrarch's Opera published in Basel, 1496 [1961,
Deyermond]. In support of his argument, he points out that
some of the sentences appear in the text of LC in the same
order as they were catalogued in the Index, and that Rojas
sometimes used two successive sentences contiguously in one
phrase.

Castro Guisasola is less certain about the influence of
Boccaccio in LC. He defers to Farinelli and Menéndez Pelayo's presentation, while he personally recognizes Fiammetta as a source. As in the case of Petrarch, he reproduces passages from Boccaccio's works which have a counter-
part in LC.

As for the humanistic theatre, Castro Guisasola does
not feel that Menéndez Pelayo's treatment [1910] is conclu-
sive, except for the analogies with Poliscena. With respect
to the Italian Renaissance comedy, Castro Guisasola agrees
with Menéndez Pelayo that LC preceded this literary development. Furthermore, he states that LC has no relation with
Orfeo (1471) by Poliziano and Timone (1480) by Boiardo.

When it comes to Castilian literature, the most substantial influence which Castro Guisasola finds derives from
the Libro· de buen amor, especially in the figure of Celestina. But he is not convinced by the numerous similarities
which Menéndez Pelayo [1910] discovers in the two works.
Castro Guisasola also finds traces in LC from the poets of
the reign of Juan II, Alfonso V, Enrique IV, and the Reyes
Católicos. Furthermore, he agrees with Foulché-Delbosc
[1902] about the influence of Juan de Mena's Laberinto. As
for the description of the perversity of women, the influence
is clearly that of El corbacho. Linguistically, however,

Castro Guisasola sees an important connection between LC
and the Cárcel de amor by Diego Fernández de San Pedro.
From the study of the sources of LC, it can be con-
cluded that the work is basically in the manner of Terence's
comedies. But since LC was not intended for the stage, no
attention was paid to its length nor to the "excessive crudeza
de los hechos." The extensive borrowings of sentences and
moralizing from the most renowned writers reveals the author's deference to the taste of his times.

1925

Millé y Giménez, Juan, "Acerca de la génesis de la Celestina," Revue Hispanique, LXV (1925), 140-145.
Millé y Giménez suggests that the fundamental conception of LC could have been inspired from one of the stories
in the collection Sales Españolas, Madrid, 1890, edited by
Paz y Melía. This collection contains the "Cuentos que notó
don Juan de Arguijo." Arguijo lived during the reign of Isa-
bel la Católica. The death of Vargas in one of the cuentos
reminds us of Calisto's death both in deed and in concept.

1929

Spitzer, Leo, "Note sur La Celestina," Revista de Filología
Española, XVI (1929), 59-60.
In this note, Spitzer shows an instance of Rojas' in-
debtedness to Aristotle's Ethics [Chapter 1].

1930

Spitzer, Leo, "Zur Celestina," Zeitschrift für Romanische
Philologie, L (1930), 237-240.
Spitzer emphasizes that the motifs he finds in LC belong to the Middle Ages and not to the Renaissance. He sees
a relationship between Calisto's speech and Act I, Scene II
and medieval treatises on love. To prove his point, Spitzer
quotes from medieval French texts from Gelzer's Nature
studie. He makes references to the Minnepoesie in discussing Calisto's preference for his beloved to the glories of the
other world. Calisto's adoration of Melibea, "Melibeo soy,"
belongs to the tradition of provençal poetry. As for Sempronio's protest against historical nobility, it is found already in St. Thomas Aquinas.

1932

Küchler, Walther, "Die erste bekannte Ausgabe der Comedia
de Calisto y Melibea," Romanistiches Jahrbuch, VI (1956),
315-323. (This article was actually written in 1932 and later
found among Küchler's papers.)
    Küchler reaffirms that the outstanding source of LC is
the Libro de buen amor. Küchler maintains that Rojas based
his book not only on observation of reality but also on his
literary knowledge, which he transformed so as to give it an
illusion of reality.

1933

Eberwein, Helena, "Zur Bedeutung der erweiterten Celestina-
fassung," Zur Deutung mittelalterlicher Existenz. Bonn,
1933.
    Miss Eberwein points out that in the medieval tradi-
tion the surrender of a belt, Melibea's cinturón, implies that
the lady is surrendering her love.
    As for the use of magic, Celestina and the lovers
form a pact, that of lovers and a witch, often found in medieval tales. These tales are the literary and historical basis of the Tragicomedia. The use of magic, in this case,
could not be omitted because it contributes a mysterious atmosphere which aggrandizes the skill of the go-between.

1938

Rösler, Margarete, "Beziehungen der Celestina zur Alexius-
legende," Zeitschrift für Romanische Philologie, LXVIII
(1938), 365-367.
    In addition to the already discussed source, Miss Rös-
ler sees a connection between Pleberio's lament and the legend of Alexius. In most versions of the legend, the mother
comes to the body of Alexius while the father is lamenting.
Miss Rösler finds it peculiar that in LC Pleberio is alone.
But since he does mention the mother, Miss Rösler feels
that Rojas has merely made a thoughtless use of his source.

1939

Dávalos, Balbino, "Las dos elegías que engendraron La Celestina," Letras de México, II (1939), 7-8.
    Dávalos publishes his own translation from the elegies
of Propertius (Elegy V, Bk. IV) and Ovid's satire "Est
Quaedem - Quicumque volet cognoscere Lenam," both of which

allude to a go-between and which he believes helped awaken
in the mind of Rojas the idea of LC.

Miranda, Edelmira Esther, "Safo en La Celestina y en la
'Imitación de diversos' de fray Luis de León," Boletín de la
Academia Argentina de Letras, VII (1939), 577-584.
          Miss Miranda states that Rojas' quotations from Sap-
pho are taken from Mena's work and from Ovid's Epistle XV,
which he probably read in Latin. As for Fray Luis de León's
work, she does not consider Rojas a source even though the
poem cited offers some similarities with LC.

1942

Alonso, Amado, "Sobre antecedentes de La Celestina," Revista de Filología Hispánica, IV (1942), 266-268.
          Alonso sees no connection between the function of Cel-
estina and the old woman who aids the lovers in the Historia
de los amores de Bayad y Riyad, published by Alois Richard
Nykl. The role of the old woman who often comes to the aid
of the lovers in Arabian tales does not correspond to the social function performed by Celestina, because the "celestinesco está en ayudar por oficio y con espíritu demoníaco."

1943

Sánchez-Castañer, Francisco, "Antecedentes celestinescos en
las Cantigas de Santa María," Mediterráneo, I (1943), 33-90.
          Sánchez-Castañer boasts that he is the first scholar
to point out the thematic concordances between LC and the
Cantigas of Alfonso X, particularly "Miracles performed vol-
untarily by the Virgin" (LXIV) and "Miracles performed by
images" (CCCXII).
          He asserts that the first literary sketch of the Celes-
tinesque type in "lengua romance" is to be found in the Can-
tiga LXIV. The chief difference between the text of the Cantigas and the characterization in Rojas' work lies in that the
former used several old women as go-betweens to aid the
Caballero while in the Tragicomedia these are narrowed down
to one: Celestina.
          In the Cantiga CCCXII, he finds outlined the charac-
ters of Calisto and Melibea.

1944

Grismer, Raymond Leonard, The Influence of Plautus in
Spain before Lope de Vega. New York, 1944.

Grismer studies the relation of the Plautine plays to
what he calls "the novels of the Celestine genre." He notes
that the use of an argument, which was sometimes preceded
by a prologue, shows a possible imitation of Latin comedies.
So does the fact that the name Tragicomedia was first used
in Plautus' Amphitryon. On the other hand, he points out
that the aside, used so effectively by the clever servants of
the Plautine plays, is neglected in these dramatic novels, oc-
curring infrequently and without the forcefulness it has in the
Latin comedies.

Heller, J. L., and R. L. Grismer, "Seneca in the Celestinesque Novel," Hispanic Review, XII (1944), 29-48.
Certain works of a moralizing character were ascribed
to Seneca in the Middle Ages and early Renaissance. These
seem to have circulated more widely even than Seneca's genuine works. One of these is the Senecae Proverbia, translated into Spanish as early as 1482. This is a compilation
of proverbs or sententiae arranged alphabetically and drawn
from two sources. The first portion, A to N, is a collection of quotations culled from the verses of Mimes by Publi-
lius Syrus; the second part, N to the end of the alphabet,
contains a collection of maxims in prose taken from the Liber
de moribus ascribed to Seneca. The Proverbia is a major
source for the proverbs in LC.
Heller and Grismer show that the Proverbia is the
most popular source for the maxims used by both the authors
of LC and the novels derived from it. Moreover, the Publi-
lian references are more popular than those derived from the
Liber de moribus. This choice reflects a greater response
to the cynical worldly wisdom of the characters of the Roman
mimes. The authors note that greater use is made of the
Proverbia itself than of the Spanish version.

1950

Bayo, Marcial José, "Nota sobre La Celestina," Clavileño,
I (1950), 48-53.
In reviewing the bibliography dealing with the sources
of LC, Bayo deplores the emphasis given to the Latin and
erudite sources to the detriment of the influence of Castilian
writers. He finds that not sufficient attention has been given
to the reminiscences of Manrique's Coplas abounding especially in the last three acts of the Tragicomedia, though he admits that the treatment of the theme of death is closely related to stoic and agnostic tendencies.

Menéndez Pidal, Ramón, "La lengua en tiempos de los Reyes
Católicos," Cuadernos Hispano-Americanos, XIII (1950), 9-
24.
        Menéndez Pidal suggests that "las blasfemias de Calis-
to en adoración de Melibea" are directly derived from the
poetry of the reign of Juan II. He notes in particular the
connection with the Cancionero where the religious vocabulary
is used in a profane context.

1953

Vallata, Juan de, Poliodorus, ed. José María Casas Homs.
Madrid, 1953.
        Casas notes that the points of contact between LC and
Poliodorus are more numerous and more easily recognizable
than in the case of other acknowledged sources of LC.
        He outlines the parallel structures of the two works,
pointing to the similarities with Rojas' statements about his
authorship, age, and manner of composition. In addition,
the lovers, go-between, and servants play similar roles in
the development of the dramatic action of both works.
        Casas does not suggest that Rojas knew Poliodorus,
but that the similarities between the two works point to the
existence of an "ambiente dramático estudiantil." The Latin
Poliodorus belongs to the genre of Spanish humanistic comedies which has not received proper critical attention.

1954

Yndurain, Francisco, "Una nota a La Celestina," Revista de
Filología Española, XXXVIII (1954), 278-281.
        Yndurain attempts to show how the reference to the
gallo and his calling the gallinas is derived from the "Poema
del gallo," a Latin poem with which Rojas was probably familiar.

1955

Webber, Edwin J., "Tragedy and Comedy in the Celestina,"
Hispania, XXXV (1955), 318-320.
        According to Webber, it is interesting to note that the
tragedies of Seneca have not been recognized as a potential
source for LC, and yet the latter has various reminiscences
of the Senecan tragedies. For example, while the pursuit of
Hippolytus by Phaedra is the reverse of the situation in LC,
the action nevertheless follows a strikingly similar pattern.
Webber also notes verbal similarities.

1956

Gilman, Stephen, The Art of 'La Celestina'. Madison, 1956.
     Gilman penetratingly defines the thematic and philo-
sophical role of Petrarch's De remediis in LC [Cahpter 5].
He divides the utilization of Petrarch into three stages, each
stage revealing an increasing depth of thematic understanding.
Gilman disagrees with Menéndez Pelayo's [1910] denial of
Petrarch's influence on LC. Availing himself of the same
examples, Gilman discusses the extent of Petrarch's penetration into the thematic art of LC. Gilman observes that
the "horizontal commonplaces of the De remediis ... are by
their very nature adjusted to the needs of dialogic engagement, to situations involving the unmeshment of spoken consciousness." But in none of the phases does the question of
influence apply. Petrarch's work does not radiate its doctrine into LC, but rather, in order that the theme might be
expressed more effectively, Rojas assimilates concepts and
implications "to create his own century, his original version
of the theme of his time."

1958

Webber, Edwin J., "The Celestina as an Arte de Amores,"
Modern Philology, LV (1958), 145-153.
     Webber points to the existence, in the late Middle
Ages and the early Renaissance, of an amatory genre which
was related to the concept of comedy. He refers to this
genre as the arte de amores. The arte de amores need not
be wholly or exclusively dramatic, for even the sentimental
novel must be included within the concept.
     Webber shows that the generic origin of LC is to be
found in the arte de amores. Even the initial intrigue, the
love affair of Calisto and Melibea, is an appropriate choice
for an arte de amores.
     The basic story, however, existed in its original dra-
matic form in the elegiac comedy Pamphilus, reappears in
the Libro de buen amor in a narrative version, and is found
again in dramatic form in Leonardo Bruni's Poliscena. Webber notes similarities between LC and Poliscena, not only in
the basic intrigue, but also in the manner of establishing the
trajectory of the action, as well as in certain external features
of the work. From this he concludes that Rojas was familiar
with Bruni's work.

1961

Deyermond, A. D., The Petrarchan Sources of 'La Celestina'. Oxford, 1961.
    For Deyermond, the purpose of an examination of Ro-
jas' Petrarchan sources is twofold: first, it throws light on
the authorship and bibliographical problems; and second, a
realization of how far Rojas modifies his Petrarchan original
and how far he adheres to it can tell us something about his
stylistic creation and more about his moral and emotional
world.
    Rojas used the Basel 1496 Opera, which contains a
large number of Latin works and ends with an Index to the
sententia and exempla contained in the volume.   The Index
of this volume should be considered one of the Latin Petrarchan sources.
    Deyermond's conclusions substantiate earlier critical
studies which showed that Act I does not contain a single
verifiable borrowing.   It is clear therefore that its author did
not use the Index of Petrarch's Opera.
    Acts II-XVI of the original version, however, contain
53 definite borrowings from the Index to the Opera, and on
nine occasions Rojas borrows a group of sententiae or exempla which are consecutive in the Index but not in the text
of Petrarch's works.   Again, Deyermond's findings substantiate earlier studies which show that Rojas mostly used the Index alone, but sometimes looked up references in the text
and extracted additional material from it.   Deyermond establishes Rojas' dependence on the Index as a primary source
when consecutive entries are used.   The Index was used independently, in the customary medieval way, as an autonomous list of sententiae.   Thus, it is as much a source in
its own right as are any of Petrarch's Latin works.
    In the 1502 version, the evidence is of the same na-
ture as that for the Comedia.   Deyermond finds 17 definite
borrowings from the Index.   The independent use of the Index
predominates to an even greater extent.
    In the 16-act version, most of the borrowings come
from the "A" section of the Index.   Deyermond supposes
that Rojas was familiar with the Index for some time and
that he was especially interested in what Petrarch had to say
on adversitas, amor, and amicitia.
    Independently of the Index, De Remediis, Book I, was
Rojas' most important single Petrarchan source, particularly
in the Comedia.   The curiously undigested form in which the
borrowings from De Remediis, Book I, and the Preface of
Book II, are used by Rojas in the Tragicomedia, suggests

that by 1502 Rojas was either less able or less willing to
fuse a borrowing with the original work so as to make the
whole original. De Rebus familiaribus is a major source for
the 1502 version.

Deyermond states that De Remediis, De Rebus familiaribus, and Bucolicum Carmen are the only works whose text
is directly used by Rojas. Rojas may have been familiar
with the Canzoniere and I Trionfi, but he makes no textual
borrowings from them in LC.

In a few passages, LC is markedly Petrarchan in tone
without actual borrowing or reminiscence. At the beginning
of Act IV, for example, in Celestina's complaint against old
age and her denunciation of wealth and youth, Rojas takes
Petrarchan material and blends it for his own purposes so as
to produce a scene which is original and convincing, and
whose ultimate moral tendency diverges sharply from Petrarch's Christian thought. Usually, however, when Rojas
wanted to express Petrarch's views, he preferred to do so in
Petrarch's own words. It is clear from the number of conscious borrowings that Rojas had Petrarch's Opera before
him as he wrote. Mere reminiscences are scarce in individual passages but Petrarch's attitudes are reflected in the work
as a whole. The unevenness in the distribution of borrowings
in the acts suggests that Rojas borrowed spontaneously as he
wrote. Celestina's speeches contain the greatest number of
borrowings. Sixty-four of the borrowings occur in the
speeches of the low-life characters, and 33 in those of the
aristocrats, a proportion which for Deyermond refutes Menéndez Pelayo's views on Rojas' supposed pedantry in his use
of Petrarch.

Deyermond sees no conscious design in the absence of
Petrarchan borrowings in Act I. He thus disagrees with Gilman [1956] who feels that Rojas purposely kept such borrowings out of Act I on the grounds that they were out of place
in it, while he found them suitable for the rest of LC.

Rojas uses Petrarch in three ways. He takes over
specifically Petrarchan views on life--which come entirely
from Book I and the Preface of Book II of De Remediis; he
uses Petrarch's general proverbial or moral philosophy; and
he follows Petrarch's stock of classical allusions. But while
Petrarch is his chief source of material and responsible for
much of his sententiousness, he does not influence Rojas'
style. Most important, though, Rojas drew heavily on Petrarch for his outlook on life, his work does not simply reflect Petrarch's views.

Deyermond, A. D., "The Text-book Mishandled: Andreas

Capellanus and the Opening Scene of La Celestina," Neophilologus, XLV (1961), 218-221.

Deyermond states that the prestige and diffusion of
Andreas' treatise De Amore, Book III, was such that it would
almost certainly be familiar to a Spanish university student
of the second half of the fifteenth century.

Deyermond finds a good deal of evidence in Calisto's
opening speech that the author of Act I made a conscious use
of Andreas' dialogues.

Gilman, Stephen, and Michael J. Ruggerio, "Rodrigo de Reinosa and La Celestina," Romanische Forschungen, LXXIII
(1961), 255-284.

An inventory of the belongings of Rojas' wife, Leonor
Alvarez, includes nine books not mentioned in the published
catalogue of Rojas' library [1930, Valle Lersundi].   One of
these is Rodrigo de Reinosa's Coplas de las comadres.   A
close examination of this work lead the authors to believe
that it was an important source for LC, and decisively influenced the portrait of Celestina.   It seems that Reinosa
composed the Coplas in the early 1480's.

The authors are primarily concerned with showing
what the author of Act I borrowed from Reinosa's Coplas and
how he went about it.   They believe that this author combined Sancha, the local alcahueta, and Mari García, the
witch, into the composite figure of Celestina.   This alone
would indicate that the Coplas served as a source for LC
rather than the reverse (Menéndez Pelayo [1910] considered
Reinosa's work posterior to the composition of LC).   The
textual relationship between the two works is so striking that
the derivation is self-evident.

There are many specific parallels in the description
of Mari García with details of Celestina which Pármeno com-
municates in Act I.   But there are signs of an apparent re-
ordering of material which indicates that the author of Act I
changed and adapted the Coplas according to his own artistic
purposes.

Three indications point to the Coplas as a source for
Act I:
    1. Celestina combines brujería and alcahuetería.   In the
       Coplas Reinosa apportioned these two professions among
       three separate types.   All continuations or imitations,
       however, continue the single character established by
       Celestina.
    2. Pármeno's description of Celestina systematically gath-
       ers references, to the art of repairing maidenheads,
       which are widely dispersed in the Coplas.   It indicates

a reorganization of material.
3. The Coplas are more copious in their listing, less accurate in spelling, and several items are given full
   nomenclature, whereas Act I is more accurate in spelling, and only gives an abbreviated form.
   The authors consider the parallels between the two
texts decisive.

Lida de Malkiel, María Rosa, Two Spanish Masterpieces:
The 'Book of Good Love' and 'La Celestina'. Urbana, 1961.
       See Note, Chapter 1, Malkiel, 1961.

Pabst, Walter, "¿Ay tal mujer nascida en el mundo?, Zur
göttlichen Abkunft der Celestina," Homenaje a Dámaso Alonso.
Madrid, 1961, pp. 557-576.
      According to Pabst, the scene of Melibea's suicide co-
incides in more than 12 particulars with the suicide of Dido.
For example, both occur at dawn; in both cases the suicide
sends a female messenger; both use pretexts to keep relations and servants away. The most remarkable similarity is
in the scenic background. Both take a last look at the sea,
the harbor, the ships. There is no artistic preparation or
necessity in LC for this final landscape. It is evidently a
literary allusion to Virgil.
      So is Pleberio's allusion to the ships he had built.
This echoes the Aeneid, (Bk. IV, 537 ff.) where Dido la-.
ments, "Why did I allow these ships to be rebuilt?" Pleberio's phrase, again, has no function, antecedent or importance in the work--it is merely a classical echo.
      It is also notable that in both Virgil and Rojas the
the cause of all the miseries, Venus and Celestina, are absent when the two women commit suicide. From these analogies, we conclude that there is an inner connection between Venus and Celestina. Celestina exhibits suggestions
of the non-human, the super-human. She is the final metamorphosis of Venus.
      There are analogous echoes from the Aeneid in the
coming together of the lovers. Pabst points to a number of
details, for example Dido pities and harbors the shipwrecked
Trojan; Melibea pities Calisto and gives him her belt. Venus
gets the assistance of Amor; Celestina that of Sempronio,
etc.
      Celestina is no longer Venus, but she derives from
Venus. However, she derives not only from Virgil's Venus,
but also from Boccaccio's Venus in Elegia di Madonna Fiammetta. Pabst also details Rojas' indebtedness to Bocaccio's
Venus. Rojas secularized and humanized the numinous fig-

ures of Virgil and Boccaccio.   Instead of evil striking from
above (vertically), it now strikes horizontally, from man to
man.   The goddess has been degraded to witch and cheat.

Trotter, G. D., "The Coplas de las comadres of Rodrigo de
Reynosa and La Celestina," Homenaje a Dámaso Alonso.
Madrid, 1961, pp. 527-537.
       Trotter also establishes that a close textual resem-
blance exists between the Coplas and LC, and he too points
to the passage in Act I where Pármeno describes Celestina's
way of life.   His feeling is that one author plagiarized the
other, but he is unable to commit himself further since the
pliegos contain little or no textual evidence of their date of
composition or place of printing.   According to Trotter, it
is impossible to solve this problem of textual filiation unless
further discoveries are made.

1962

Castro, Américo, 'La Celestina' como contienda literaria.
Madrid, 1962.
       For Castro's view of LC as a rupture with the me-
dieval tradition, see Chapter 6.

Lida de Malkiel, María Rosa, La originalidad artística de
'La Celestina'.   Buenos Aires, 1961.
       Roman comedy--Terentian comedy in particular--
served as model for a great number of technical devices
found in LC.   But it did not contribute to the story, the tone,
or the depiction of characters and milieu.   Rojas exhibits a
fundamental artistic divergence from his models which has
not been properly understood by most scholars.   LC, however, is in close relation with the elegiac comedy in its use
of a contemporary setting.
       Humanistic comedy offers LC an example of stylistic
variety in the use of the aside and in the conception of time
and place.   The flexible conception of time and the great
mobility in the action allow a realistic dramatic development.
Many humanistic comedies are primarily cuadros de costumbres of contemporary life.   Much in evidence are their tendency to satire, not because they were conceived with a didactic aim, but simply because they enjoyed exposing human
weaknesses and vices, especially of clerics and women.
Humanistic comedy allowed a reworking of these themes in
an entirely new manner, and an assimilation of situations
and elements from other sources.   LC shares the technical,
linguistic, and thematic elements of the humanistic comedy,

but it offers several characteristics which are in contrast to
it, the most obvious is the elaborate style of its prose and
its spiritual concept of love.

For Mrs. Malkiel, a comparison between LC and its
predecessors enables us to appreciate the complexity and
originality of Rojas' art, in spite of its varied literary indebtedness.

The authors of LC, using as a model the Roman drama which has no scenic indications, treat the stage directions artistically, incorporating them into the dramatic text.
Elegiac comedy indicated stage directions in the narrative
sections. Humanistic comedy together with Roman comedy
served as a guide for the use of dialogued stage directions
in LC.

Mrs. Malkiel divides the dialogue into several typical
forms and determines the literary antecedents for each type.
For the rhetorical tone, the authors of LC used Plautus as
a departure, but they gave it great variety of content and extended its use to all types of characters and situations. Humanistic comedy, following the example of Plautus and Terence, assigned a significant role to the tirade and to the
moralizing and erudite exhortation. In LC, the long tirade
or invective is designed to suit the particular character who
utters it. Terence is responsible for the short lines of dialogue, but humanistic comedy showed the authors of LC how
to use it in a realistic manner. As for the use of the monologue, elegiac comedy and the sentimental novel of the Renaissance gave the authors of LC a model for the depiction of
inner conflicts.

The cinematographic technique which allows mobility
in space derives directly from the conception of space of the
humanistic comedy and indirectly from the medieval scenario
and from a free interpretation of the ancient classical theatre.
The free conception of time is inherited from medieval drama.

It is the weight of courtly tradition which causes the
protagonists to proceed as if the possibility of marriage was
denied to them a priori. The structure of the roman courtois
determines the trajectory of the love story in LC. The authors of LC allow a traditional situation to function within a
realistic framework. This external motivation is based on
the chivalric-sentimental literature and is closely related to
other situations in Act I--all of which have the same literary
filiation. The use of magic is a contribution of the elegiac
Latin poets.

In Rojas' handling of irony, Mrs. Malkiel finds that
both Roman comedy and Greek tragedy--which she believes
Rojas knew--played an important role.

The doubling of characters occurs frequently in Roman comedy, where it underscores the characterization or complicates the intrigue. Elegiac comedy also affords examples of doubling. For the device of repetition of situations, however, LC is indebted to the roman courtois. Humanistic comedy resorts to duplication of characters for superficial theatricality and animation. Doubling in LC, on the other hand, is transformed into an essential part of the dramatic presentation.

The Tragicomedia makes use of the sentimental literature of its time for the portrayal of its hero. Calisto's delight in exhibiting his suffering is a distinctive trait of the troubadour lyric and of the sentimental novel. The genesis of the inactive lover is to be found in Graeco-Roman comedy but in LC the character differs from the type found in Plautus and Terence. Actually, the authors of LC inherited the ineffectual, sensual lover from humanistic comedy. Fiammetta is the most important source for Calisto. Traditionally, the victim of love was a woman. But it took all the weight of the love lyrics and the sentimental novel to enable the authors of LC to assign the role of the irrational lover to a man. If the tradition of Roman comedy set the type of the idle lover, Boccaccio's Fiammetta was the decisive model for the individualization of the character. Piccolomini's Historia de duobus amantibus, however, exercised a completely negative influence on the Tragicomedia. There could be no greater contrast than between Calisto and Eurialo. As for Diego de San Pedro, LC derived from his protagonists the ineffectual lover whose life is spent "no sólo en amar sino en mirarse amar."

There is decidedly no literary model for the character of Melibea. But the authors did incorporate into the characterization single traits found in sentimental literature from antiquity to the fifteenth century. Mrs. Malkiel finds clear and decisive contacts with Euripides' Hyppolitus. The traditional love situation of LC, however, has its roots in the medieval poems under Ovidian influence. The sentimental novel contributed many details to the portrayal of Melibea, the most important of these being the death that she chooses. The circumstances of her death, however, coincide with those of Dido's.

The character of Celestina displays a general similarity with that of the lena and servus fallax, but it is basically different. The lena of Plautus and Terence abhors her profession, whereas Celestina shows singular dignity and professional pride. Furthermore, the essential role of Celestina is that of seduction, whereas the Roman slave is needed

for planning a clever plot. He endangers his life purely as
a literary convention, whereas Celestina does so to satisfy
her avarice. Only in her secondary traits can Celestina be
compared to the lena of Roman elegy, namely in her dealings
with the supernatural. Elegiac comedy, the fabliaux and the
roman courtois develop the character of the go-between,
which anticipates the essential activity of Celestina: the coming and going between hero and heroine until their passion is
fulfilled. The imitation of Pamphilus introduced the note of
avarice in the Libro de buen amor, but only Rojas saw the
tragic potential of avarice, previously conceived as a humorous trait. The Corbacho contributed to the particular vision
of reality and its stylistic expression found in many passages
of LC. As for humanistic comedy, it gave dramatic freedom
to LC, an interest in the lower classes in the development
of the action but not in the portrayal of characters.

The tradition of Plautus and Terence, reinforced by
the Latin comedy of the Middle Ages and of the Renaissance,
suggested to the authors of the Tragicomedia the substantial
role of the servant, as well as some situations and traits.
But LC departs from the inherited concept of the servus
fallax as an instrument of his master. Rojas substitutes for
the slave a person who is artistically elaborated in his concrete individuality.

As for the mochachas, there is an implicit condemnation of the courtesan in Roman comedy. But in LC, the authors exhibit a positive attitude. The Libro de buen amor
and the Corbacho give Rojas a point of departure for some
of his dramatic scenes, especially the envy and hatred of the
courtesans toward Melibea. Humanistic comedy introduced
the possibility of artistic sympathy for the courtesans, and
it showed the way for a progressive incorporation of the mochachas into the drama.

According to Mrs. Malkiel, Centurio has none of the
characteristics of the miles gloriosus and the lenus of Roman comedy. On the contrary, his basic characteristics are
alien to his supposed prototype. His model is not to be
found in Latin literature but in the Spanish reality of Rojas'
time. His immediate success is proof that readers recognized in him a real type from contemporary society.

1963

Ayllón, Cándido, "Petrarch and Fernando de Rojas," Romanic Review, LIV (1963), 81-94.

Ayllón emphasizes that Rojas, though utilizing Petrarchan material, is able to express his own feelings and atti-

tudes through his characters. For Rojas' thematic and philosophical indebtedness to Petrarch, see Chapter 5.

Berndt, Erna Ruth, Amor, Muerte y Fortuna en 'La Celestina'. Madrid, 1963.
        Miss Berndt discusses in detail the traditional literary
elements whic helped form Rojas' concept of the theme of
Love, Death and Fortune [Chapter 5]. Her book is essentially a summary of the cultural environment which Rojas inherited.

Heugas, Pierre, ed. La Célestine. Paris, 1963.
        According to Heugas, LC is a work belonging to the
erudite tradition of the fifteenth century. Rojas followed the
example of the first author in the use of his sources and in
his adherence to fifteenth-century values. His orginality consists in the fact that the sources are translated into good romance and properly integrated into the work's moral aim.
LC was written to be read aloud before a public of clerics
who knew that poets were to be read for edifying purposes
[Chapter 6].

1964

Wardropper, Bruce W., "Pleberio's Lament for Melibea and
the Medieval Elegiac Tradition," Modern Language Notes,
LXXIX (1964), 140-152.
        Wardropper sees Pleberio's lament as springing from
both the tradition of the Latin planctus and the epic elegy in
the vernacular. The epic introduced a note of personal grief
and Pleberio, like his epic predecessors, is concerned with
his personal loss [Chapter 5]. The fifteenth century, on the
other hand, expressed its grief by giving a perfect consolation to the mourner. The good death capped the good life.
Jorge Manrique expressed the art of living well and dying
well, assenting the orthodox Christian answer to the problem
of death. The elegiac tradition, however, allowed Pleberio
an areligious expression of grief.

1966

Richthofen, Erich von, "El Corbacho: las interpolaciones y
la deuda de La Celestina," Homenaje a Rodríguez-Moñino,
Vol. II. Madrid, 1966, pp. 115-120.
        It has been established that there are strong thematic
and stylistic resemblances between the Corbacho and LC, especially the latter's first act. Both authors are writing in

reproval of loco amor. This leads to the speculation that
both works belong to the "corriente talaverana." The fact
that many late additions were composed for the Corbacho
and that Act I of LC antedates the rest of the work puts the
end of the one and the beginning of the other close together
in time. Richthofen strongly encourages further investigation.

Toro-Garland, Fernando de, "La Celestina en Las mil y una
noches," Revista de Literatura, XXIX (1966), 5-33.
        Toro-Garland shows that Rojas could have found char-
acters similar to those he depicts in the Arabic tales of A
Thousand and One Nights. No one, he argues, has given
enough weight to this collection as a source of materials for
Rojas. Toro-Garland bolsters his argument with copious illustrations.

                            1967

Whinnom, Keith, Spanish Literary Historiography: Three
Forms of Distortion [Inaugural Lecture]. Exeter, 1967.
        The substance of Whinnon's remarkable lecture, as
indicated by its title, is a very broad one. Whinnom's purpose is to correct an erroneous view of literary history
which tends to emphasize what has survived for us rather than
what mattered in the past itself.
        As far as Rojas is concerned, he should be placed in
the general stream of European literature, overwhelmingly
in Latin, rather than in a continuum of specifically Spanish
works, because such a continuum did not exist.
        With respect to the Libro de buen amor, which is
universally taken as a major source of LC, Whinnom denies
the alleged indebtedness of Rojas to the Arcipreste de Hita.
It is hardly conceivable that an amateur humanist like Rojas,
whose literary hero is Petrarch, would have taken a popular
book like the Libro de buen amor as his literary model.
Moreover, the Libro de buen amor could not have been known
to any writer at the end of the fifteenth century, for it suf-
fered an eclipse from 1449 to 1790.
        According to Whinnom, Rojas' reading was probably
far less extensive than is commonly supposed.

                            1968

Bell, A. Robert, "Folklore and Mythology in La Celestina,"
Medieval Epic to the "Epic" Theatre of Brecht, ed. R. P.
Armato and J. M. Spalek. Los Angeles, 1968.

See Chapter 5.

Groult, Pierre, "Une sources méconnue de La Celestina,"
Les Lettres Romanes, XXII (1968), 207-227.
        A source of LC which has been unjustifiably neglected
by most scholars, with the exception of Lida de Malkiel
[1962], is the "Exemplum de canicula lacrimante" in the
Disciplina Clericalis by Pedro Alonso. The points of contact between the two works are many, but most astonishing
is the resemblance between the two go-betweens.
        Alonso's Exemplum, a tale originally drawn from the
Sendebar, was modified in later centuries and reappeared in
a fifteenth-century version by Sánchez de Vercial.
        Though enumerating the points of contact with the
source, Groult assigns greater significance to the elements
which Rojas added to the tale [Chapter 6].
        The Exemplum of Pedro Alonso, according to Groult,
is the source of LC which has furnished all the essential
elements of both the characters and the theme of the drama.
Four different versions of this Exemplum exist and it is
quite reasonable to suppose that the authors of LC knew all
four. The version by Sánchez de Vercial, however, is the
one that is closest to the theme of LC, and is probably its
immediate source.

                                1969

Heugas, Pierre, "Variation sur un portrait: de Mélibée à
Dulcinée," Bulletin Hispanique, LXXI (1969), 5-30.
        Heugas notes that the description of the physical
beauty of Melibea given in Act I, while conforming in its details to medieval literary convention, offers us an example
of a parody of that convention. This first author of LC
achieves this parody by juxtaposing Calisto's exalted description of Melibea with Sempronio's misogynistic responses.
Thus the dialogue between Calisto and Sempronio offers two
discordant voices and serves insidiously to demythicize her.
Sempronio's rebuttal succeeds in taking Melibea off the ped-
estal where Calisto had put her. Moreover, the anti-por-
trait of Melibea is introduced later in the work by Elicia
and Aureusa.
        Whereas the authors of LC demythicize the Lady of
medieval tradition, Cervantes uses Dulcinea to mock her
openly. The chief motif Rojas and Cervantes have in common is the portrayal of the "belle dame sans merci." But
Rojas and Cervantes also have this trait in common: both
display the same derisive attitude toward the traditionally

glorified Lady.

1970

Lorenzo-Rivero, Luis, "La Celestinesca come creación de Castilla la Nueva," <u>Duquesne Hispanic Review</u>, VII (1970), 1-4.
    See Chapter 5 and 7.

Chapter 4

THE INFLUENCE OF 'LA CELESTINA'

1895

Wolf, Ferdinand, "Sobre el drama español - La Celestina y sus traducciones," La España Moderna, LXXX (1895), 99-123.

Wolf finds that LC exhibits dramatic and artistic elements which are peculiar to the Spanish national drama and which influenced the development of the "comedia natural en prosa" and of the "comedia de costumbres," a genre which Torres Naharro was first to cultivate. He states that the influence of LC is first found in the works of Lope de Rueda and Juan de Timoneda. Wolf discusses the translations of Bülow and Germond de Lavigne, both of which reproduce in German and French even the peculiarities of the original in style and diction. But passages which are considered offensive were omitted or bowdlerized.

1899

Menéndez Pelayo, Marcelino, ed. La Celestina (E. Krapf). 2 vols. Vigo, 1899-1900.

Menéndez Pelayo lists the many Spanish works which are based on LC. He points to the more daring and licentious character of the numerous imitations of LC. He speaks as an indignant Victorian when referring to the Tebaida, Serafina, and Hipólita.

1902

Farinelli, Arturo, "Wilhelm Fehse, Cristof Wirsungs deutsche Celestinäubersetzungen," Deutsche Literaturzeitung, XXIII (1902), 2786-2794. (Review of Fehse's doctoral dissertation printed in Halle, 1902.)

Farinelli defends his own original statement that LC enjoyed popularity in Germany in the sixteenth century and that it had a great impact on German literature, in spite of

Fehse's statements to the contrary.   As proof, Farinelli
points to the fact that Wirsung saw the need to make two different translations of LC at two different times of his life.
Having examined these translations, Farinelli agrees with
Fehse that the second one shows a riper style, more careful
workmanship, and an improvement in his knowledge of Italian,
this being the language from which Wirsung probably translated.
     Farinelli contends that LC was also very popular in
Italy, thus disagreeing with Croce* who found no other reference to it in the sixteenth century than one in Geraldi Cintio's "Discorso intorno al comporre delle commedie e delle
tragedie" [1931, Mazzoni].
     *[Croce, Benedetto, Ricerche Ispano-Italiche.   Naples,
1896.]

1903

Rosenbach, A. S. W., "The Influence of the Celestina in the
early English drama," Jahrbuch der Deutschen Shakespeare-
Gesellschaft, XXXIX (1903), 43-61.
     Rosenbach attributes to LC an even greater role than
that claimed by other critics.   He states that LC influenced
and molded the dramatic art not only of Spain, but also of
Italy, France, Germany, and England, and that LC "exerted
its virile influence into the fabric of continental literature."
Rosenbach's article deals mostly with the Interlude of Calisto
and Melibea, published around 1540 [or 1525, according to
Ugualde (1954)] by John Rastell.   This is the first play in
English dramatic literature indebted to a continental source.
Rosenbach wishes to prove that this first Calisto and Melibea
in the English language is of primary significance in the development of English drama.   The story of the Interlude is
a condensed version of only the first four acts of LC.   At
the end of the Interlude, Melibea confesses her guilt to her
father but does not kill herself.   But then, she had not taken
the final step with Calisto.   Rosenbach supposes that the
translator used a Spanish text printed in Italy.   He dismisses
the attribution of the Interlude to Rastell in favor of a pupil
of Juan Luis Vives [1954, Ugualde; 1955, Schoeck].

1910

Menéndez Pelayo, Marcelino, Orígenes de la novela, Vol.
III.   Madrid, 1905-1910.
     Menéndez Pelayo surveys the field of translations of
LC.   He evaluates the translations by Wirsung of 1520 and

by Mabbe of 1631 as works which have artistic value in themselves. While the first French translation was by Jacques
de Lavardin in 1527, he considers the better one to be that
by Germond de Lavigne in 1841. As for the English version
by John Rastell, it is actually an adaptation in verse. The
German scholar Gaspar Barth translated LC into Latin in
1624 with the title Pornoboscodidascalus, preceded by an ex-
travagant introduction. Menéndez Pelayo feels that Barth was
more lucid when he worked on the translation than when he
wrote the introduction.

Menéndez Pelayo gives a detailed presentation of the
influence of LC on Spanish letters, beginning with Torres
Naharro, who shows in his theatre a preference for the sentimental and amorous aspect of LC. He distinguishes between
works influenced by LC and actual imitations. To the former
belong Lope de Rueda's El rufián cobarde, Lope de Vega's
La Dorotea and El caballero de Olmedo. Traces of LC are
also found in Cervantes and in Calderón. He devotes a whole
chapter to the works belonging to the category of deliberate
imitations of LC, beginning with Pedro Manuel de Urrea's
verse Egloga de la Tragicomedia de Calisto y Melibea of
1513.

1912

Reynier, Gustave, "La Célestine," Les origines du roman
réaliste.   Paris, 1912.

Reynier also lists the important translations of LC,
beginning with the Italian one by Alfonso Ordóñez of 1506.
His study deals with the influences of LC on French literature, beginning with Macette by Regnier. He shows that
Rojas' influence was not limited to the theatre but that
French storytellers, including Rabelais, were also familiar
with his work. Reynier points out that the least conventional character of the French comedy of the sixteenth century
is that of the go-between. This character is highly realistic
because Rojas had furnished a model "d'une verité saisis-
sante." Jean de la Taille uses the go-between in Corrivaux,
Larivey in the Veuve. The fact that Rojas chose an intermediary form between the novel and drama gave him a great
deal of freedom, whereas the French comic writers who imitated him were bound by the rules of the comic art form,
whose artificial standards made it difficult for them to match
his realism. In addition, the sixteenth century was not prepared to accept crude Spanish realism and Rojas' pessimistic concept of life, all of which explains why LC's influence
was of a secondary nature. Above all, LC helped to counter-

balance somewhat the chivalric convention and the sentimental idealism of that century.

1922

Mazzei, P., "Per la fortuna di due opere spagnole in Italia,"
Revista de Filología Española, IX (1922), 384-386.
     Mazzei disagrees with Croce's contention [1902, Fari-
nelli] that LC did not influence Italian writers of the sixteenth
century. He maintains that because of the many translations
into Italian in the sixteenth century, a certain effect was
bound to be felt in the Italian comedies of that period [1954,
Boughner]. He cites Iacopo Nardi's I due felici rivali (1513)
in which the figure of the braggart appears for the first time
in an erudite comedy. Nardi's Trasone closely follows Centurio, sometimes echoes him verbatim.

1923

Allen, Warner H., ed. La Celestina, trans. by James
Mabbe. London, 1923.
     Allen publishes Mabbe's translation of LC with a criti-
cal study of the problems of LC [Chapter 1, 1923, Allen].

Carayón, M., "L'amour et la musique sur un passage de La
Célestine," Revue de Littérature Moderne, III (1923), 419-
421.
     Carayón compares LC to Twelfth Night. As his chief
argument he uses the passage in Act II, Scene IV of LC
where Calisto asks Sempronio to sing the saddest song he
knows and compares it to Shakespeare's "if music be the
food of love, play on." The expression of love through music in Shakespeare is a development of the theme as found in
LC, though it is enriched by the poetry and intellectualism
of the English playwright. Carayón conjectures that Shakespeare may have read Mabbe's translation. He defers to
Fitzmaurice-Kelly's treatment of the possible influence of LC
on Romeo and Juliet in his History of Spanish Literature.

1924

Petriconi, H., "Trotaconventos, Celestina, Gerarda," Die
neueren Sprachen, XXXII (1924), 232-239.
     Petriconi compares the character of Gerarda in Lope's
La Dorotea to that of Celestina. He finds that the former
lacks the frankness of Celestina, and only when she is drunk
does she say the truth about herself. Her character is es-

sentially the same, but the times have changed and she be-
haves as the times require her to do.

Schevill, Rudolph, "Celestina or the Tragicomedy of Calisto
and Melibea" (rev. art.), Hispania, VII (1924), 412-414.
          Schevill reviews Allen's edition [1923] of Mabbe's
translation. He feels that Mabbe's work is worthy of being
incorporated into English literature. He notes that Mabbe
has given LC a pseudo-classical varnish, minimizing the
Christian element of the original [1939, Houck]. Because of
Mabbe's apparent aversion to Roman Catholicism, he mis-
translates all that pertains to saints, monks, church, etc.

1925

Eyer, Cortland, "Juan Cirne and the Celestina," Hispanic
Review, V (1925), 265-268.
          Eyer compares a few scenes of the sixteenth-century
work Tragedia de los amores de Eneas y de la reina Dido
by Juan Cirne to passages in LC. He finds in Dido's determination to die after her second meeting with Aeneas a parallel with Melibea's suicide. He feels certain that Cirne was
influenced by LC in his dramatic concept of Dido's death.

1926

Montesinos, J. F., "Dos reminiscencias de La Celestina en
Comedias de Lope," Revista de Filología Española, XIII
(1926), 60-62.
          Although Menéndez Pelayo had already discussed the
Celestinesque types in Lope [1910], Montesinos on the other
hand, is interested in singling out specific textual similarities. He points to a similarity between Leonor in Lope's
El galán escarmentado and Areusa's indignation in Act IX.
Celestina's discussion with Pármeno about the embaxador
francés finds an echo in Por la puente, Juana. Celestina
is actually quoted in El Marqués de las Navas.

1928

Asín, Oliver J., "Más reminiscencias de La Celestina en el
teatro de Lone," Revista de Filología Española, XV (1928),
67-74.
          Asín chooses Lope's La bella mal maridada to show
Rojas' influence. Although Marcela's need for wine and
Lope's use of archaisms could be construed as a mere coincidence, Asín argues for a direct influence. He states that

the rich folkloric element in LC may have attracted Lope.
He finds a direct reference to Calisto and Melibea in La
francesilla, El entremés de la hechicera, La cortesía de
España, and El caballero de Olmedo.

1931

Mazzoni, Guido, "Qualche accenno italiano alla Celestina,"
Rendiconti della R. Accademia Nazionale dei Lincei, VII
(1931), 249-252.
    Mazzoni gives a bibliography of Italian critics who
have discussed LC, beginning with the "Discorso intorno al
comporre delle commedie e delle tragedie" by G. Geraldi
Cintio (1504-1573), who speaks of the author of LC as an
imitator of the ancients. His study establishes that LC has
a history in Italy [1902, Farinelli] and that it exercised a
certain influence on Italian letters.

1932

Casalduero, Joaquín, "Queja de las fregonas," Revista de
Filología Española, XIX (1932), 185-187.
    Casalduero points to the relationship between Cer-
vantes' La entretenida and LC. He quotes a passage from
La entretenida which deals with the relationship between
servant and master. Cristina's speech shows a close resemblance to that of Areusa of Act IX where she depicts how
vilified the servants are by their masters.

1939

Houck, Helen Phipps, "Mabbe's Paganization of the Celestina," PMLA, LIV (1939), 422-431.
    Miss Houck compares Mabbe's translation of LC to
Rojas' text. She states that Mabbe set out to paganize the
work and to make it represent the Renaissance spirit as he
felt it. Mabbe thus eliminates the moral purpose of LC and
omits all reference to church doctrine. Though Rojas' text
offers enough classical allusions to satisfy an erudite reader,
Mabbe adds numerous classical allusions of his own. Furthermore, he secularizes, classicizes, and expurgates all references to Christianity. Mabbe's work is not faithful to the
spirit of the original and Houck ascribes this departure to
Mabbe's sociological and ideological background. Mabbe was
probably weary of piety and decided to make of LC a book
of resounding "Elizabethan prose, genial, jovial, taking no
thought for questions of theology or the soul's destiny."

1940

Jaramillo, Gabriel Giraldo, "Don Juan Rodríguez Freyle y
La Celestina," Boletín de Historia y Antigüedades, XXVII
(1940), 582-586.
    Colonial writers were familiar with the humanistic cul-
ture of Spain and influenced by the Spanish classics. A case
in point is El Carnero of don Juan Rodríguez Freyle, where
all the misogynous parts seem to have been directly inspired
by LC.

1941

La Grone, Gregory G. , "Salas Barbadillo and the Celestina,"
Hispanic Review, IX (1941), 440-458.
    La Grone demonstrates that some of the ideas, char-
acters, and ironical elements in the works of Salas Barbadillo are clearly due to LC. He shows how Salas Barbadillo
made use of the Tragicomedia, quoting passages from both
LC and La ingeniosa Elena. He believes that La ingeniosa
Elena (1614), an enlarged version of La hija de Celestina,
affords an interesting seventeenth-century commentary on LC.
He leaves no doubt that Salas Barbadillo had assimilated
much of the irony found in the Tragicomedia. Reminiscences
of LC and the interpretation that Salas Barbadillo had given
it can be found in almost any one of his satirical works.
The Celestina type appears regularly in his satirical sketches.
Though Salas Barbadillo presents the ideas and knowledge of
life that he had gained from LC in a completely new and
original form, his work is clear evidence that LC was still
very much alive in Spain one hundred years after its first
appearance.

1953

Custodio, Alvaro, "La Celestina y la literatura estatal del
Siglo de Oro," Cuadernos Americanos, LXX (1953), 262-275.
    Custodio states that a work like LC did not find a
continuity in Spain because of the pagan spirit that reigns in
it.   The literature that follows is a "literatura estatal"
where everything is resolved through Christian dogma.

1954

Boughner, Daniel C. , The Braggart in Renaissance Comedy.
Minneapolis, 1954.
    The figure of the braggart in LC antedates his appear-

ance in Italian comedies. In Iacopo Nardi's I due felici
rivali (1513), Trasone's boasts bear a suspicious resemblance to the absurdities of Centurio. It seems, therefore,
that a reversal of direction has taken place by which Spanish
literature contributes to the Italian literary scene.

Ugualde, Louis, "The Celestina of 1502," Boston Public Library Quarterly, VI (1954), 206-222.
         The moral tone of the English Interlude of Calisto and
Melibea of 1525 suggests the possibility that it was written
by a pupil of Juan Luis Vives who at that time was teaching
at Oxford. The Interlude marks the first contact of English
and foreign literature.

1955

Schoeck, R. J., "The Influence of La Celestina in England,"
Boston Public Library Quarterly, VII (1955), 224-225.
         A majority of scholars attribute the Tudor Interlude
of 1525 to John Rastell, thus opposing the hypothesis advanced by Ugualde that it was written by a pupil of Juan Luis
Vives. Furthermore, Schoeck avers that the Interlude does
not constitute the first English play indebted to a foreign
source.

Ugualde, Louis, "A Reply," Boston Public Library Quarterly,
VII (1955), 226-227.
         According to Ugualde, the attribution to Rastell re-
mains uncertain, since it would seem that the similarity of
the moralizing addresses as well as the references to heresy
in Rastell's work and in the Interlude offer no stronger argument than that given by the colophon which states that Rastell
printed the work, but which does not give the me fieri fecit
he used in Gentleness and Nobility.
         As for foreign influences, Ugualde corrects his earlier
statements by stating that the Interlude represents the first
English contact with Spanish literature.

1956

Gilman, Stephen, The Art of 'La Celestina'. Madison, 1956.
         As far as Gilman is concerned, the imitations of LC
remain imitative and do not initiate a Celestinesque genre.
For him, a meaningful continuation would have involved an
evident formal trend toward novel or drama. Feliciano de
Silva and the others are simply continuators and their more
or less successful imitations do not reveal a conscious point

of view.

1959

Bataillon, Marcel, "Pour une histoire exigeante des formes:
Le case de La Célestine," Proceedings of the Congress of
International Comparative Literature Association, ed. W. P.
Friedrich. Chapel Hill, 1959, pp. 35-44.

Bataillon establishes that LC is the first of a long line
of works belonging to what he defines as the Celestinesque
genre. These are works in dialogued prose, not intended for
the stage, but for a reading aloud in cultured male circles.
Hence the bold dialogue.

The form of the genre is closely connected to and influenced by its content. A case in point is the particular
use of the aside in this genre, which though derived from
Roman comedy, tends to underline the cynical travesty of
the muttered insolence. All characters are prey to moral
turpitude. Even the passionate Calisto is worthy of contempt. Language and characters both stress the author's
moral intent. The abundance of proverbs, sentences and
maxims underscores the author's irony, since these are ut-
tered by the least worthy characters. It is only from the
point of view of the moral purpose that we can interpret in
a coherent manner the content and literary technique of this
genre.

It would be interesting to discover why this literary
form did not prosper in other countries when the prototype
itself did. Are we to suppose that the form is tied to
Spain's history? In other words, the case may require a
totally Spanish explanation.

Lida de Malkiel, María Rosa, "De Centurio al Mariscal de
Turena: Fortuna de una frase de La Celestina," Hispanic
Review, XXVII (1959), 150-166.

Mrs. Malkiel studies the successive artistic elabora-
tions of Centurio's phrase (Act XVIII), "Yo te juro por el
sancto Martilogio de pe a pa, el braço me tiembla de lo que
por ella entiendo hacer." The tone of the phrase was modified in Floresta española (1574) by Melchor de Santa Cruz,
where it is spoken by a titled gentleman who is about to engage in battle. After Floresta was translated into French in
1600, the phrase, "temen las carnes del estrecho en que las
ha de poner el coraçon," became so diffused in French comedies that it gained proverbial proportions, until it came to be
commonly attributed to Mariscal de Turena (1611-75). However, in the latter's case it was not his lack of temerity but

his reflexive nature that spurred the attribution.

Satrústequi, José María, "La Celestina en la literatura popular vasca," Revista de Literatura, XVI (1959), 146-158.
    Satrústequi finds evidence in support of the thesis that
LC had a place in the oral tradition of the Basque people,
thus offering proof of contact between the latter and the rest
of Spain.
    His argument is based on libelous verses found in the
Actas Notariales of 1619 belonging to the Archives of the
Cathedral of Pamplona, in which Celestina, Areusa, and Elicia appear. Though offering many parallels with the original with emphasis on the laboratory of Celestina, the author
adds new ideas or reproduces situations of LC in a cruder
manner. The verses as a whole reveal that their author not
only knew the Tragicomedia well, but also assimilated the
psychological features of its characters.

Sisto, David T., "The String in the Conjurations of La Celestina and Doña Bárbara," Romance Notes, I (1959), 50-52.
    Sisto finds a parallel in the brujería of Celestina and
Doña Bárbara (by Rómulo Gallegos), especially in their use
of a piece of string or yarn in their conjurations. Both wom-
en use these pieces of yarn to obtain power over the men
and the spirits they are dealing with.

1961

Bataillon, Marcel, 'La Célestine' selon Fernando de Rojas.
Paris, 1961.
    Bataillon states that the imitations of LC offer a key
to the understanding of the moral and social theme on which
LC is based. The elements, both stylistic and moral, repeated in the imitations [Chapter 5] clearly reveal that the
contemporaries of Rojas saw in his work what has escaped
modern critics, namely a condemnation of the locos enamorados and of hypocrisy.
    Bataillon goes on to establish a relationship between
the lover Don Quijote, who sends Sancho to his Dulcinea, and
Calisto who uses Celestina to obtain Melibea. He assumes
that Rojas' Act IV and the original Act I were present in
Cervantes' mind when he was giving form to the dialogue in
the Sierra Morena, although it must be granted that the novelist also had in mind the whole series of lovers who de-
scended from Calisto. The reason the commentators of Don
Quijote have not noted the Don Quijote-Calisto analogy, argues Bataillon, is that the nineteenth-century scholars denied

that Rojas condemns the locos enamorados.

As for the relationship between the Caballero de Olmedo and LC, Bataillon sees Don Alonso as an anti-Calisto.
The real link with LC is Fabia, who practices the same art
as Celestina.   Fabia's presence, speech, and actions parody
Rojas' work.   This is a literary bouquet that Lope throws
to a discriminating audience.

Deyermond, A. D., "La crítica de La Celestina de Jacques
de Lavardin," Hispanófila, V, No. 13 (1961), 1-4.

Lavardin, not finding the moral of LC to his own liking, creates for his translation (1577) a new character,
Aristón, brother of Alisa, for Act XXI.   Aristón guides Pleberio to a Christian acceptance of death.

For his translation Lavardin composed a preliminary
epistle which draws heavily on Rojas' discussion of Act I in
the Letter.   Lavardin's imitation of Rojas is important because it shows that Rojas' literary criticism was acceptable
in another country, at another time, and by a man whose
moral concepts differed greatly from those of the Tragicomedia.

Lida de Malkiel, María Rosa, Two Spanish Masterpieces:
'The Book of Good Love' and 'La Celestina.'   Urbana, 1961.

See Note Chapter 1, Lida de Malkiel, 1961.

1962

Lida de Malkiel, María Rosa, La originalidad artística de
'La Celestina'.   Buenos Aires, 1962.

For Mrs. Malkiel, a study of the imitations and
adaptations gives us a clue to the reaction of the public which
lived close in time to LC, and an understanding of the cultural ambience of the time.

The imitations of LC adopted its original use of stage
directions but in different proportions.   The modern adaptations, however, in their effort to reduce the original work
to present-day theatrical proportions, exhibit a considerable
reduction in the use of directions and monologues.

LC introduces various types of dialogue in Castilian
literature, with emphasis on the short conversation.   In the
earliest imitations, the rhetorical phrase still prevails, but
the short dialogue appears in the later imitations, while in
the modern adaptations it is transformed into rapid rhythms.
Except for the Dorotea, the imitations remained faithful to
their model in the use of monologues, whereas the adaptations all agree in the suppression of monologues.   All the

imitations are partial to the use of the aside.

The imitators of LC did not comprehend the elasticity of its conception of place. The adaptations present a more static and conventional spatial opposition between characters. They also interpreted in a variety of ways the singular conception of time in LC. The more recent adaptations, however, are more concerned with shortening the action than with reproducing the conception of time of the original.

The imitations extend the use of classic references, commonplaces and sentences. They also augment the number of secondary characters to add animation to the action, thereby creating non-organic episodes. The adaptations, instead, are concerned with the physical limitations of the theatre, and therefore omit scenes and characters.

Irony is so inherent in the structure of LC that however independent its imitations are and however they shorten the original text, they always preserve some of the ironical situations of LC. A reading of the more recent adaptations raises the question whether their authors understood the verbal irony of the Tragicomedia. By eliminating whatever seems superfluous to the modern concept of theatre, many effects of anticipation, correlation, and contrast are destroyed.

Doubling is fairly rare in the imitations, except for the multiplication of secondary characters, designed to enliven the dialogue. Doubling was one of the least admired aspects of LC in the adaptations, which aimed at speeding the action.

The conventional figure of the lover prevails in the imitations, but the character of Calisto does not maintain its complex equilibrium. His melancholy and withdrawal reach ridiculous proportions. The imitators inflate the literary side of the lover, especially Calisto's affection for the sacro-profane hyperbole. The adapations, however, omit important passages in order to shorten the text.

The complex figure of Melibea is simplified by the imitators who tend to portray a more conventional heroine who lacks the vital and resolute character of the original. All 'the imitations omit her revolt against the accepted social norm. They all end with the marriage of their heroines, which the latter demand as a condition for their surrender. The Comedia Eufrosina is the only one of the imitations which traces the sentimental evolution of the heroine in a masterful manner. The adaptations do not follow a single interpretation, but often the need to shorten the original is detrimental to the characterization.

The figure of the father is either obedient to the origi-

nal conception or considerably different from it. During Rojas' time, the preoccupation with honor stifled all desire for
familial tenderness both in the authors and in their readers.
All the more original does the conception of the father appear in LC. In the adaptations, the figure of the father suf-
fers the most radical change.

The figure of the mother, trusting and loving, owes
little to literary tradition and did not influence later literary
treatments. In the imitations, the character of the mother
received little attention. Some of the adaptations eliminate
the character altogether, as was customary in the Spanish
theatre of the Golden Age; others fail to retain the traits of
the character as it was conceived.

The conception of Celestina differs widely in the imitations. Some eliminate her; others delight in portraying her
love affairs. Sometimes they emphasize isolated scenes because of the picturesque element in them. But one significant departure in some of the imitations is the introduction
of the love letter--a literary tradition which Rojas had dis-
carded--whereby the servant carries on the intrigue, thus un-
dermining the dramatic role of the alcahueta. The character
which fascinated the public becomes in most continuations inessential and frivolous. In the adaptations, for the most
part, Celestina has lost the detailed characterization and the
peculiar dramatic and stylistic power which she had in the
Tragicomedia.

In the imitations, the intervention of the servants is
of greater importance than in LC, marking a return to the
original seruus fallax. The number of servants is increased,
functioning like a chorus around the master. The emphasis
is on the vulgar ambience. There is no effort to individual-
ize the character of the servants. The adaptations generally
simplify the moral contrast between the two pairs of servants
in LC. The figure of Lucrecia becomes inessential to the
drama in the imitations, where she is deprived of her autonomous characters. The adaptations either eliminate her or
considerably diminish her role.

The imitations differ from the original in the treatment of the courtesans. In the original, they have a more
extensive and varied role than the ruffian; in the imitations,
the latter attracts most of the attention. Furthermore, their
number increases and by becoming accessory to the scabrous
scenes they lose their organic role. The adaptations alter-
nate between omission of the courtesans and a lively presentation of them.

In the imitations, although incorporated into the intrigue and enriched with modalities from other characters,

Centurio loses his original unity of character. The tendency
was to amplify the bravado and to add scenes of brutality
and assorted sordid elements. Few of the adaptations, however, retain this character, probably reluctant to introduce a
new character toward the end of the drama, especially since
they want to shorten the text.

It is obvious that both the imitators and adapters, although relishing all the possibilities that the portrayal of the
lower class offered, pay more attention to their noble characters. This was also to be true in the case of the theatre
of the Golden Age, of Shakespeare, and of Molière. It is
clear that Rojas was far ahead of his time in his social attitude.

Oostendorp, H. Th., El conflicto entre el honor y el amor
en la literatura española hasta el siglo XVII. The Hague,
1962.
        The imitations of LC reflect the important changes
that took place under the influence of neoplatonic ideas which
favored the free choice of the marriage partner and which
considered marriage as the desired solution for a love relationship. Some of the imitators concur with Rojas' conservative stand [Chapter 6], namely Sancho de Muñón, Sebastián
Fernández, and Pedro Manuel de Urrea. These imitators
emphasized the social equality of the lovers but condemned
their rebellious attitude toward paternal vigilance. Only
Torres Naharro sides with the lovers. But, as a whole, the
imitators are intent on legalizing the love of their protagonists by resorting to the secret marriage.

1963

Brault, Gérard J., 'Célestine': A Critical Edition of the
French Translation (1527). Detroit, 1963.
        Brault presents a critical edition of the Célestine
based on the anonymous 1527 translation into French. The
purpose of this edition is to make the influence of LC in
France better understood.

        LC influenced Nicolas de Troyes, who incorporated
verbatim two sub-plots of LC into his Grand paragon des
nouvelles nouvelles (1536). Lavardin's translation should be
remembered in any study on the emergence of the femme
d'intrigue and the miles gloriosus in late sixteenth-century
drama.

Heugas, Pierre, ed. La Célestine. Paris, 1963.
        Heugas reviews the works that exhibit the influence of

LC. He agrees with Bataillon [1961] that LC is the source
for Lazarillo. Lazarillo's biography is inspired by Pármeno's. It exhibits the same concept of time and place as does
LC. LC thus opens the way to the novel and leads to Cervantes.

McPheeters, D. W., "Cervantes' Verses on La Celestina,"
Romance Notes, IV (1963), 136-138.

    McPheeters attempts to interpret the meaning of Cervantes' verses on LC appearing at the beginning of Don Quijote: "Libro, en mi opinión, divino/ si encubriera más lo
humano."

    The word humano carries the meaning of lechery and
sensuality. Cervantes is censuring the sexual immorality of
the work. The contrast humano-divino adds a baroque element to the verses and reflects a Neoplatonic concept much
to Cervantes' liking.

1964

Picoche, Louis, "Gérard J. Brault, ed. Célestine" (rev.
art.), Romance Philology, XVIII (1964), 251-252.

    Of the three French Renaissance translations of LC
(1527, 1577, and 1633), 19 different editions appeared. Picoche would like to see a synoptic edition of the Spanish text
and these three translations. This would put at the disposal
of French Hispanists the various interpretations of cruces in
the Spanish text.

Scoles, Emma, "La prima traduzione italiana della Celestina:
Repertorio bibliografico," Studi di Letteratura Spagnola.
Rome, 1964.

    Miss Scoles sets out to establish the number of Italian editions based on Ordóñez' translation of 1506. The aim
of her study is to discover which Italian editions actually
existed, which are extant, and which are simply the result
of equivocal information.

    A case in point is the 1505 Venice edition of LC which
though mentioned in catalogues was never seen by any scholar.
Miss Scoles advances the hypothesis that this is actually an
erroneous entry for the 1525 Venice edition. Similarly, the
1514 Venice edition was an erroneous entry for the 1514 Milan edition by Claricio.

    As a result of Miss Scoles' bibliographical research,
it can be stated with certainty that 13 Italian editions were
based on Ordóñez' translation [Chapter 2, 1964].

1965

Martínez Lacalle, Guadalupe, "A Manuscript Version of
Mabbe's Celestina." Revue de Littérature Comparée, XXXIX
(1965), 78-91.
This is a detailed description of a manuscript of
Mabbe's translation in the possession of the Duke of North-
umberland. Of special interest are the differences between
the MS and Mabbe's printed version. The MS bears numerous marginal annotations, chiefly alongside passages referring to religion. They throw considerable light on the
changes which Mabbe made from his early drafts to the final
printed text. The MS is much closer to the Spanish original
than is the printed version, suggesting that Mabbe tried to
remove the flavor of translation and to produce an English-
sounding work. The marginal notes are often found at points
where the differences are the greatest.
Miss Martínez suggests that this MS is a fair copy of
Mabbe's first draft, and that Mabbe revised this copy at a
later date in preparing it for the press.

Trotter, G. D., "The Date of the Comedia Thebayda," Modern Language Review, LX (1965), 386-390.
An examination of text, typography, and illustrations
convinces Trotter that the Comedia Thebayda was written and
printed between late 1519 and early 1521. This conflicts with
Mrs. Malkiel's dating, which places this work before 1504.
If the 1519-1521 dating is correct, the Comedia Thebayda
cannot compete with Urrea's Penitencia de amor (Burgos,
1514) for the honor of being the first prose imitation of LC.

1966

Guerra, Conde, "Gil Vicente y La Celestina," La Estafeta
Literaria, No. 343 (1966), 8, 9.
Gil Vicente received his greatest intellectual influence
from Rojas. In his Barca do Inferno (1517), he recreates
Celestina in the character of Brígida Vaz, except that we
meet Brigida in the afterlife recounting her dealings on earth.
LC was not permitted by the Inquisition to circulate
in Portugal, even though it circulated freely in Spain. Guerra suggests that Gil Vicente's admiration for Rojas was so
great that he wrote his Barca do Inferno in order to enable
his countrymen to become acquainted with Rojas' work
through his own imitation.
Gil Vicente's supposed relationship with Rojas in Salamanca will remain a conjecture until further facts are un-

earthed about him.

McPheeters, D. W. , "Una traducción hebrea de La Celestina
en el siglo XVI," Homenaje a Rodríguez-Moñino, Vol. I.
Madrid, 1966, pp. 399-411.

    McPheeters examines "Un Poema del amigo del poeta
cuando virtió un tratado de Melibea y Calisto," written in
Hebrew by Joseph ben Samuel Tsarfati, who, like Ordóñez,
was in the service of Julius II. His translation of LC has
not been found, but McPheeters translates Rabbi Joseph's in-
troductory poems (1507 or 1508) and shows that, contrary to
the opinion held by Mrs. Malkiel, the translator shared fully
in the Christian moralizing attitude of his contemporaries toward LC.

    The poem also exhibits an anti-feminism similar to
that of Rojas himself, and proves how alive this medieval
tradition was at the height of the Renaissance.

Pérez, Luis C. , "Coplas desconocidas del tema celestinesco,"
Homenaje a Rodríguez Moñino, Vol. II. Madrid, 1966, pp.
51-57.

    Pérez has discovered a sixteenth-century "Copla que
hizo tremar a una alcahueta que auia engañado ciertos cau-
alleros trayéndolos en traspassos engañosamente." He believes that this copla belongs to a well-established medieval
tradition of the Celestinesque genre.

1967

Purcell, H. D. , "The Celestina and the Interlude of Calisto
and Melibea," Bulletin of Hispanic Studies, XLIV (1967), 1-
15.

    According to Purcell, the Interlude is an adaption--
and not, as is often stated, a truncated translation--of the
21 act LC. The adapter's skill has been underrated, says
Purcell, though his versification is admittedly faulty. The
Interlude was written for the entertainment of Sir Thomas
More's household. Didactic in its intention, it is a departure
from the allegorical Morality of the period--a departure
which found no imitators, however.

1968

Mendeloff, Henry, "On Translating La Celestina into French
and Italian," Hispania, LI (1968), 111-115.

    It is difficult, says Mendeloff, to render in a transla-
tion the threefold character of dialogue in LC: medieval

rhetoric, popular language, folkloric proverbs and sayings.
The task is further complicated by the anomalous juxtaposition of disparate levels of diction.   The translator will succeed only if he is able to convey the Latinisms, the rhetoric,
and the popular aspects of the style.   Strict adherence to
twentieth-century canons is incompatible with a convincing
translation.

    With this in mind, Mendeloff finds serious shortcom-
ings in the translations by Doyon (1952) and Alvaro (1943).
Closer in spirit to LC is the 1527 French translation edited
by Brault.

1969

Hanrahan, Thomas, S. J., "Sin, the Celestina and Iñigo
López de Loyola," Romance Notes, XI (1969), 385-391.
    An examination of the Ejercicios Espirituales reveals,
according to Father Hanrahan, that the source for the description of sin was found in LC.   The psychological process
of temptation which St. Ignatius of Loyola describes in his
Ejercicios offers similarities with the case of Melibea which
are more than accidental.

Chapter 5

'LA CELESTINA' AS A WORK OF ART

1825

Martínez de la Rosa, F., Obras literarias, Vol. II. Paris, 1825, pp. 353-354.

Martínez de la Rosa states that LC contains all the seeds of drama and that it inspired the creation of other works which are more properly defined as drama.

1838

Moratín, Leandro Fernández de, "Orígenes del teatro español," Tesoro del teatro español, Vol. I. Paris, 1838.

For Moratín, LC is the original source of the Spanish comedia. He calls it "one of the most classical works" that Spanish literature has ever produced.

1841

Lavigne, Germond de, ed. La Célestine. Paris, 1841.

Lavigne considers LC the mother of Castilian drama. He claims that the work was intended for the stage and that it was capable of being performed.

1849

Ticknor, George, History of Spanish Literature. London, 1849, pp. 239-248.

Ticknor defines LC as a dramatized romance rather than genuine drama. Its style consists for him in an idle and cold display of learning.

1894

González Aguejas, Lorenzo, "La Celestina," La España Moderna, VI, No. 67 (1894), 78-103.

González Aguejas is one of the first scholars to engage

in a discussion of the merits and defects of the five intercalated acts in LC and their influence on the structure and
style of the work.   The question has been whether the additional five acts which first appear in the 1502 edition enhance
or detract from the dramatic development of the action and
psychological motivation of the characters.   González Aguejas
is of the opinion that these acts are stylistically and dramatically unnecessary to the work and that in fact they are an in-
trusion which breaks the essential integrity of the story.

1895

Soravilla, Javier, La Celestina.   Madrid, 1895.
       Soravilla considers LC as a sketch which was jotted
down in 15 days by an inexpert hand.   The result of this effort, however, is not a work which can be read lightly, for
it exhibits great passions, high moral and aesthetic qualities,
and a beauty of style inherited from Arabic writings.
       As for the characters, Soravilla finds Melibea admir-
ably drawn, Celestina the dominating force of the work, the
very incarnation of Mephistophelis, and Centurio the best defined of all the characters.
       Soravilla compiled an alphabetical list of maxims,
thoughts, and sentences of each act.   This compilation of
maxims is to be considered a stylistic guide to the beautiful
and pure Castilian language.   Moreover, he points out that it
is these very sentences and maxims which heighten the whole
work and which distinguish it from licentious books.

Wolf, Ferdinand, "Sobre el drama español - La Celestina y
sus traducciones," La España Moderna, VII, No. 80 (1895),
99-123.
       Wolf maintains that epic qualities still dominate in LC,
as evidenced by the loquacity of its characters, and by the
episodic breaks in the action which delay its rapid dramatic
course.   He feels that in spite of its unwieldy exterior form,
its division into 21 acts, the work has dramatic tone, dramatic life, and dramatic action.   The characters are presented in this action and through it.   LC was written at a
moment of transition when the separation between genres was
not well defined.   Thus it is the prototype of the "género
novelesco" of national Spanish drama.   LC gave to Spanish
drama a basis in the popular and a national character.

1899

Menéndez Pelayo, Marcelino, ed.   La Celestina (E. Krapf).

2 vols. Vigo, 1899-1900.

Menéndez Pelayo defines LC as a play because everything in it is of an active nature and is not narrative in spirit.   LC has contributed an entirely new form of dialogue to
modern literature.   He considers it the masterpiece of Spanish realistic comedy.

1900

Foulché-Delbosc, R., "Observations sur La Célestine," Revue Hispanique, VII (1900), 28-80.

According to Foulché-Delbosc, the additional five acts
are a tasteless display of erudition.   He feels that in breaking the stylistic harmony of the original 1499 edition with an
excessive use of sentences, maxims, and classical references,
the "adicionador" [Chapter 1] revealed his lack of literary
talent.   Moreover, he feels that the "Tratado de Centurio"
destroys the unity of the work.   Whereas this unity in the
Comedia was achieved through Calisto's death after one
scene of love, in the Tragicomedia it is destroyed by lengthening the love episode to one month.

1902

Foulché-Delbosc, R., "Observations sur La Célestine," Revue Hispanique, IX (1902), 171-199.

Foulché-Delbosc blames the "adicionador" of 1502 for
making of Melibea a very sensuous woman in Act XIX as
against the timid virgin of the original Act XVI.

1904

Desdevises du Dezert, M. G., "La comédie de Caliste et
Melibée," Revue des Cours et Conférences, XII (1904), 739-
756.

Desdevises du Dezert analyzes the most important
parts of LC, quoting these in French and Spanish, to give
the reader a feeling for the beauty and the intensity of the
work.

He does not find any redeeming qualities in the characters.   They follow each other's example in all the villainies
they perpetrate and seem confident that self-interest excuses
all actions and that cowardice is the governing law of life.

1910

Menéndez Pelayo, Marcelino, Orígenes de la novela, Vol.

III.   Madrid, 1905-1910.

Menéndez Pelayo denounces Celestina as an "abismo de perversidad" when he states that among the types of absolute perversity created by artists not one equals her, not even Iago. She embodies what he calls "positivo satanismo" which is the practice of evil for evil's sake. Menéndez Pelayo is overwhelmed by the abominations which Celestina is capable of committing and is both repelled and fascinated by her satanic greatness. Sempronio and Pármeno are for him the type of confidant, or gracioso. They introduce for the first time the parallelism between the loves of the masters and those of the servants. As for Melibea, she is the tempestuous woman in love who has no reason to exist other than love itself.

Menéndez Pelayo feels that the rhetoric of the characters does not lessen the depth of their sentiments. He notes that there is a deliberate effort to write well. But he states that each character does not speak according to his role. However, the Renaissance is not known for its sobriety of style; hence the amplifications and the verbal overabundance of LC. But the vulnerable point of LC is the repetitious dialogue which detracts from the dramatic tension.

In judging the Tragicomedia, he singles out as the principal weaknesses of the five additional acts the unnecessary display of erudition and the insertion of an episodic and useless intrigue which in no way modifies the dénouement. Still, he finds in the longer version beauties which none other than Rojas was capable of creating.

1912

Reynier, Gustave, "La Célestine," Les origines du roman réaliste. Paris, 1912.

According to Reynier, Rojas' talent lies in the portrayal of his characters. Particularly notable is the intensity of life in Celestina, her power to corrupt, her sensuality, and her cupidity. The figures of the two lovers stand apart from the inferior characters and are heightened by the juxtaposition.

The form that Rojas chose is an intermediate one between the novel and drama and this gave him a great deal of freedom to express his realistic genius.

1913

Cejador y Frauca, Julio, ed. La Celestina. Madrid, 1913.

Cejador agrees with Menéndez Pelayo's definition of

Celestina [1910], and he defines her as "un caso sublime de
mala voluntad." She is like Iago, but more human. Cejador
is impressed by the monstrosity of the pact with the devil and
the magic potions Celestina prepares.

As for the intercalated material, Cejador discards one
by one the elements added by the "corrector" Proaza, who,
striving for a more refined and rare erudition, succeeded only in coarsening the character portrayal and making an indiscriminate use of refranes. Furthermore, the additional acts
destroy the most admirable element of the Comedia, namely
the sudden change from comedy to tragedy. He rejects the
additional episode as useless, supporting the general view
that the Comedia is aesthetically superior to the Tragicomedia.

He states that the Spanish Renaissance is born with
LC and with it, the Spanish theatre. But as a work of art,
LC is better suited to reading than to staging because it does
not follow theatrical conventions. He calls the work a pure
drama: it is not "representable por tan puro drama como
es y pura vida." Cejador considers it the first work where
popular speech is successfully integrated with erudite speech.
But the popular speech is still reserved for the lower classes.

Echalar, Bernardo de, "Fernando de Rojas: La Celestina,"
Estudios Franciscanos, XIII (1913), 96-109.

Echalar defends Celestina against the critics who have
found her distasteful. For him, the character of Celestina
is not merely a literary invention and an imitation of Trotaconventos but a social reality. The whole work itself is an
amalgamation of two types of literature: the erudite and the
realistic.

1914

Azorín (Martínez Ruiz, José), "La Celestina," Valores literarios. Obras Completas, Vol. II. Madrid, 1959.

Azorín makes light of the formidable and weighty interpretations of Celestina's character. Azorín maintains
that the originality of LC consists in the fact that for the first
time we find ourselves in the presence of a psychologist: a
writer who creates, animates, and develops characters. All
of these psychological processes unfold in the atmosphere of
a palpitating reality.

As for the style, there is in LC, according to Azorín,
the stylization of the spoken language, the ennoblement of
daily speech, but the author goes beyond the norm of good
taste in his use of oratory. The overabundance of classical

references, sentences, and reflections has weakened the
gracefulness and spontaneity of the original Comedia.

Finally, in Celestina Azorín sees simply a very astute
woman. Her pacts with the devil, her unguents, herbs, etc.,
are all part of the picturesque, not the demonic as Menéndez
Pelayo and the Cejador believed.

1923

Allen, Warner H., ed.   Celestina, trans. by James Mabbe.
London, 1923.

Allen avers that the additional five acts improve the
structure of LC. In the original version, Calisto falls off the
ladder by chance. This is a flaw. When Rojas revised his
work, he made the fall of Calisto depend on the natural desire of Elicia and Areusa to avenge the death of Celestina and
of their lovers. Thus Calisto's ungoverned passion becomes
the real cause of his death. At the same time, Allen does
not deny that some of the added elements are infelicitous.

House, Ralph E., "The Present Status of the Problem of Authorship of the Celestina," Philological Quarterly, II (1923),
38-47.

House is another critic who feels that the demonic role
of Celestina has been overestimated--he refers in particular
to Menéndez Pelayo--and that undue emphasis has been placed
on the claptrap of witchcraft with which he surrounds herself.
It is the sight of Calisto that causes Melibea to love him.
Her passion is what drives her to take a decidedly active part
in her ruin, and unrepentantly follow her lover in death.
Thus human nature succumbs to its own passion.

Although the additions contain some of the most admirable passages of the Tragicomedia, House concedes that as a
whole they do not maintain the high standard of excellence of
the primitive version. He notes that what was a subtle humor
in the Comedia becomes a noticeable striving for comic effect
in the Tragicomedia.

In the additions, the plot becomes complicated and the
dramatic motives change. Areusa and Elicia want revenge;
Sosia and Centurio come into the picture. Centurio sends a
cripple in his stead to kill Calisto. Calisto dies from the attack of Traso. The drama of passion becomes a comedy of
intrigue. A difference does exist between the simple plot of
the Comedia in which human passions lead their victims on to
their destruction and the complicated intrigue of the additions
in which each character deceives the other in order to gain
his ends: Areusa inveigles Sosia into betraying the plans of

his master; Centurio is tricked into a promise to kill Calisto.
Generally speaking, the characters of the Comedia do
not pay attention to natural phenomena, but in the Tragicomedia references are made to "suaves plantas," "fresca
verdura," and "deleytosas estrellas."

As for the tone of the Comedia, there are only a few
passages in which a comic intent is discernible--a pun is
found in I, when Sempronio says, "no vayas por lana e ven-
gas sin pluma." The development of a sinister plot leaves
little room for comedy. Although the themes are rich in
comic possibilities, Celestina's humor scarcely goes beyond
the bounds of geniality of expression. In spite of the rarity
of downright comic passages, however, House calls the author a humorist with a light touch, because he never allows
a humorous situation to develop into buffoonery or hyperbole.
In the Comedia, none of the characters plays anything approaching a comic role. House makes a distinction between
the use of humor in the Comedia, where it is more subtle,
and that of Tragicomedia, where a striving for comic effect
is in evidence, for example the extensive additions to the
eulogy on wine in Act II. More significant in this respect is
the part of Centurio who plays throughout a comic role.
Centurio is a rejuvenated miles gloriosus. This cowardly
braggart becomes one of the stock characters in the theatre.

In the use of satire the comic element is slight. Satire is an inherent part of the argumentation where Sempronio
censures the vices and weaknesses of women to distract Calisto from his passion. In Areusa's tirade against mistresses
who mistreat their servants the connection with the plot is incidental. The tirade of Calisto against the judge who sen-
tenced his servants is considered a satire on the judicial
class. The satire on the clergy's immorality is introduced
with a frequency that makes it significant.

1924

Petriconi, H., "Trotaconventos, Celestina, Gerarda," Die
Neueren Sprachen, XXXII (1924), 232-239.
Petriconi looks upon Celestina as a Spanish national
figure. According to him, the author has personalized her
by giving her a personal biography through Pármeno and her
own reminiscences. His go-between thus develops into a
character.

1925

Maeztu, Ramiro de, Don Quijote, Don Juan y La Celestina.

Madrid, 1925.

Maeztu calls Celestina "la santa del hedonismo" because her mission is to satisfy the whims of others.   For her
there is no other God than pleasure.   She represents egotistical knowledge because she sees in people only the weaknesses
which she can exploit.   Therefore he defines her as "el saber
egoista y el saber utilitario."

1928

Reischmann, Karl, Die stilistische Abwechslung in der span-
ischen Tragikomedie 'La Celestina'.   Bonn, 1928.
Reischmann presents without comment a catalogue of
certain elegant peculiarities of Rojas' style, under the following general categories: Stylistic variety in number, article,
noun, adjective, adverb, preposition, conjunction, pronoun,
verbs, expression of concepts, and use of synonyms.

Unfortunately, Reischmann does not make use of his
catalogue for any discussion of Rojas' style.

1929

Castro, Américo, "El problema histórico de La Celestina,"
Santa Teresa y otros ensayos.   Santander, 1929.
Castro conceives the pattern of LC as a binary one,
in which two worlds are juxtaposed: the one represented by
Calisto and Melibea; the other, by Celestina and the servants.
These worlds are separate and never interpenetrate.   Celes-
tina acts as an intermediary between them.

The conflict between servants and masters is reas-
serted by the inner pattern of the novel.   This pattern is a
constant series of oppositions between the upper and the lower
class modes of feeling: the opportunistic Sempronio contrasts with the idealized Calisto; the vulgar Areusa, with the
refined Melibea.   The cleavage echoes the social world of
Rojas' time, when the medieval hierarchy of classes was beginning to break.   The author of LC perceives that the beautiful unity of the medieval world was a thing of the past.

The tragic dénouement of LC is inspired by Italian
humanism.   For Castro, "la postura trágica y vital de Fernando de Rojas es humanístico-renacentista."   There is no
evidence in the work of ethical or moral values.

As for the use of magic, Celestina's contact with the
devil is purely accessory.

1932

Küchler, Walther, "Die erste bekannte Ausgabe der Comedia de Calisto y Melibea," Romanistiches Jahrbuch, VI (1956), 315-323. (This article was actually written in 1932 and later found among Küchler's papers.)

Although our attention is focused on Celestina, we should not forget that the author named the work after Calisto and Melibea. Küchler considers the work a dramatized form of a novel, a "Lesedrama," which was never meant for the stage.

Calisto at first appears without any individual traits, but he gradually becomes more individualized. Küchler feels that Melibea is a more real person than Calisto, though her characterization follows some conventional literary lines. Celestina is the world of brutality and meanness, the embodiment of the principle of evil.

Küchler denies that the story of Calisto and Melibea is realistic. Their love has been transformed into a poetic experience.

Calisto's disappearance from life is a passive experience while Melibea's is induced by her own will. She rejects her upbringing, and her surrender comes of her own free will, as does her suicide. She shows her freedom even though it leads to her destruction. It is an act of defiance against the arbitrariness of fortune.

Again, we find expressed in Küchler's article the idea that the additions weaken the dramatic impact of the catastrophe.

Rauhut, Franz, "Das Dämonische in der Celestina," Festgabe zum 60. Geburtstag Karl Vosslers, Vol. I. Munich, 1932, pp. 117-148.

Rauhut reviews the judgments on LC which have been stressed in different centuries according to the particular preoccupations of the period. While the Romantic age stressed the gigantic stature of Celestina and the function of the demonic element, more recently, beginning with Azorín, stress has been placed on realism. The realism to be observed in LC is not the typical slice of life, but rather what Rauhut defines as spiritual truth, "seelische Wahrheit," where each person is an individual, each speaking in his own individual way.

Celestina spouts worldly wisdom which she uses as a weapon and tool of her trade. She is a cynic, has no human feelings and puts all her faculties to the service of greed. It is her dispassionate cynicism that gives her a demonic

quality, not her summoning of the devil. She acquires a superior force, which may be called demonic, within the context of a realistic world and experience.

Rauhut tries to define the demonic after reviewing the
various meanings from the ancient Greeks to Paul Tillich.
He agrees with Menéndez Pelayo that Celestina is the abyss
in person. Thus she becomes more than her individual self
and acquires the stature of a myth. Connected with this is
the witchcraft which she practices. Her witchcraft scenes
are important because they show that the devilish powers are
at work in the love story. She is an individual, with an individual destiny and an individual end, and she is at the
same time a mythical presence, the symbol of the demonic
in this work. However, while the demonic force of love and
fate is entirely serious, the demonic character of Celestina
is attenuated by the comic element, which gives her a grotesque aspect.

As for the additional acts, Rauhut believes that these
injure the original concept of the Comedia. They soften the
frightfulness of Fate and give a realistic motivation to Calisto's death by making it hang on vengeance. If, however,
Rojas wrote the additions, it is clear that he no longer understood his own original concept.

1939

Arciniega, Rosa, "La Celestina, antelación del Don Juan,"
Revista de las Indias, V (1939), 258-277.
    For Arciniega, Sempronio is the most repulsive figure
of the drama. He represents the utmost in degradation.
Celestina, on the other hand, is the most human character,
she is life itself. She is used as a bridge between the desires that move both lovers.

Croce, Benedetto, "La Celestina," La Critica, XXXVII
(1939), 81-91.
    According to Croce, the sentiment that fills LC is
that of the "forza irruente, prepotente, irrefrenabile, travol-
gente e paurosa" of sensual love. The comparison between
the two lovers of LC and Romeo and Juliet has become a
literary commonplace started by romantic German criticism
and later accepted by Spanish scholars. Croce considers the
similarities to be extrinsic and superficial. Juliet conse-
crates her love with the rite of marriage while Melibea for-
gets every law and every duty "nell'ebbrezza dei sensi."
Romeo has a spirituality lacking in Calisto, who also is in-
ebriated by the "sensuale bollore."

Croce discovers dignity in Celestina. She has the dignity of one who does what nature has charged her with and she does it well. She wants to stay outside the sphere of morality. Croce finds a similarity of tone and style in the most varied and different situations. The work defies those who want speech to be adequate to the station of the speaker and appropriate to the action. Yet in LC the style sounds spontaneous and normal, proving that these realistic percepts are not infallible.

For Croce, even if there were two authors in the physical sense, "poetically" they are one, for the entire LC springs from a unified poetic concept.

Houck, Helen Phipps, "Mabbe's Paganization of the Celestina," PMLA, LIV (1939), 422-431.
Miss Houck speaks of Rojas' style as sober, stark, forcible, intense, and concentrated.

1940

Poston, Lawrence Sanford, Jr., An Etymological Vocabulary to the 'Celestina', A-E. Chicago, 1940.
Poston presents a study of all words in LC from A to E, exclusive of proper names. He gathers all information from the current edition of the Diccionario de la Academia and from specific etymological studies. The etymologies of words beginning with A are studied in full. In the B to E section, the etymologies are stated briefly. He attempts to indicate the exact meaning of a word in a particular context and to note which words appear only in certain contexts or forms. He makes special note of all locutions as well as all phrases or expressions which present difficulty in translation.

1941

Madariaga, Salvador de, "Discurso sobre Melibea," Sur, LXXVI (1941), 38-69.
While the medieval dispute was raging as to whether Woman is an instrument of the devil or the idealized angelic creature of the troubadours, we have the creation of a beautiful and unforgettable figure: Melibea. She loves like a human being, errs like one, and like all human beings pays for her errors with her life. She is neither angel nor devil. She is a woman. LC signifies nothing more than the discovery of woman in a modern sense. Melibea is curious, impulsive, cautious. She is the woman totally in love.

Calisto personifies the troubadour. He remains within the tradition of courtly love. In Celestina, on the other
hand, we see the picture of woman as propagated by the misogynist monks of the Middle Ages.

1943

Cirot, G., "La Célestine de Paul Achard," Bulletin Hispanique, XLV (1943), 98-100.
    While LC is a splendid prelude to the Spanish drama
begun by Juan del Encina, it also opens the way to the series
of pícaros who will dominate the Spanish novel. As a result,
LC exhibits a confusion of different genres which set it apart
from other literary works.

Giusti, Roberto F., "Fernando de Rojas. Su obra de humanidad española y de arte renacentista," Boletín de la
Academia Argentina de Letras, XII (1943), 121-142.
    Rojas is able to convert the Celestinesque type into a
well-defined human character. Celestina does not exhibit the
monstrous and diabolic qualities previous critics have attributed to her. She is simply a human being who practices
a profession like any other, "vivo de él, como cada cual ofi-
cial del suyo, muy limpiamente."
    As for his language, Rojas was able to find a rhythm
for his dialogue which is flexible, short, incisive.

1944

Grismer, Raymond Leonard, The Influence of Plautus in
Spain before Lope de Vega. New York, 1944.
    Grismer states that LC and most of its continuations
were never intended for stage production. He applies the not
unfamiliar term "dramatic novel" to these works.

1946

Green, Otis H., "On Rojas' Description of Melibea," Hispanic Review, XIV (1946), 254-256.
    Green demonstrates that Calisto's description of the
physical attributes of Melibea falls clearly within the medieval concept of Natura naturans. Green links Calisto's initial
statement concerning Melibea's beauty, "en dar poder a Natura que de tan perfecta hermosura te dotasse," to the full
amplification of Calisto's praise which appears later in the
act.
    The physical description served to justify the experi-

ence of love, and it was a medieval practice to present the
physical attributes in a given order--going from head to foot.
Familiarity with these medieval practices would have shown
to many critics that the initial tribute to Melibea's beauty,
with its reference to God and Nature, and the later physical
description are part of an elaborate medieval scheme.

1947

Frank, Rachel, "Four Paradoxes in the Celestina," Romanic
Review, XLVIII (1947), 53-68.
          It is Miss Frank's opinion that Rojas' apparent techni-
cal weaknesses are not artistically unaccountable of psycho-
logically eccentric, but rather that they reflect "a spirit intensely ambitious to express the contradictions of his time
without compromise." She proceeds to interpret the four
paradoxes of the work within their literary context.
          Calisto, who as a character is worthy of Melibea's
love and yet so absurd a figure that his servants mock him,
is finally slain by a comical whim of destiny. It seems that
the broad outlines of Calisto's conduct correspond to a standard treatment of male characters which the sentimental novel usually followed. This genre offered a literary precedent
for treating a male character in a considerably less dignified
light than the female character.
          The second paradox involves Melibea's change from
discreet woman to a defiant proclaimer of a woman's right
to love outside of marriage. Similarly, this new type of
heroine has its root in the sentimental novel, where the husband is typically unloved by his wife and is set off against
the lover. Lucretia of the Historia de duobus amantibus by
Piccolomini offers a framework of literary tradition for the
seeming iconoclasm of Melibea's sudden metamorphosis.
          The third paradox is found in the way Melibea and
Calisto conduct their love affair, behaving as though actual
obstacles to their marriage existed. But the reason for this
is that for both of them true love for a spouse is inconceivable. Their love must fulfill itself outside marriage to preserve its purity. Since it is destined to be sinful, it invites
the scene of foreboding with the summoning of the devil.
The incantation performed by Celestina symbolizes the evil
which pervades the whole book.
          And finally, Rojas accords his lower class characters
the ability to look within themselves and reflect upon their
actions. He allows them to speak as though they were members of the aristocracy. With the idealized speech and
thoughts of the poor, Rojas tries to raise them to the level

of the rich in a process of equalization.   The novel does not
place the two worlds of servants and masters side by side
[1929, Américo Castro]--one heroic, one prosaic--but causes
them to interpenetrate and to blend in a common humanity.

1950

Menéndez Pidal, Ramón, "La lengua en tiempos de los Reyes
Católicos," Cuadernos Hispano-Americanos, XIII (1950), 9-
24.
      According to Menéndez Pidal, the anonymous author of
the first act imposes a style of expression on the continuator.
It is the elegance found in the first act which guides the continuator in recreating the conversational language of the various circles of a society "entre cortesana y universitaria cual
era la de la docta Salamanca."   The great innovation of LC
lies in the creation of a prose dialogue.
      The moment of linguistic transition is visible not only
in the style of LC but also in the adaptation of the religious
language to a profane context and in its archaic grammatical
forms.   But the dialogue of LC inaugurates the tendency to
"naturalidad y cristalina trasparencia" which characterizes
the language of the sixteenth century.

O'Kane, Eleanor, "The Proverb: Rabelais and Cervantes,"
Comparative Literature, II (1950), 360-369.
      Miss O'Kane illustrates the mastery of Spanish writers
in the use of the proverb as an effective literary device.
With examples from the Corbacho and LC, she shows how
skillfully these writers exploited the stylistic and psychological resources of the proverb.   For instance, the proverb,
"el mozo del escudero gallego que andaba todo el año des-
calzo y por un día quería matar al zapatero," becomes in
LC, "¿quieres decir que soy como el mozo del escudero
gallego?"   Here in perfect harmony we find adaptation, allusion, and psychological development.

1951

Orozco Díaz, Emilio, "El huerto de Melibea," Arbor, XIX
(1951), 47-60.
      According to Orozco, the garden plays an essential
role in the development of the Tragicomedia.   For the moment the lovers meet in the garden, it becomes the only possible world for them.   The garden participates as a witness
to their love.   It is the first dramatization of a participating
landscape that Spanish literature offers.

1952

Asensio, Manuel, "El tiempo en La Celestina," Hispanic Review, XX (1952), 28-43.

Critics have noticed a discrepancy between the normal flow of time and the development of events in LC, as exhibited by Melibea's sudden surrender to passion. According to Asensio, however, Rojas had an integral and precise vision of the world he had created and conceived his world within a logical, concrete, and real time.

Although it is his intention to prove that the action of LC is conceived within a real time, Asensio concedes that a separation of time exists between the first garden scene and the rest of the work. This initial scene would constitute the prologue of the work, allowing a few days' time to pass before we witness the scene in Calisto's room. Asensio maintains that the structural lines of the original Comedia are clearly defined: A prologue in which the love is born; the first garden scene; and, after a certain lapse of time, the three days of continuous action during which we see the consequences of this love. Thus, the separation of time that necessarily exists between the first garden scene and the rest of the work does not negate that the whole was conceived and executed with great respect for human truth.

His solution to the avowed temporal contradiction is the insertion of a few days between the first chance meeting and Calisto's return home, which in turn initiates three days of continuous action. According to Asensio, the fact that the whole of LC is conceived and executed within a real time supports the thesis of single authorship for the whole work.

1953

Asensio, Manuel J., "A Rejoinder," Hispanic Review, XXI (1953), 45-50.

Asensio persists in his basic argument that the love of Calisto and Melibea was born before the encounter in the garden; that time elapsed between a first meeting and the encounter in the garden and that further time elapsed between the garden scene and Calisto's revelation of his love to Sempronio.

Gilman, Stephen, "A Propos of 'El tiempo en La Celstina' by Manuel J. Asensio," Hispanic Review, XXI (1953), 42-45.

While Asensio defends the non-existence of any temporal contradiction in LC, Gilman accepts the possibility that in fiction two separate times may coexist. Gilman notes

that the text offers evidence against an hiatus between the
first and the second scene.   Moreover, the intensity of the
lover's passion can be explained within the well-established
literary tradition of passionate love at first sight.

Gilman, Stephen, "Diálogo y estilo and La Celestina," Nueva
Revista de Filología Hispánica, VII (1953), 461-469.
        According to Gilman, the existence of the additions re-
veals Rojas' awareness of the nature of his own art.   The
words which he added emphasize the internal direction of the
language.   It is a spoken language, "en cuanto está escrito
como si saliera de una vida y se dirigiera hacia otra--cada
palabra se sostiene en un yo y un tú."   Dialogue for Rojas
is the encounter of two lives.
        In Gilman's view, style, topics, and action "vienen a
prestar consciente servicio" to the first and second person
which constitute Rojas' artistic paradigm.

Green, Otis H., "Celestina, Auto I: 'Minerua con el can',"
Nueva Revista de Filología Hispánica, VII (1953), 470-474.
        Green suggests a textual emendation for "Minerua con
el can" to read "Minerva con Vulcán."   He attributes the error to the 1499 printer who, imagining a parallel with the
preceding "con el toro," interpreted the text to read "con el
can."
        Menéndez Pidal has already corrected "Eras y Crato
médicos," which ought to read "Erasístrato médico," and
pointed out that "piedad de silencia" is an erratum for "piedad
de Seleuco."

Green, Otis H., "La furia de Melibea," Clavileño, IV (1953),
1-3.
        According to Green, Melibea's fury is provoked by a
lack of humility on the part of the aspiring fenhedor--a quality prescribed by the rules of courtly love.
        By refusing to obey the courtly tradition, Calisto be-
comes nothing more than a "loco enamorado" who embarks
on the road of his own destruction, since the author's explicit purpose is to admonish "los locos enamorados ... que a
sus amigas llaman e dizen ser su Dios."
        The traditional code required the fenhedor to keep his
feelings secret.   It follows that when the lover neglected to
follow the accepted rules, he could expect a reaction similar
to Melibea's fury.

Petriconi, H., "Die Schuldfrage," Die Verführte Unschuld.
Hamburg, 1953.

In Petriconi's view, one cannot speak of a seduction
in Melibea's case. She gives herself freely to Calisto; and
he is not guilty of her downfall. As for the lovers' death,
it cannot be regarded as retribution for their guilt; it occurs
out of aesthetic necessity, like that of Romeo and Juliet.

Samonà, Carmelo, <u>Aspetti del retoricismo nella 'Celestina'.</u>
Rome, 1953.
        Samonà's thesis is that in spite of its originality, the
style of LC adheres to a culturally determined and well-defined rhetorical tradition. Rojas' style reflects the new climate of buen gusto, devoted to rhetorical moderation. We
see him bound through his literary education by the very elements which are going through a period of crisis. And yet
his originality breaks through the ornamental and precious
manner to which he is bound.
        Samonà examines the traditional stylistic elements
which contributed to the artistic expression in LC and evaluates their suitability for expressing a particular world of
ideas and feelings. He finds that Rojas gave an intimate and
personal tone to the aristocratic language he used, thus
achieving a lyrical equilibrium between a rhetorical and a
realistic tradition.
        The attitude of the author toward the traditional rhe-
torical forms is one both of respect and criticism. We see
that in the process of changing from impersonal and stylized
forms into "affective" and "personal" ones, lies one of the
interesting stylistic problems of the work. Rojas himself
has undergone a process of questioning and evaluating the
rigid code of traditional literary values. These values have
undergone a process of purification in LC.
        The additions of 1502 indicate a conscious attempt to
remain faithful to the spirit of the original. Underneath the
aesthetic incongruities of some erudite enumerations and
sententious disgressions lies a fundamental stylistic unity
which renders the thesis of dual authorship untenable.

1954

Adinolfi, Giulia, "<u>La Celestina e la sua unità di composizi-</u>
one," <u>Filologia Romanza,</u> I (1954), 12-60.
        Love is at the center of Rojas' dramatic conception.
It is neither a symbol nor an abstraction but a carnal experience. The sense of guilt which Rojas associates with love
shows itself in the tragic end of the lovers and their collaborators, and also in the desperate bitterness which pervades
the world he has created. This dramatic conception of love

is exacerbated by a fundamental pessimism and an integral fatalism.   In LC people are irretrievably drawn to love; hence we see a drama of human weakness and not a drama of seduction.   Celestina's strength lies in her ability to arouse in the heart of men the passion which will lead them to destruction.   The perversion of the protagonists results from their own moral weakness, from their congenital inability to struggle.

Rojas structures his work with dimensions of time and space which allow him to portray his characters within a deeper perspective [Gilman, 1945].   The narrative element is not mechanically inserted in the dramatic discourse, but springs from it, and is therefore deeply connected to it. What gives impetus to the tension and drama is the reflections, sentences, and erudite references and proverbs.   This sententiousness is the distinctive character of Rojas' art.

In the Tragicomedia, Rojas rethinks the world of the Comedia in rational, logical moralizing terms.   What had previously been a source of emotion, of drama, of poetry, now becomes an object of reflection.   Rojas entered this reflective stage with Pleberio's monologue.   The structure and tone of the additions reveal the presence of Rojas in a new awareness of himself as a poet.   The temporal dimension he had originally created for his characters becomes accentuated.   He prolongs the life of his protagonists, creating a pause wherein he describes and contemplates the painful condition of two lovers, "il loro angoscioso gioire di amore." The new moralizing interest creates Calisto's monologue after his servants' death, when he is reminded of his honor. Rhetoric here is an instrument of dramatic tension.

In the more extended and reflective view of his work, Rojas can fully realize and develop what he had sacrificed in the Comedia.   In the Tragicomedia, Act XIX, the author abandons the economy of the love scene of the Comedia for the sake of lyrical expression.   Love is still earthy but it is also abandonment and tenderness, with nature participating in the lovers' fulfillment.   And yet this scene maintains a profound unity with the original text and a coherence with the motifs of the whole Comedia, thus testifying to the unity of conception of the whole work.

The two narrative nuclei in the Tragicomedia--the lengthening of the love episode, and the development of the underworld--both reveal an intrinsic unity with the original Comedia.   In the one we have abandonment to pleasure; in the other, the desire for vengeance.   It is through the very failure of this vengeance that Calisto's death becomes more clearly accidental.   Furthermore, this new development al-

lows a more individual characterization of Elicia and Areusa.
But here again the author remains faithful to his original creation. This is especially evident in Elicia's characters. As
for Areusa, all the aspects of her character reappear confirmed and developed. Her independent spirit is reaffirmed.
Once again, the two versions show a perfect continuity of development as we watch the author relive with a more critical
awareness the world and the characters of his Comedia.
        The author added Centurio not only as an instrument
of vengeance but to give life to a world suffering from the
loss of its principal characters. Centurio, however, remains
a caricature, a grotesque figure. We miss in him the ambiguity of the other characters, which made them real and
undefinable.
        An examination of the additions points to the intimate
and profound coherence that exists between the two versions.
The language of the additions is to be viewed with respect to
the text where they have been inserted. Adinolfi notes that
the verbosity and sententiousness of the additions are already
anticipated in the original parts. Their aesthetic value is
dictated by the dramatic moment in which they are inserted.
One cannot consider their particular character a new element
or a stylistic departure from the tone of the original.
        The additions consisting of a word or phrase show
Rojas' preoccupation with language and the clear awareness
he had acquired of his own stylistic devices. Adinolfi agrees
with Gilman that the brief variants accentuate the intimate
function of language in the Comedia; they identify the person
to whom the speech is directed.
        Both the diversity and persistence of motifs which ex-
ist in the two stages of the work clearly show that Rojas was
the creator and revisor of his work. Rojas manifests his
own personality even in the parts which differ from the rest.
The facts known about his life, viewed along with the historical conditions of his time, offer definite proof for attributing
the complete work to him.

Criado de Val, M., "Melibea y Celestina ante el juicio de
Don Quijote," Anales Cervantinos, IV (1954), 187-198.
        According to Criado de Val, the initial conception of
Melibea belongs to the first author and stems from the medieval courtly tradition. But the theme is transformed by
Rojas: to the original conventionalism, Rojas adds realistic
details, as in the description of Melibea by Areusa.
        Whereas the original author of Act I limits his criti-
cism to the social danger of the go-betweens and deceitful
servants against a costumbrista setting, Rojas "plantea la

cuestión trágicamente." In LC we have the classic problem
in Spanish life of how to establish a love relationship. The
tragedy in the life of Calisto and Melibea is brought about by
an error of method, since they fail to comply with the Spanish manner of becoming acquainted.

Gilman, Stephen, "The 'Argumentos' to La Celestina," Romance Philology, VIII (1954), 71-87.
          In this article, Gilman discusses the aesthetic inade-
quacy of the arguments of the edition of 1499 when compared
to those accompanying the additional acts of 1502. In the
1499 edition of LC, the anonymous author of the general argument overstresses the moral intention of LC, while the individual arguments overstress the plot. On the other hand,
the author of 1502 offers passages of self-criticism and
some insight into the intention behind the additions.

MacDonald, Inez, "Some Observations on the Celestina,"
Hispanic Review, XXII (1954), 264-281.
          Miss MacDonald deals with two of the questions which
still remain unanswered: Why do Calisto and Melibea need-
lessly carry on a clandestine affair; and why does Calisto
employ Celestina.
          Miss MacDonald states that the answer to these ques-
tions is to be found in the literary convention in vogue at
the end of the fifteenth century and not in modern prejudices.
First of all, Rojas sets out to demonstrate the evils of "loco
amor" as Juan Ruiz had done before him. He stresses the
dangers into which love throws its victims but which, though
wholly evil, is enticingly delectable. The whole force and
glamor of love is that it is secret and that its sole aim is
fulfillment. This idea belongs to the traditional view that
love has nothing to do with marriage. Secondly the very
violence of Calisto's love prepares the ground for Celestina's
intervention: Calisto succumbs to the violence of instantane-
ous passion, while Melibea remains untouched by it. Therefore Celestina is necessary to the situation as Rojas understood it. Both Calisto and Melibea are victims of love, but
Melibea is the victim of the superior and evil forces which
Celestina commands.

McPheeters, D. W., "The Element of Fatality in the Tragicomedia de Calisto y Melibea," Symposium, VIII (1954),
331-335.
          McPheeters deals with the role played by adverse
fortune in the development of the Tragicomedia.
          He maintains that the reference to the loss of a falcon

was traditionally intended to portend misfortune.   In fact,
Pármeno's speech makes the loss of the neblí the first step
in the concatenation of unfortunate happenings which will lead
to tragedy.

Calisto's infractions of courtly decorum in the initial
scene are also a significant portent.   Calisto is doomed because he disregarded the first four steps by which a lover in
the medieval courtly tradition hoped to become a fenhedor or
silent admirer of his lady.

Also, there are numerous references throughout LC
to falling, especially falling from high estate as part of the
inevitable turning of Fortune's wheel.   The additions confirm
the two bad omens mentioned above.

Trotter, G. D., "Sobre 'La furia de Melibea' de Otis H.
Green," Clavileño, V (1954), 55-56.

Contrary to Green's interpretation of Melibea's fury
[1953], Trotter maintains that Melibea's rejection is the central point of the dramatic plot.   The vehemence of rebuff is
necessary to exhibit Celestina's diabolic greatness.   Celestina's triumph affords her a dramatic stature which would
have been denied her had Melibea shown a willingness to re-
ciprocate Calisto's love.

Calisto may not have adhered to the ritualistic nature
of courtly love, but neither does Melibea exhibit the decorum
of the courtly lady.   She follows the universal laws of the
woman in love.

According to Trotter, the meaning of the first scene
must be sought within the artistic scheme of the entire work,
i. e. , in the fundamental relationship between man and woman,
and certainly not in the stylized relations of the drut and of
his lady.   The love of the protagonists of LC has no relationship to the complicated protocol required by the cultivated
tradition of the Frauendienst.   The two lovers obey nothing
but a mysterious and omnipotent passion which annihilates
them by the nature of its own fury.

Ugualde, Louis, "The Celestina of 1502," Boston Public Library Quarterly, VI (1954), 206-222.

The dramatic dialogue of LC is a vivid representation
of human conversations in which the comic and the tragic al-
ternate.   The creation of this new form of dialogue is one of
the chief merits of the book.

Rojas has delineated for the first time the parallelism
of love among nobles and among servants.

Although some critics have considered LC as an
apotheosis of love like Tristan and Isolde, Ugualde sees it as

a tragedy in which love surges as a mysterious and terrible deity.

As for Celestina, she is moved only by greed--the very greed which leads her to her destruction.   But one cannot help admire her astuteness and the manner in which she governs and dominates other lives.

1955

Gilman, Stephen, "Fortune and Space in La Celestina," Romanische Forschungen, LXVI (1955), 342-360.

It is Gilman's opinion that Rojas did not intend to indicate the geographical identity of his city [Chapter 7]; he allowed it to appear only in the off-hand remarks of his characters.   Just as he named these characters generically, so too the city seems purposely nameless.   This is an aspect of Rojas' art.   The work as a whole lacks references to specific land- or sea-scapes, for "he gives us a brief glimpse of that wide expanse of space discovered by the Renaissance as the new circumstance of the individual."   The only concrete reference is made by Melibea when looking at the navíos.

Gilman's thesis is that Rojas was a supremely conscious author and that in the 1502 additions, he reveals himself as aware of the most intimate details of his art.   And yet the question remains unanswered as to why he makes his single reference to horizontal space and why he chooses Melibea to carry it.   Gilman maintains that the answer to these questions will lead us into the thematic substance of LC. Gilman proposes that "Melibea's sentence was written precisely because Rojas wanted to refer to the space of landscape and horizon--what might be called disinterested space-- at the climax of his action."   This is a kind of tacit recognition of the decisive role played by space in LC.   Rojas substitutes a continuous three-dimensional trajectory for scenic limitations.   And wherever barriers exist--walls, doors-- these serve as obstacles to the desires of the characters, but not as scenery or other indications of aesthetic foreshortening.   It is this spatial freedom which gives such a deceptive illusion of identifiable reality to the fictitious reality.

Gilman identifies the fall through space as a recurrent event in the work and as an underlying preoccupation in the minds of the characters.   In LC, we have the ever-present danger of vertical space or death by falling.   The physical vertigo is complemented by the moral vertigo in the same character, who fears both "la cayda en el espacio" as well as "la cayda de fortuna."   Because Calisto's death is accidental, the note of retribution or punishment that a fall from

Fortune implied in the medieval world is distinctly absent, for
"the Goddess Fortune has departed from the scene and left
mere mechanical chance in her place." The manner of death
that Rojas chooses for his characters implies that "man has
been left alone in an alien universe, an universe in which dimensions are the heirs of Fortune." Fortune and space become one. Gilman points to other instances in the Prologue
and in the acrostic which carry the note of thematic vertigo,
reflecting the thematic importance of Space and Fortune in
the work. This demonstrates to us that "failure--a fall or
spatial death in one form or another--is inherent in the very
aspiration."

    "The landscape of Melibea's death is inevitably a land-
scape of Fortune transformed into space--with faraway ships."
Gilman sees a connection between Melibea's scenery of suicide and the marine backgrounds of Renaissance and pre-Renaissance painting. The ships in the faraway horizon "represent Fortune newly converted into dimensional exposure." He
uses Breughel's Icarus (ca. 1554) as an example of the "alien,
inattentive space which Icarus has attempted to conquer and
which in its naked height and distance reduces him to the size
of an insect. For both Breughel and Rojas, then, a fall and
faraway ships represent Fortune's new dimensionality. Each
has tried to express the theme of human insignificance in a
world agonizingly indifferent to its enormity."

Webber, Edwin J., "Tragedy and Comedy in the Celestina,"
Hispania, XXXV (1955), 318-320.
    For Webber, the fall from happy estate heightens the
effect of the descent, especially when introduced suddenly in
the midst of the heroes' romantic obliviousness.

1956

Earle, Peter G., "Love Concepts in La cárcel de Amor and
La Celestina," Hispania, XXXIX (1956), 92-96.
    Earle defines the Tragicomedia as a sentimental work
which aims at renovating a literary genre through the elimi-
nation of some elements, the parody of others, and the re-
generation of still more. Most of the parody in LC is directed at aristocratic customs and manners.
    Earle compares LC to the Cárcel de amor (1492).
He lists similarities in plot, but also some fundamental differences. In both books love is identified as a malignant supernatural force. The lover's passion is a form of idolatry
grown out of the Provençal concept that the lady is infinitely
superior to her pretender. Similar in both lovers are the

effects of turbación, but Calisto is much more human than
Leriano. A comparison between Laureola and Melibea shows
that an improvement in character-creation is in evidence.
From the beginning, a confusion of emotions and moral re-
straints is perceptible in Melibea, whereas Laureola remains
impervious to passion.

Both the Cárcel de amor and LC reveal trends of
thought historically identifiable. The Cárcel is written exclusively from the aristocratic viewpoint. The characters in
it are one-dimensional. Their visision of the world is pessimistic. On the other hand, LC's complexity, the many-sided-
ness of its characters, the conflicts of ideas and emotions,
divorce it from the conventional species of the sentimental
novel. For it brings "a clear vision of inner and external
realities, a human revelation rather than a moral teaching."

Gilman, Stephen, The Art of 'La Celestina'. Madison, 1956.
Gilman defines Rojas' stylistic innovations and guides
us to a fuller understanding of Rojas' creative process, his
artistic and creative awareness. Gilman sees "style, topic
and action join in a conscious subservience to the first and
second persons which conclude Rojas' artistic paradigm."
Rojas develops only stylistic elements which contribute to the
development of the dialogic situation in interlocking the tú and
the yo of human conversation. He eliminates everything
which need not penetrate the consciousness of the speaker.
Each speech exists in function of the speaker and the listener
and not for the instruction or entertainment of the reader.
All life in the work is dedicated to dialogue. Dialogue is for
Rojas the language which results from the meeting of two
lives. Clarity is a necessary ingredient to dialogue. Rojas'
notion of vital clarity is almost always additive and it is
therefore related to the process of revision of 1502. There
his efforts are directed toward an adequate relationship between the word and its speaker or listener. He seeks to
complete, to clarify the dialogic direction. Gilman defines
the art of LC as "that of a vital dialectic guided skilfully towards a plenitude of meaning and on a scale ranging from
stylistic clarity to thematic fulfillment." The chief ingredi-
ents of Rojas' spoken language are clarity and logic. "The
vital authenticity of the dialogue is accomplished by placing
logic and lesson on the surface of spoken language."

Rojas practices a new type of decorum: a dialogic
decorum which guides the rise and fall of style without inter-
fering with the autonomous encounter of two or more lives.

Gilman studies the individuals in LC as they are related to each other in dialogue, and not apart from it. The

characters reveal their own consciousness through dialogue.
Rojas, however, has given Celestina a characterization which
is denied to others. The interpolations point to Rojas'
heightened interest in Celestina.

While from Rojas' dialogic artistry emerges each of
the lives, engaged as they all are in a struggle of consciousness, from his structural artistry emerges a particular frame
of spoken consciousness. Each act examined separately ac-
cents a phase or state of consciousness of the central individual. The structure is sustained by an intentional ordering
of consciousness. In a detailed analysis of the first 12 acts,
Gilman demonstrates the structural order or direction of each
act to support his initial concept of the act "as a unit of dialogic consciousness as designed without dependence on the
third person." The structure of the acts was calculated to
unify the progression of the dialogue. The dialogic situations
of each act are the equivalents of scenes. Since Rojas' whole
artistry is non-theatrical, or a-theatrical, it is not surpris-
ing that his situations do not adhere to a scenic structure.

As for space, there is a three-dimensional quality in
LC which permits absolute freedom of movement. Rojas,
however, eliminates all external artifacts that do not of their
own weight penetrate the consciousness of the speaker. Col-
or, too, is introduced in relation to the dialogic obligations
of each situation. Time serves to set apart the structural
units or dialogic situations. The work moves within a bal-
anced geometry of space, object and light which orders the
disparate consciousness of the speaker.

For Gilman, Pleberio's lament is a thematic epilogue.
His is the consciousness of the survivor, surviving against
his will, and his words reflect the broken perspectives of
sentiment which alone are left to him. Rojas' thematic innovation: he has reduced Fortune from an allegorical personage to its temporal and spatial media of operation. And by
doing so, he substitutes human lives for literature's previous
didactic and exemplary concern with man. Love, too, is converted from mythological inevitability to intimate sentimental
awareness. Love furnishes sentiments ranging from deleite
to gloria. Love, the primary force in almost all the characters, can supply its own inner defense against Fortune
which has become time and space. "Each of the characters
of LC lives consciously within his own individual juncture of
duration and dimension, of sentiment and argument, of experience and necessity. This is what happens to Fortune and
Love when submitted to a dialogic art; this is the very core
of Rojas' theme."

Rojas' utilization of Petrarch's De remediis is closely

connected with the thematic need of the work itself.   The
presence of Aristotle and the absence of Petrarch in Act I
coincides not only with tentative theses but also with characters who are not yet fully engaged in conflict, not yet fully
involved in dialogical situations.   The entry of the De remediis into LC coincides with a new possibility of irony and
with the engagement of consciousness in dialogue on a level
more profound than that of mere argumentative discussion.
"The Stoicism of Petrarch helps invoke ironically the anguished (or cynical) anti-Stoic awareness of the speakers."
In the fifteen acts of LC, the De remediis offers the possibility of irony and the patterning of character.   "His horizontal structure and his doctrinal emphasis on the free consciousness of the subject help Rojas to build in irony the
several consciousnesses of his characters and to order them
artistically in terms of a few elementary determinants."

Petrarch's contribution to LC can be divided into three
distinct phases.   First, it is missing in Act I where the new
consciousness is not yet fully engaged in dialogue.   Second,
it appears in the Comedia where an ironical comedy of conscious life comes into being, availing itself of the patterns
of awareness and confrontation of life already contained in
Petrarch's work, the author freeing himself from vertical
didacticism.   The patterns of character in LC involve the
same two factors that are so decisive in Petrarch, the inner
consciousness and the general pattern or commonplace Stoic
doctrine.   From these elements, Rojas creates an ironical
comedy of conscious life.   And finally, the references to
Petrarch diminish in the 1502 additions.   Rojas utilizes what
is implied in De remediis.   Hence we have the thematic adaptation of the Prologue.   In none of these phases does Gilman
find the notion of influence applicable.

The traditional generic schism cannot be applied to
LC because "the unprecedented psychology of consciousness
of the inhabitants of LC is alien to both the novel and the
drama."   The stylistic originality of LC lies in its dialogic
artistry, whereas the generic artistry of the work lies in the
reversal of the usual structure of drama.   In drama, we find
action framed with suitable scenes and divided into a traditional number of acts; in LC, we find the work framed into
acts and divided into dialogic situations.

LC exhibits a unique self-shaping life and is therefore
ageneric.   But in the additions of 1502, there is an indication of generic modification.   The third person (él) missing
in the Comedia, appears for the first time in the Tragicomedia, openly contributing to and prearranging a sequence
of action.   Rojas, aware of the process of continuation, of-

fers the first indication of segregation of novel and drama,
leaning towards comedy.   Gilman points to incipient changes
of characterization and action and new techniques in dialogue
and structure where dialogue is designed not for its own sake
but for the listeners a departure from dialogic consciousness.
There is a trend toward a dramatic ordering in Acts XV,
XVII, and XVIII, while Acts XVI and XIX offer novelistic
features.   The generic innovation of 1502 is that Rojas allows us to witness the emergence of the two major genres of
the comic century: novel and drama.   It is apparent from
the purely comic and theatrical elements, the novelistic and
lyrical experiences and sentimental amplitude, that Rojas now
knows his characters in the third person.   But for Gilman,
the work remains externally ageneric, even though his artistry led Rojas to a deep understanding of the meaning of novel
and drama.   The arguments of 1502, too, furnish their own
evidence of Rojas' increased awareness of the relationship of
creator to created.   Certain observations in these arguments
serve to illuminate the intent of the artist.   For Gilman,
"the added acts clarify the whole in the same manner that the
interpolations, large and small, clarify the parts."   The evidence of the interpolations points to Rojas' awareness of the
need for clarity.   For Rojas, clarity is indispensable to dialogue.   The additions and emendations reveal his striving for
clarity and his perception of obscurities resulting from the
lack of adequate relationship between the word and its speaker
or listener.   Rojas' concept of clarity seems to be related
to the whole process of revision in 1502.   His is a process
of creative completion.   Therefore not only does he add in
revising, but all that is added seems to grow out of what was
already there.   Thus we see search for stylistic clarity leading him to thematic fulfillment.

Green, Otis H. , "Lo de tu abuela con el ximio (Celestina:
Auto I), Hispanic Review, XXIV (1956), 1-12.
        Green examines the statement made by Sempronio and
endeavors to show that this ribald joke, "Lo de tu abuela con
el ximio, testigo es el cuchillo de tu abuelo," is part of a
medieval and Renaissance tradition.   He feels that in 1499
this phrase would have been no more insulting as a jest than
"¡Tu madre!"   Green points out that throughout the Middle
Ages there was an increasing tendency to connect the ape
with sexual desire.   In the Renaissance, the narrative tradition of the lustful ape received new impetus from the redis-
covery of the ithyphallic ape of the ancients.

Spector, Norman B. , "The Procuress and Religious Hypocrisy," Italica, XXXIII (1956), 52-59.

For Spector, Rojas' characterization of Celestina offers the fullest exploitation of the dramatic possibilities found
in other literary portrayals of the type, and her machinations
take on a demonic quality.

Celestina is the complete procuress. The stereotyped
traits of the classical lena: her greed, the absence of pity
for the lover whom she despoils, the magical powers of the
Ovidian sorceress, together with the buhonera's bag of tricks,
are depicted with consummate vividness. But all of these
traits are concealed behind her hypocrisy and show of piety,
which serve to outline more clearly the monstrous corruption
of her character.

For his portrayal of Celestina, Rojas was well served
by Christianity, with its emphasis on virginity and chastity,
and by the Spanish social sense of sexual sin, for these provided him with the basis for a new conception of the role of
the procuress. She corrupts the young and innocent and
gains access to them by means of her false piety. In Rojas'
hands, Celestina becomes a great threat to Christian morality.

1957

Garrido Pallardó, Fernando, Los problemas de Calisto y
Melibea y el conflicto de su autor. Figueras, 1957.

Garrido Pallardó feels strongly that LC was written
for the stage, and believes that the work could be presented
within the framework of the medieval stage. As for the rhetorical quality of the work, he points out that Rojas was
aware of the aesthetics of style and that throughout there is
an effort to adhere to the principle of clarity, "abrevia e ven
al fecho."

Gilman, Stephen, "The Fall of Fortune: from Allegory to
Fiction," Filologia Romanza, IV (1957), 337-354.

Gilman reaffirms the thematic equation of Fortune and
Space in LC. For him, the falling in LC is "a visible sign
of a replacement of the moral universe of traditional commonplaces by a barren dimensional universe excruciatingly
indifferent to man's concerns. It is a sign ... of fecund
transition from Middle Ages to Renaissance."

Russell, P. E., "The Art of Fernando de Rojas," Bulletin
of Hispanic Studies, XXXIV (1957), 160-167.

Russell singles out the ways in which comedy and humor enter into Rojas' art. Stress is laid on the cowardice

of Sempronio and Pármeno in Act XII. Here Rojas is adher-
ing to a comic tradition which thought cowardice funny. Humor, on the other hand, is often linked with the note of defiance, which seems to be characteristic of many of the characters in LC. Rojas' pessimism is so corrosive, however,
that he leaves us with the belief that no value is to be attributed even to these acts of defiance.

Quijano Terán, Margarita, 'La Celestina' y 'Otelo'. Estudio
de Literatura Dramática Comparada. Mexico City, 1957.
        Miss Quijano Terán examines the structure and char-
acters of LC and compares these to Othello. Miss Quijano
Terán holds that LC should be considered a drama even
though Rojas is inartistic in the handling of his characters.
She sees Rojas as a moralist more intent on pointing a lesson than in elaborating the psychology of his characters. As
for Celestina, she finds her unconvincing and inconsistent.
        Though the comparison was first suggested by Me-
néndez Pelayo, she feels there is no significant likeness between either the situation or the characters of the two works.
Miss Quijano Terán concludes that Shakespeare, Othello and
Iago are infinitely superior to Rojas, LC and its protagonist.

                              1958

Alvarez, Guzmán, El amor en la novela picaresca española.
The Hague, 1958.
        For Alvarez, LC belongs in the periphery of the pi-
caresque genre. The reason the servants of Calisto are
servants and not pícaros is that Calisto is not the typical
master found in the picaresque novel.

Ayllón Cándido, "Death in La Celestina," Hispania XLI
(1958), 160-164.
        According to Ayllón, Rojas reveals through the dia-
logue and action of his characters a profound concern with
life and death. The characters are in a great hurry to en-
joy life, unaware of the fact that their very destruction lies
in their impetuosity. Intimately related to the theme of
death are the two forces of love and avarice. Celestina
ironically fails to realize the avaricious wishes of both Sempronio and Pármeno. Her greed leads her to her violent
death. On the other hand, the author's irony is at work in
the accidental death of Calisto, while Melibea's choice of
death ennobles her character.
        Ayllón concludes that "with Pleberio immersed in
tragedy, LC bitterly reveals Fernando de Rojas' pessimistic

presentation of the relation between love and death."

Webber, Edwin J., "The Celestina as an Arte de Amores,"
Modern Philology, LV (1958), 145-153.
          Webber states that the dramatic nature of LC cannot
be explained solely in terms of Terentian comedy, and much
less can it be explained in terms of Senecan tragedy.
          Webber believes that Rojas set out to compose an arte
de amores [Chapter 3] in dramatic style, and that for his
dialogue form he drew upon a variety of available models,
including Terence, Plautus, Seneca, possibly the Pamphilus,
and one or more Italian humanistic comedies. Webber enu-
merates several features of LC which reveal the manner in
which Rojas combined the concept of the arte de amores with
elements from all of the above.

1959

Loehlin, Marian R., "Celestina of the Twenty Hands," Hispania, XLII (1959), 309-316.
          Miss Loehlin discusses Celestina's relationships and
contacts with each member of the lower class and her handling of each one until each is under her command and will.
Miss Loehlin points out how Celestina's method of dealing
with the upper classes differs from her treatment of the lower classes and reveals her perspicacity. She keeps members of her own class a little lower than herself. But she
is humble in her relationship with her superiors.
          Celestina's hands are an important key to both her
life and her death. Her techniques are controlled by her
dexterous hands. The modulations of her hands reflect the
variety of her abilities, but the one time she renounces the
mobility and dexterity of her hands--in her refusal to share
her reward--she meets her death.

Russell, P. E., "Celestina," Times Literary Supplement
(July 10, 1959), 411.
          According to Russell, Pármeno's statement, "todo era
burla ·y mentira," is in fifteenth-century terms a declaration
of orthodoxy, not of skepticism. The text shows that the authors were fascinated by the subject of the occult. Russell
contends that Melibea is the victim of a commonplace form
of sorcery, philocaptio. The text clearly indicates that she
was not in love from the start.

"Star-Crossed Lovers," Anon. rev., Times Literary Supplement (June 19, 1959), 368.

The conjurings of Celestina are seen here as nothing
more than mockery and lies, especially since they all end
with the witch threatening the devil himself.   Celestina's conjurings were simply a deception which impressed her clients.
The introduction of spells and invocations does nothing to advance the plot.   Melibea is in love with Calisto from the
start.

1961

Basdekis, Demetrius, "Romantic Elements in La Celestina,"
Hispania, XLIV (1961), 52-54.
          Basdekis sees LC as a work containing all the basic
elements of Romantic literature.   The core of LC's romanticism lies in its treatment of love: a pristine love whose ultimate manifestation is death.   Evidence for the mal du si-
ècle element is found in Calisto's melancholia.   There is,
too, the use of the supernatural, which occupies an important place in formal romanticism.   Celestina's obsession with
the supernatural almost invariably channels itself toward the
satanic.
          The rebellion of the individual against organized so-
ciety is noticeable in Celestina herself.   The individualism
of characters seems to be propelled by an enigmatic force.
The introspective Calisto is the foremost representative of
that individualism.

Bataillon, Marcel, 'La Célestine' selon Fernando de Rojas.
Paris, 1961.
          Bataillon distinguishes in his study the original act
from the tragicomical superstructures created by Rojas.   The
anonymous author showed little interest in the lovers Calisto
and Melibea.   The drama of the first act is the seduction/ of
Pármeno by the arguments of Celestina.   Attention is centered on Pármeno and his moral defeat through an inimitable
use of logic.
          In his superstructures, Rojas continues the morality
of the first act.   LC originally is and will continue to be a
moralizing work [Chapter 6], written "en represión de los
locos enamorados que vencidos en su desordenado apetito,
a sus amigas llaman e dizen ser su Dios, assimesmo fecha
en aviso de los engaños de las alcahuetas e malos e lisonjeros sirvientes."   Bataillon shows that in most cases Rojas
expands on what his forerunner had done in Act I.   Bataillon
seeks confirmation of this interpretation by comparing LC
with its imitations [Chapter 4].   Similarities in thematic and
stylistic treatment between LC and the adaptations allow us

to interpret LC in the way Rojas intended, namely a condemnation of los locos enamorados. Bataillon examines the
artistic devices which bring out LC's moral point of view.

Bataillon's textual analysis addresses itself to elements which betray the moral character of the work and its
didactic intention. For him, Rojas uses the art of moralizing for a literary divertissement rather than puritanical ser-
monizing. This artistic purpose, however, does not erase
from LC its character of morality or cancel out its didactic
intention.

Bataillon places LC generically with the arte de
amores, as suggested by Webber [1958]. But Rojas went beyond this generic type and created the Celestinesque genre.
Bataillon singles out the fundamental stylistic devices which
make up this new genre. The use of tú, although it has a
Roman origin, has a different meaning in LC, especially
when used between servant and master--a familiarity which
borders on insolence. The use of tú is widespread in the
continuations and imitations. Another technique, the systematic use of asides, "hablar entre dientes," expresses the
duplicity of base characters. This duplicity is accentuated
by their constant use of proverbs and philosophical sentences
--the wisdom of which is little practiced by them. Again,
while the aside in Plautus and Terence was a mere convention, in LC (where it is to be vaguely heard by the person
involved) the aside is used to express betrayal, the betrayal
of "malas mujeres and falsos sirvientes." The imitations
similarly make widespread use of the aside. Unquestionably
this aside entre dientes translates a well-defined moral and
social relationship between servants and masters, revealing
the impudence of the former and the naiveté of the latter.

Another comic device contrasting with the use of the
aside is the words spoken too loud. This too is used for a
moral purpose. Another piquant aspect of the dialogue is
the sophistic use of proverbs and maxims. The discrepancy
between the nobility of the maxims and the base character of
their speakers forms part of the moral intent of the work.

It is only in this century that Calisto has been seen
in his true light, worthy of contempt and not of sympathy.
Miss Frank [1954] noted the grotesque manner in which Rojas treated him. For Bataillon, Calisto is an "obsédé ridicule." His amorous obsession destroys in him all noble or
delicate thoughts. His death reflects Rojas' reprobation of
his particular madness. Even his prodigality is a sign of
weakness. Calisto is a tragicomic character, not a hero.
His sudden death does not modify Rojas' condemnation of his
sensual obsession. It exemplifies the destiny awaiting the

slaves of disorderly passion.

In the 1502 additions, Rojas takes up again states of
mind and moral themes which he had already treated in the
Comedia "sans les épuiser." The parts of LC which modern
critics have found inferior and disconcerting, especially in
the additions of 1502, Rojas' contemporaries not only found
meaningful but also imitated, as the continuations of LC show.

The moral and social theme on which the action of
LC is based is the degradation of a nobleman and of his love
by his unworthy servants, who are perverted by virtue of
their association with the underworld.

Celestina's intervention into the action is brought about
by Sempronio. Her intervention becomes appropriate in the
logic of an intrigue where the servants play an important
role, a role which touches on the world of prostitution where
Celestina is the key character. Rojas is attacking a social
and moral problem by presenting this world.

Rojas accentuates the correlation between the baseness
of the servants and the ridiculous trust Calisto puts in them.
The additions of Act XII emphasize that the noble characters
are blind; the servants, cynical.

In the longer version Rojas expands his moralizing to
include the seduced girl and her family. The couple Calisto-
Melibea did not interest the author of the first act. To Rojas alone belongs the personal drama of Melibea. It is this
aspect of LC that misled Romantic scholars to connect it with
Romeo and Juliet. But, according to Bataillon, Rojas has
deliberately avoided the question of marriage.

Melibea's rejection of Calisto's advances and her fury
with Celestina illustrate Piccolomini's maxim that love is
implicit in a woman's vehement rejection. Rojas suggests
with Melibea's fall "une faiblesse profonde et déjà tentée."
Melibea does not go through any real crisis of conscience.
This is the aspect of her characterization that Juan de Valdés
found objectionable. But Rojas wants to suggest that a seem-
ingly pure girl is infinitely fragile as soon as she is exposed
to the workings of "l'amour coupable," and her fall does not
necessarily result from the devil's intervention.

Melibea's parents serve a definite function in the
structure of the work. Through them, Rojas depicts the
blindness of the upper social strata to anything that does not
belong to their world. Rojas probably realized the imbalance
in the role of Pleberio [Chapter 6] within the play; that is
why he introduced a long scene between Pleberio and Alisa
in the new Act XVI. According to Bataillon, "Rojas se dé-
cide à mettre en plus vive lumière les parents de Melibée,
pour faire d'eux plus nettement des personnages ridicules,

aussi comiques, dans leur genre, que le Calisto du premier
auteur."

The second love scene which Rojas inserts in the 1502
edition is an exaltation of Love. The description of the garden is a lyrical representation of the sensual abandonment
that is to follow. Here again, the imitators did not remain
insensitive to the lyrical contemplation of a nature which
harmonizes with passion. Rojas uses this lyricism to give
a more refined, langorous tone to his heroine which contrasts
with the amorous obsession of Calisto. The presence of Lucrecia, however, degrades the pleasure, giving the scene a
Celestinesque tone.

Rojas remains faithful to the initial purpose of the
Comedia, which was conceived as a moralité by its first author. Melibea's perdition was not explicit enough in the 16-
act version where she could be considered a victim of circumstances. The Tragicomedia clarifies Melibea's behavior
and her family's blindness. The ephemeral triumph of the
deleite was prolonged in order to be better scrutinized and
better judged, not to be glorified. Thus Rojas put to profit
the advice of those who wanted to see the love episode
lengthened.

Rojas' Celestina was not intended for the stage, even
though it inaugurates true comic prose dialogue. Gilman
[1956] has already noted the expressive power of the dialogue.
The elegance of the prose comes through in a reading aloud,
which, as Proaza's verses indicate, was the delivery Rojas
intended.

Deyermond, A. D., The Petrarchan Sources of 'La Celestina'. Oxford, 1961.
        For Rojas' use of the Petrarchan sources, see Chap-
ter 6.

Deyermond, A. D., "The Text-book Mishandled: Andreas
Capellanus and the Opening Scene of La Celestina," Neophilologus, XLV (1961), 218-221.
        Basing himself on the use made of Capellanus' dia-
logue [Chapter 3], Deyermond suggests that the author of
Act I intended us to assume a previous acquaintance between
Calisto and Melibea. It is apparent from his words that Calisto prepared for a hoped-for encounter with Melibea by
looking up appropriate speeches in De Amore. This would
be in keeping with his foolish and pedantic character. He
uses the textbook approach, but he fails to get the hoped-for
textbook response.
        If we suppose the author of Act I to be a student writ-

ing for a student public, the presentation of the hero who is
unexpectedly let down by a standard authority opened up possibilities of comic development for readers who, like Calisto,
were familiar with the De Amore.

Dulsey, Bernard, "La Celestina, ¿versión larga o corta?,"
Hispanófila, IV, No. 11 (1961), 23-28.
		For Dulsey, there is no real tragedy in the longer ver-
sion.   The lovers meet with no real impediments to a lawful
union, and the proofs of Calisto's acceptability as a suitor are
many.
		Dulsey considers the Comedia superior because of its
verisimilitude, its dramatic impetus and its brevity.   The
reader can no longer feel compassion for the lovers in the
Tragicomedia because they are slaves of passion and forget
the only legitimate solution--matrimony.

Lida de Malkiel, María Rosa, Two Spanish Masterpieces:
The Book of Good Love and La Celestina.   Urbana, 1961.
		See Note Chapter 1, Lida de Malkiel, 1961.

Moreno Báez, E., "La obra y el autor," Nosotros y nuestros
clásicos.   Madrid, 1961, pp. 140-150.
		Moreno Báez maintains that Melibea's passion is inex-
plicable without the intervention of the supernatural.

Russell, P. E., "La magia como tema integral de la Tragicomedia de Calisto y Melibea," Homenaje a Dámaso Alonso.
Madrid, 1961, pp. 337-354.
		Russell maintains that witchcraft is an integral ele-
ment of the Tragicomedia.   Both the author of Act I and Rojas give great importance to the contacts that Celestina maintains with supernatural powers and to her pact with the devil.
Yet the theme of witchcraft, though important, holds a secondary place because it begins to function as a result of Calisto's disorderly passion.   The action stems from Calisto's
made love, before any intervention of sorcery.

1962

Aquirre, J. M., Calisto y Melibea, amantes cortesanos.
Zaragoza, 1962.
		Aguirre writes his book in support of the overt decla-
rations of the incipit and the assertion of Otis H. Green et
al. to the effect that LC is directed against the "desordenado
apetito" of courtly lovers--the "errada casuística provenzal"
which exalts the religion of love.   Aguirre gives a docu-

mented survey of the characteristics of courtly lovers in the
tradition, and shows that LC is firmly implanted in this tra-
dition--without prejudice, however, to the "realidad humana"
which Trotter, among others, insists upon.   Indeed, Aguirre
is convinced that the pictures of courtly love which we obtain
in literature were themselves rooted in social reality, not
mere literary game.

The dictum which Aguirre quotes from Andreas Capel-
lanus--"declaramos y mantenemos como firmamente estable-
cido que el amor no puede ejercer sus poderes entre dos
personas unidas en matrimonio"--explains in full why there
is no question of marriage between Calisto and Melibea.   He
rejects Bataillon's view that Calisto ignores marriage because
he is driven by sheer sensuality.   If that were the case, why
wouldn't he offer marriage to gain his ends and then escape?
No, Rojas is interested only in showing the great moral danger inherent in love customs of his day, created by the code
of courtly love.

Without the "añadidos" to the text (including Act XXI),
the latter might well appear to exalt courtly love: Calisto's
death might be attributed to misfortune, while Melibea's
death would be praised.   The crucial passage which determines that LC is an attack on courtly love is Pleberio's lament of Act XXI.   Here finally the author reveals his moral
intention.   Pleberio's indictment of love, which repeats the
commonplaces of the courtly tradition, proves that LC was
"specifically written against the doctrines of courtly love"--
as, indeed, Salas Barbadillo had already seen.

Barbera, Raymond E., "Sempronio," Hispania, XLV (1962),
441-442.

After Celestina, Sempronio is the most vital character of the work.   For Barbera, Sempronio is the Spanish
Iago because within him lies "a detached malevolence that
delights in surveying his victims and remorselessly exposing
their weaknesses," especially Calisto's.   In the exchanges
between Calisto and Sempronio, Calisto emerges as the dupe.
It is through Sempronio that Rojas delineates the major characters.   Sempronio seems to thrive on exposing the foibles
and weaknesses of others.

On the other hand, Celestina's actions throughout the
work betray a basic aim: to function in her trade with the
greatest possible return.

Castro, Américo, 'La Celestina' como contienda literaria.
Madrid, 1962.

For Castro, form, style, and character portrayal in

LC all derive from Rojas' vision of destructive "contienda" between the old and the new values [Chapters 6 and 7]. "Su perfil y su estructura son irregulares, su estilo es sinuoso y tensamente dinámico." Formal irregularity reflects ethical chaos in this work. Love, which had been "pacific concordance" in the work of the Arcipreste de Hita, is now strident disharmony. In this chaotic world, the accidental death of Calisto cannot be viewed as tragic. Actually, only Celestina is a tragic figure, though a deformed one. Her death is grandiose: she dies rebelling against the destiny that destroys her.

Calisto is less interesting: "solitario, monocorde y unidimensional." Areusa and Elicia are more vital, Areusa in her refusal to serve "señores" and Elicia in her escape from the house of Celestina. After the latter's death, Elicia undertakes to live her own life in freedom. As for Celestina, she is "a being as closed and absolute as Calisto" --obeyed but solitary, living in "la regia soledad de un soberano."

Rojas destroys old literary forms, but in the process he creates a new one: the technique of literary "perspectivismo." His characters are humanized. They are viewed differently by different characters. Rojas does not comment on Celestina, for example. We discover her through dialogue.

Devoto, Daniel, "Un ingrediente de Celestina," Filología, VII (1962), 98-104.
        Devoto finds in the Diccionario de la Academia that the "mantillo de niño"--which Pármeno identifies as one of the ingredients in Celestina's laboratory--is the fetal caul which sometimes covers the head of the newborn. The caul is believed to have had extraordinary powers.
        With this example, Devoto shows that where the meaning of certain words has been forgotten, the text has been misinterpreted. He points to the many translations where this passage was misinterpreted or omitted.
        The folkloric significance of the fetal caul vividly demonstrates that the magic in LC is not mere ornament.

Fernández, Dominique, "Retour à la Célestine," La Nouvelle Revue Française, X (1962), 518-521.
        Miss Fernández sees a connection between the character of Celestina and that of Brecht's Mother Courage. Both women have nourished a great dream: the former, one of pan-eroticism; the latter, one of pan-pacifism. And both have seen their dream crumble under the disintegrating force

of time. But each one, stoic in the face of disaster, continues to struggle to the last moment against the fear of old
age and the anguish of death.

Lida de Malkiel, María Rosa, La originalidad artística de
'La Celestina'. Buenos Aires, 1962.
            Mrs. Malkiel presents a comprehensive review of
critical studies, beginning with the views of seventeenth-century critics. It is important to note that in the centuries
closest to LC no one denied its dramatic nature, whereas
neoclassic criticism termed it a dramatic novel, a name
which gained wide acceptance through the prestige of German
Romantic scholarship. However, Menéndez Pelayo [1910]
formulates a sensible and irrefutable defense of the dramatic
nature of LC. For Mrs. Malkiel, many of the problems of
LC are simply the problems of its critics who could not dis-
associate themselves from the prejudices of their century
when coming to grips with a book of the fifteenth century.
Gilman [1956], in a novel critical approach, sees Rojas as
conscious of the problem of the literary genre of his work
and making an effort to resolve it. Gilman classifies LC as
a work of "pure dialogue" deriving from both the novel and
drama and containing elements of both. Gilman's analysis
of the dialogue shows, according to Mrs. Malkiel, that LC
recreates human speech in such realistic terms that from the
point of view of language it reaches with rare perfection the
dramatic ideal of suggesting reality. Gilman created the
category of pure dialogue because he could not place LC within the modern concept of drama. A less restricted concept
of drama--one which would include different types and especially the medieval drama from which LC is a direct des-
cendant--would show that LC is not an individual expression
of a unique species, but rather the expression of a forgotten
one: the basic medieval dramatic form. What has misled
critics is the artistic duality of Spanish works--the external
cultivation of classical forms and the internal adhesion to
earlier and diverse techniques. LC exhibits this artistic duality; it is an admirable improvement on medieval drama.
            In defining Rojas' artistic originality in his reelabora-
tion of literary themes and techniques, Mrs. Malkiel supports
her critical observations with her extraordinary erudition.
Again, only a bare summary of her observations and conclusions will be given. This task is simplified by the fact that
she follows the same procedure in dealing with each of the
aesthetic elements of LC. Each dramatic or artistic technique is viewed against its literary source or tradition
[Chapter 3], after which Mrs. Malkiel presents her own eval-

uation of Rojas' artistic process.   Finally she discusses how
Rojas' contribution was viewed and used by his imitators and
by twentieth-century adaptations [Chapter 4].

Rojas shows his independence from and artistic superiority over literary tradition in his handling of dramatic techniques.   He incorporates the stage directions into the dramatic text, where they serve as a running commentary on
the action, and contribute to the dynamic texture of the work.
Action develops naturally in LC with the characters moving
from one place to another while engaged in dialogue or in
monologue.

Mrs. Malkiel notes a technical discrepancy in the use
of the stage directions between Act I and the rest of the work.
In Act I, the reason for and the place of the encounter between Calisto and Melibea are given in the argument, outside
the dialogue.   Rojas seems anxious to rectify this technical
discrepancy by revealing this information in the conversation
between Calisto and Sempronio in Act II.

Rojas' handling of stage directions derives from the
Roman theatre but differs from the latter's simple announce-
ment of change and movement.   Although Rojas' technique accentuates the variety of uses initiated by medieval Latin comedy, he incorporates his stage directions into the drama in
a more systematic and organic manner.   The indications
dealing with description of interiors and change of place do
not serve a purely informative function.   They usually express individual feelings and reactions.   Their function is to
advance the action and to allow the characters to express a
subjective point of view.

One of Rojas' audacious innovations is the rhetorical
element in the speeches of both the lower and the upper
classes.   The rapid, lively dialogue is another important innovation.   The long tirade or invective, designed to suit the
particular character who utters it, forms part of the structure of the work.   The new uses, variety and importance assigned to various types of dialogue constitutes one of the
most important contributions of LC.

The aside is used in LC to reveal the intimate thoughts
of those who utter it, and generally stands in contrast to
what is being expressed aloud.

The dynamic scenario which allows mobility in space
and continuity in time is a continuous cinematographic technique which gives extraordinary verisimilitude to the comings
and goings of the characters.

Time in LC is a selection of illustrative segments
which do not coincide with the continuity of life.   Each one
of the chronologically different parts of LC shows a visible

difference in the use of time.   In Act I, the reader must infer events which have not been portrayed.   In Acts II-XVI,
the characters make more explicit references to the past.
In the "Tractado de Centurio," the expression of time is more
precise and insistent.
        Each incident in LC shows logical and psychological
verisimilitude, except for three instances: the chance encounter in the garden, the intervention of the go-between, and
the use of magic.   Two of these belong to the "antiguo auctor."   These two events lack the realistic motivation so typical of Rojas' work.   The "antiguo auctor" chose to give a
poetic light to the first chance encounter of the two protagonists.   Mrs. Malkiel states that the illicit love is not motivated by a social disparity between the two portagonists.   It
is the selfish character of Calisto and the special quality of
his impatience and his passion which best justify the intervention of Celestina.   However, Melibea's behavior is incompatible with the realism of the rest of the action and with the
moral values of the time.   Melibea's behavior is anti-histor-
ic since the secret marriage was a common practice in Rojas' days.   The authors of LC wanted to portray the effects
of engulfing passion in a situation belonging to the literary
tradition of the roman courtois.   That is why both lovers
proceed as if the possibility of marriage were denied to them
a priori, and why their situation does not harmonize with the
realistic portrayal of the contemporary social ambience.   In
view of the realistic motivation which controls the action, the
lovers' situation has no justification or function within the
drama.   Rojas accepted the imperfect motivation because it
allowed him to give prominence to Celestina.   This external
motivation based on the chivalric-sentimental novel or poems
is closely related to other aspects of Act I.   It is obvious
that these derive from a different aesthetic tradition.   In the
rest of the work, however, the traditional themes are integrated into the realistic key of the Tragicomedia and marvel-
ously articulated in it.
        The use of magic represents another departure from
realism.   But Rojas, not wishing to discard the element of
witchcraft originated by Roman elegies, inserted it in the
drama by juxtaposing the supernatural machinery with the
natural events.   This is Rojas' homage to antiquity.
        Chance, which causes Calisto's death in the Comedia,
is removed from the dramatic structure of the Tragicomedia.
The interpolator integrated Calisto's death into the action
and carefully motivated it, because accidental death is an insufficient reflection of divine justice.   Art needs cause and
effect in order to display verismilitude.

Tragic irony in LC is an organic element and not a
stylistic adornment. Peculiar to the Tragicomedia is the
ironical contrast between | human calculations and the fatal
concatenation of events which defies all human effort. In
Pleberio's obliviousness to the concept of honor upheld by the
traditional paternal figure, our expectations are ironically
foiled. But the play of irony is even more abundant and intense in the "Tractado de Centurio" than in the Comedia.

The duplication of characters, sayings, and situations
is one of the systematic procedures of the Tragicomedia.
For example, Pármeno and Sempronio are replaced by two
other servants, Tristan and Sosia. A characteristic of this
technique is that although situations, sayings, and characters
are repeated, they are neither complete duplicates nor exact
opposites. Centurio compensates for the disappearance of
Celestina, but contrary to Celestina, he ridicules his profession and his honor. Still, the grotesque and tragic Celestina
lives on in the grotesque and comical Centurio, so that the
interpolator achieves unity by means of variation.

The art of characterization in LC is so advanced that
it encompasses not only the characters' reality but also their
imaginative life.

The fact that all the characters speak in sentences and
proverbs and that some of them use historical and mythological references proves that erudition has an essential stylistic
and dramatic function and is not accidental pedantry. Through
the use of erudition LC is organically connected with the rhetorical medieval tradition and its cult of amplification. The
erudite allusion is also used for character portrayal. LC
attempts to maintain a stylistic equilibrium between the rhetorical and the popular.

The basic note of Calisto's character is his selfishness, which affects his conception of reality, his ethical
judgment and his social behavior. Calisto is the enamored
dreamer, detached from social reality. His propensity to
inaction allows him to witness passively the efforts of others
to obtain his beloved. This inaction brings out the traditional servants' role in the success of their master's love. Calisto's egoism takes the form of withdrawal and mental flight
into a world of imagination. His eloquence is part of his
mental flight. With this, Rojas emphasizes the exalted frame
of mind of the useless dreamer. When confronted with danger, the dreamer, enslaved to his inner world, either escapes or overreacts to reality. Religion is the only tie that
connects him to society. But for him God is only a powerful tool needed for the success of his love. His amorous
obsession causes in him a confusion between the sacred and

the profane.   Calisto's confusion does not reflect Rojas' own
attitude toward Christianity.   Calisto's literary allusions and
sacroprofane hyperboles designate him as a courtly lover.
The penetration of literature into his character as lover shows
the sentimental introspection in which he revels.   His delight
in exhibiting his suffering is a distinctive trait of the troubadour and of the sentimental novel.   Calisto is "empapado de
literatura."   His words echo the cerebral direction of his
love.   That is why he did not become the archetype of the
lover.

In contrast to Calisto, Melibea lives within a well-
defined social and family life.   She is conscious of her social and filial duties.   Her chief concern is her honor.   Her
desire to conceal her love affair is an aspect of her conception of honor.   Since her roots are in a social order, the
concept of honor establishes a conflict between passion and
duty which is unknown to Calisto.   The relationship between
the two protagonists corresponds to the traditional code of
courtly love, where the love raises the vassal to the social
rank of his beloved.   In breaking her ties with her society
and family, Melibea demonstrates her resolute character and
her consuming passion.

Melibea's religious faith is sincere, in contrast to the
frivolous religiosity of Calisto.   But her decision to take her
own life combined with the offer of her soul to God reveals
a conventional view of religion.

Mrs. Malkiel does not find in the lovers' garden scene
the delight in the senses noted by some critics.   For her,
Calisto is too meditative and Melibea too concerned with the
social norms for a total abandonment to passion.

Deception is inherent in Melibea's character.   It is
developed but not created by the clandestine nature of her
love.   Whereas Calisto, the dreamer, is spontaneous and
truthful, Melibea, all action, is distrustful and cunning.   Her
deceptive nature, however, does not affect the decisive actions connected with her love and with her death.

Calisto is in love from the start.   Melibea, on the
other hand, evolves from her first violent rejection through
a total surrender to her lover down to her freely-willed
death.   The magic powers aside, Melibea's love has a plaus-
ible motivation with respect to her own character, which is
both passionate and imaginative.   At the beginning, her attitude toward Calisto stands between rejection and attraction.
Her submission and surrender to love destroy her defensive
arrogance and impatience but not her natural modesty.   The
overheard conversation between her parents reaffirms her
commitment to her love.   It is at this moment that she dis-

covers the intimate and moral meaning of her love. This
discovery completes the trajectory of honor in Melibea. She,
who was concerned with her reputation, discovers an individual honor--a situation which remains unique in Spanish literature. In this light, it is logical that the question of marriage be disregarded. Her love becomes the only law she
obeys and that is why she is ready to justify with her death
her law of love and her new conception of honor. Melibea is
the heroine in love who, without the aid of natural or supernatural forces, through her own inner development, evolves
from rejection to total surrender.

The interpolations of 1502 fully develop the dramatic
tension by setting up a contrast between the apprehensive and
reasonable character of Pleberio and the blindness of his wife
and the resolute character of his daughter. This development reinforces the pessimistic view of the world as a chaotic struggle. The details of Pleberios' character inserted
into the Tragicomedia are a prelude to the attitude of love
and compassion he exhibits at the end. His lament is devoid of a moral condemnation of his daughter and of concern
for the loss of his honor. His attitude, however, does not
reflect the accepted Castilian social norm. While it is possible that Rojas' background as a converso was responsible
for this point of view, it cannot be denied that Rojas may
have wished to present a character exhibiting universal human values.

Rojas' women are more passionate and energetic and
even more cruel than the men. Alisa is the grand lady,
proud of her social position. Act XVI emphasizes the blindness and pride of the mother who is totally unaware of her
daughter's rebellious nature. The figure of the trusting and
loving mother owes little to literary tradition; it is a Biblical vestige which stands in full contradiction to the Spanish
concept of the mother's role [Chapter 7].

Celestina's chief dramatic function is to bring about
the seduction of Melibea. But her character cannot be reduced simply to that of an avaricious alcahueta. Her popular religiosity is devoid of feeling and morality and amounts
to no more than a few proverbial phrases. Celestina is
deeply rooted in society and functions as an instrument of
social cohesion. She dies as she lived, with the full involvement of the citizenry. Her only positive moral note is her
professional pride. But her moments of indecision and her
weaknesses tend to humanize her. She is not the quintes-
sence of evil critical tradition has made her to be. The
magic of Celestina is a decoration in the Latin manner. Rojas, as a dramatist, motivates all the incidents. Her spe-

cial gift lies in the presence of mind with which she captures
the attention and will of her interlocutors.

The servants in LC have an individual life which is
concretely portrayed.   They function with all their personality
and add their own conflicts to the drama.   Sempronio and
Pármeno obey Calisto out of personal interest.   One of the
basic ironies of the Tragicomedia is that the role of counsel-
or is assigned to the character guilty of cowardice and fool-
ishness.   In Pármeno, the sense of inferiority of the adoles-
cent is an essential part of his character.   He sees the world
through his corrosive astuteness.   What separates Sosia and
Tristán from the other two servants is their moral character.   The bitter irony of the Tragicomedia is that, while Sosia and Tristán are loyal to him, Calisto does not take them
into his confidence.   And yet, it is an indiscretion on their
part that kills him.   Lucrecia is prudent and faithful.

As for the mochachas, their character traits are reversed in the additions of 1502.   From the point of view of
character, the continuity between Elicia of the original text
and that of Areusa of Acts XIV, XV, XVII, XVIII, as well as
the continuity of Areusa of the original text and that of Elicia
of the interpolated acts, is so obvious that it is best to disregard the change of name and to concentrate on the unity of
character.   Gilman and Morby have pointed to a significant
change in Areusa from passive in the Comedia to dynamic in
the Tragicomedia.   At the same time, the quarrelsome and
practical Elicia has acquired a capacity for sentimentality
and eloquence, which was a distinctive trait of Areusa in the
Comedia.   The irony of the Tragicomedia is that the heart-
less courtesan, Elicia (Areusa in the interpolations), who led
Crito, Sempronio and Sosia on, is now in love with Centurio,
although she is aware of his cowardice and baseness.   The
authors of LC exhibit a positive attitude toward the courtesans.   The irony is that while the two courtesans are indirectly responsible for the death of the protagonists, the latter do
not even know of their existence.

Whereas the characters so far are highly original vari-
ations of preexisting literary types, Centurio is a new creation based on Rojas' observation of the contemporary social
scene.   From this absolutely original character spring the
later literary braggarts; Rojas himself copied no model.

In Centurio we find a paradoxical contrast between his
tameness and the frightfully dangerous figure he pretends to
be.   Also, he assumes a chivalrous sentimental attitude of
protection toward his lady.   In the violent and excited world
of the Tragicomedia, he is one of the few characters who is
calm and in control of himself.   He lacks the passionate vio-

lence expressed as love in Calisto and Melibea, as avarice
in Celestina, and as rancor in the mochachas. He poses as
the professional ruffian and his involvement with the others
is based on this lie. What redeems him aesthetically is his
power of imagination. He is not the typical exploiter of
women. He candidly admits his inability to earn and to save
money. But in spite of his cowardice and his peaceful intentions, chance turns his lies into truth and Calisto dies finally
because of his intervention. This turn of events reveals
once again the bitter irony that runs through the Tragicomedia.
        Centurio provides the only humorous note of the Tragi-
comedia. His jokes reveal that he really does not take himself seriously. His bullying and his ridicule of his own bra-
vado--in short, his self-awareness--is his essential characteristic. His psychological ambivalence, which has nothing
to do with caricature, is the most significant proof of the
revolutionary attitude of the Tragicomedia vis-à-vis the lower
classes.
        Even the fiercest critics of the interpolated acts rec-
ognize the artistic merit of Centurio. But Mrs. Malkiel
finds it inexplicable that he has been unanimously attributed
to Latin sources, namely the miles gloriosus. The braggart
of Roman comedy is a real soldier, rich and powerful, who
considers himself irresistible to women. The only thing Centurio has in common with him is his cowardice and boastful-
ness, but both are presented in quite different ways. His
speeches do not offer a single reminiscence of Roman comedy.
Furthermore, Centurio shares none of the characteristics of
the pimp or lenus of Roman comedy. The enthusiastic ac-
claim with which this new character was received is owed in
part to the fact that readers recognized in him a real type
taken from Rojas' contemporary society. Incidentally, the
readers' affection for the low characters in general offers
evidence of a growing disaffection with the erudite tradition
and a change of direction in artistic comprehension.
        LC was above and beyond the artistic comprehension
of its readers. The change of title to La Celestina testifies
to the fact that the public was incapable of understanding the
complex equilibrium of the work, reducing it to its comical
elements and denying it is tragical essence.

1963

Ayllón, Cándido, "Petrarch and Fernando de Rojas," Romanic Review, LIV (1963), 81-94.
        Ayllón reviews Rojas' indebtedness to Petrarch. He

examines a number of borrowings in order to understand Rojas' use of Petrarch and to ascertain how effective he was in
adapting Petrarch to his own ends.

Rojas employs Petrarch effectively to develop his own
themes.   Through Petrarch, he expresses his own bitterness
and pessimism.   Rojas' genius enabled him to vitalize in dynamic dialogue some of Petrarch's more static lines.   Whereas in Petrarch these lines were abstract considerations of
many problems, in Rojas they became an essential part of
his energetic and human characters.   Rojas was able to use
Petrarch both artistically and philosophically because neither
the structural situations nor the characters were hindered
by the use of these borrowings.

The Prologue of the 1502 edition reveals a thematic
and philosophical preoccupation similar to that of the Tragicomedia in its totality.   Thematically, it sets the stage for
the action of the work.   Philosophically, it expresses a despairing view of life and the world--everything is negatively
depicted in terms of struggle and antagonism.   It is the bitter view which culminates in Pleberio's lament where the
meaninglessness of the world is emphasized, in spite of the
stress on Epicureanism in the Tragicomedia.

Berndt, Erna Ruth, Amor, Muerte y Fortuna en 'La Celestina'.   Madrid, 1963.

Miss Berndt places the major themes of LC within
their historical context.   She establishes which literary elements influenced Rojas' treatment of the themes of Love,
Death, and Fortune.

The theme of Love is influenced by both the mysogin-
ist and courtly tradition.   The discussion between Sempronio
and Calisto exhibits all the elements of an antifeminist treatise.   Sempronio himself represents the life of the senses.
Physical pleasure suffices to give him a will to live.   Calisto, on the other hand, represents the courtly lover who seeks
to transcend the life of the senses.   Calisto adopts in his
speech the stylistic hyperboles of the poets of the Cancionero.
Calisto's rhetoric is an affectation which makes him look ridiculous.   Rojas attacks Calisto's effusions through Sempronio.   Sempronio's attitude toward his master's love discloses
the author's ironical intention.

The theme of Death is expressed in the "impaciencia
vital" of the characters, who are afraid of dying before having fulfilled their desires.   The inexorability of death is a
constant consideration which affects their actions, hence their
"prisa por el vivir," for death annihilates man's individual
will.

The theme of Fortune in LC is connected with that of
fate.   This power which controls human events remains indifferent to the passions of man and simply follows its own
inmutable course.   The tragic irony in Rojas' work is that
the characters, striving for their goals, actually find themselves on the road to destruction.   The world has reserved
for them the opposite of what they had been striving for.
Pleberio's final words are a lament over the fate of man.

Heugas, Pierre, ed.   La Célestine.   Paris, 1963.
      For Heugas, the structure of LC is a series of auton-
omous dialogues connected by a very fluid conception of time
and space.   The original author of Act I gave Rojas the fully-
developed character of Celestina.   Rojas assigns to Celestina the major role in a series of temptations and "semi-
temptations": Melibea, Lucrecia, Sosia through Areusa,
semi-temptation of Areusa.   Rojas thus remains faithful to
the process of temptation initiated in Act I with Pármeno.
      The theme of the love of the masters is supported by
that of the servants.   But due punishment is foreseen for
those who provide assistance to illicit love.   On the other
hand, though the characters are to exhibit the author's didactic purpose, they are human creations rather than moral
types.
      Rojas remains faithful to the doctrine of decorum in
his use of language and style; his dialogue is in the direction of the natural without being vulgar.   But the juridical
element in the language shows that LC is the work of a
bachiller.
            Irony gives the work a human dimension.
      Heugas agrees with Gilman [1956] that the additions
clarify the whole without altering its basic concept.   The
lovers' indifference to their servants' death, however, underscores their guilt and justifies the intervention of Fortune,
which the fifteenth century regarded as dependent on divine
Providence.   It is logical therefore that Calisto's death
should be caused by the ridiculous machinations of the underworld, to which he had turned for the success of his love.
      Heugas objects to Gilman's interpretation [1945] of the
fluidity of time and the limitation of space because these existential concepts deprive the work of its moral significance.
Heugas suggests that a reasonable amount of time has actually elapsed to maintain the standards of decorum.   Certain
liberties are taken in dealing with time and space.   The
scene is not fully described; it must be subjectively imagined
through the few allusions and concrete indications.   In LC
we have the poetic stylization of time and space.   Rojas cap-

tures a poetic essence of reality similar to perspective in
Flemish paintings.

Act XII contains the core of the reaction. Here is
the first garden scene and the punishment of Celestina and
the servants.

Leo, Ulrich, "Die Literarische Gattung der Celestina,"
Romanische Forschungen, LXXV (1963), 54-80.
　　　Leo blames Mrs. Malkiel [1962] for using historical
perspective to determine the genre to which LC belongs; and
Gilman [1956] for forcing LC to comply with his precon-
ceived idea that LC is a unique genre: the "dialogue." Leo
wants to use the "immanent" approach--simply seeing the
text as it is. His conclusion is the paradoxical one that Rojas did not find a form adequate to what he wished to express. LC was meant as a psychological novel: the quasi-
dramatic dialogue chain was not the best form for this great
plan. "A subtle spirit like Rojas simply has too complex
and too finely-shaded things to say--he would like to break
through the shackles of direct speech; but he cannot." Both
the sense of inner time as different from objective time and
the continuous change of place are better suited to the novel.
The film would be adequate, and Leo is even tempted to call
LC a "filmed novel."

As for the implausibilities of LC: the failure to mention marriage; Pleberio's silence when Melibea addresses him
from the tower; the absence of any allusion to damnation after suicide--all show Rojas ruthlessly sacrificing probability
for artistic purposes. Hence Leo calls him one of the most
"modern" psychologists of the Middle Ages. Such breaks
with probability occur in the greatest novels. Other novelistic elements are the slow linear motion of the action and
the love of detail and nuance.

Leo supposes that Rojas used the dialogue because he
simply continued a work he found.

1964

Barbera, Raymond E., "Calisto: the Paradoxical Hero,"
Hispania, XLVII (1964), 256-257.
　　　Rojas wanted to present in the figure of Calisto an
"unhero" through whom he could express his own pervasive
pessimism. A young man himself, Rojas chose as his hero
another young man, but one who is eviscerated, without
courage, without moral fibre. The work as a whole, however, succeeds because of Rojas' success with the characters
of Celestina, Sempronio and Pármeno and with their social

ambience.   As is evidenced by the shift in the very title of
the work, it is Celestina who holds the center of the stage,
rather than Calisto in whom Rojas had poured his own pessimism.

Flightner, James A., "Pleberio," Hispania, XLVII (1964),
79-81.
     Most critics have limited their treatment of the char-
acter of Pleberio to a consideration of his final monologue.
Actually, however, Pleberio's importance is established long
before he makes an entrance.   He represents the strength of
the family institution.   He is ever-present in the consciousness of the other characters as the powerful antagonist who
can terminate in an instant their intrigues and their very
lives.
     Pleberio is also the tender father.   He bears a kin-
ship to Celestina in his concern with old age and material
well-being.   Toward those who have deceived him, however,
he shows an inexplicable magnanimity.   His protest against
deified love goes far beyond the sphere of sensual love--
Celestina's territory.   In behalf of all men, he inveighs
against love, the world, and fortune, all of which control
man's destiny.

Gilman, Stephen, "Fernando de Rojas as Author," Romanische Forschungen, LXXVI (1964), 255-290.
     Gilman sees Rojas as a man conscious of his art,
who looks back on his work and attempts to explain it by revising it.   "It was precisely his acute consciousness of possibly dangerous originality which led him to employ the various protective strategies of the prologue material."   The
text itself gives us insights into Rojas' sense of himself as
an author.   An investigation of the language in LC allows us
to know Rojas in a way which transcends the level of intention.   The use of certain words will take us from the style
to the man.   For example, the word solo in Pleberio's
speech points to intellectual and personal solitude.   The word
gozo, a key word, represents the triumph of consciousness.
Pleasure is the foundation of an intense relationship between
otherwise lonely consciousnesses.   Gilman thus establishes
a relationship between the life of Fernando de Rojas and the
lives which he created.   Rojas does not write directly about
converso problems because he creates characters whose existence reflects Rojas' own resentment, cowardice, deceit,
and cynicism.   This is how Rojas obliterates himself in his
own masterpiece [1963, Chapter 7].

Reynolds, John J. , "La moça que esperava al ministro
(Celestina: Aucto III)," Romance Notes, V (1964), 200-202.
        Reynolds points out that in order to interpret correct-
ly the passage in Act III where Celestina, accompanied by
Sempronio, asks Elicia whether the girl who was waiting for
the cleric has left, the reader has to turn back to the inci-
dent in Act I when Sempronio's unexpected arrival while Crito was with Elicia causes some confusion in Celestina's
household.   Celestina is actually asking whether the house is
unoccupied and whether Crito, who had been hidden from
Sempronio, has left.   But, in order not to arouse any suspicion in Sempronio, Celestina invents a girl waiting for a
cleric and asks whether the girl, meaning Crito, has left.

Toro-Garland, Fernando, "Celestina, hechicera, clásica y
tradicional," Cuadernos Hispano-americanos, LX (1964),
438-445.
        Toro-Garland maintains that Celestina is an authentic
witch.   He classifies Celestina as both a hechicera and a
bruja.   But as sorceress and witch Celestina is essentially
a literary creation.   She probably would not favorably compare with the practicing witches of her time.   Celestina's
principal activity is that of a procuress, for which she is
more dependent on her psychological insight than on the magic arts.   Celestina could carry on her activities as a go-between without having to summon the devil.   Magic traditionally played a role in matters of love both in literature and
in the popular mind.   The medieval world was a world interested in magic and Rojas knew it.   And although Celestina's psychological powers and skill were sufficient to
achieve her aim, the absence of supernatural powers would
have represented a departure from the "realidad imaginativa"
of Rojas' time.
        Celestina had to be both a witch and a sorceress to
constitute a real literary character for her contemporaries.
The later Celestinas operated as trotaconventos who occa-
sionally sought the assistance of a witch.
        Rojas created a character whose major strength lies
in her psychological powers.   The use of magic would be
eliminated without altering either the action or the structure
of the work.   The conjurations afforded Rojas the opportunity to display his erudition by giving a classical character
to a popular figure.

Wardropper, Bruce W. , "Pleberio's Lament for Melibea and
the Medieval Elegiac Tradition," Modern Language Notes,
LXXIX (1964), 140-152.

The epic elegy stressed personal rather than public inconsolability. The elegy frequently presents man in a moment of truancy from religious orthodoxy. Pleberio, like his
predecessors in the epic poems--Charlemagne and Gonzalo
Gustios--is concerned with his personal grief. He condemns
death's unjust and arbitrary actions. The tradition of the
epic elegy is responsible for the fact that Pleberio does not
fall back on orthodox Christian resignation. His note of personal grief does not reflect a Jewish attitude to death.

Rojas' work demonstrates the ability of unrestrained
sexual love to spread disorder to the whole of society. Cupidity in the form of avarice and lust reigns in the world,
and is the cause of disorder and destruction. This reign of
destruction is the disorder which Pleberio laments in his
elegiac peroration.

Rojas sees man powerless against the forces of the
Satanic Trinity: Fortune, World, Love. The anguish of man
in spite of and beyond the consolation of religion is a major
theme of LC. Elegiac poetry allows man to express his ex-
tra-religious anxieties, his own grief as a man who sees the
capricious destiny to which he is subjected and against which
he must struggle.

1965

Barbera, Raymond E. , "A Harlot, a Heroine," Hispania,
XLVIII (1965), 790-799.

Barbera denies the contention of Gilman and Malkiel
that Celestina acts out of character when she fails to gauge
the anger of her accomplice. For Barbara, Celestina is as
intelligent here as she is throughout. She dies, in fact, because her confederates sense their own inferiority.

"I believe," writes Barbera, "that it is Rojas' somewhat disguised intent to 'enthrone' Celestina." Rojas names
his hero and heroine; yet by a steady comic attack on Calisto,
the latter is hollowed and obliterated, until the work assumes
its new and rightful title after its true heroine, Celestina.

Rojas reacts to his hostile and dangerous environment
by lavishing his attention, not on the ostensibly heroic nobleman, but on a harlot and her entourage. Celestina is a
quasi-defiant member of society. She embodies a criticism
of society in her courage, vigor, and assertiveness. She is
the new anti-hero. Rojas, himself a victim of society, un-
derstands that true humanity can exist in a character like
Celestina, while inhumanity can go disguised under idealistic
concepts.

Foster, David William, "Some Attitudes Towards Love in the
Celestina," Hispania, XLVIII (1965), 484-492.
    The play exhibits four basic attitudes toward love,
each one represented by a principal character.
    In Calisto we find the rhetoric of courtly love. He
expresses his love with all the stereotypes of the upper-class
tradition, including the profession of the religion of love.
But in Melibea's presence, Calisto becomes simply a lustful
man. This conflict between ideal sentiments and libidinous
passion, underlined by Sempronio's comments, is a basic
irony in Rojas' work.
    The principle of simple nature is illustrated by Sem-
pronio, who accepts the pleasurable biological necessity of
love.
    Melibea is portrayed as a Christian lady whose initial
purity comes to be replaced by total abandonment to desire.
Her rejection of Calisto's advances at the beginning of LC
does not stem from Calisto's failure to follow courtly formulas, but simply from her Christian virtue. There is no
semblance of courtly affectation in Melibea.
    As for Celestina, she is a proponent of hedonistic love.
For her, love is the motivating force of mankind and of the
universe. But her violent end shows that no human emotion
can lead to a successful and stable existence.
    The disaster which overtakes Calisto and Melibea is
due to the fundamental dichotomy between love as they preach
it and love as they practice it.

Goldman, Peter B., "A New Interpretation of 'comedor de
huevos asados'," Romanische Forschungen, LXXVII (1965),
363-367.
    Without rejecting Gillet's suggestion [1956] that "en-
comendador" is a preferable reading and that the phrase indicates wifely infidelity, Goldman links the phrase to Rojas'
knowledge of Jewish customs. At the death of a relative,
mourners were accustomed to eating eggs. Eating eggs is
therefore to be taken as an indication of grief. The grief
which is meant here is that of Celestina's husband, witness-
ing her numerous infidelities. Garrido, Pallardó's suggestion [1957] that Celestina is a converso would bolster this
hypothesis.

Green, Otis H., "The Artistic Originality of La Celestina,"
Hispanic Review, XXXIII (1965), 15-31.
    This is essentially a review of Mrs. Malkiel's book
[1962].
    On the question of Calisto's failure to consider mar-

riage, Green gives an answer in accordance with his moral
interpretation of LC as a whole [Chapter 6]: "The breaking
of both the Christian and the courtly codes by Calisto (the impatience, the bawd, the magic) was necessary to increase the
guilt of the lovers (destined to punishment from the first) and
to speed the action."

As for Celestina's magic, it must be taken seriously.
For example, it is magic which transforms Melibea's fury into a fainting spell at the mention of Calisto's name.   This,
says Green, does not destroy the motivation.   The function
of magic, which is, after all, a mortal sin, is to build up
the tension toward the final catastrophe.

Green, Otis H., "Did the 'World' 'Create' Pleberio?,"
Romanische Forschungen, LXXVII (1965), 108-110.
Commenting on Pleberio's lament, "Del mundo me
quexo porque en si me crió," Green takes issue with Gilman's
view [1956] that this is a cry of cosmic despair.   Mundo is
not the equivalent of the universe, it is not natura naturata,
it is simply the world of human affairs.   Pleberio complains
of the world as a man in and of the world; better, he says,
if instead of nourishing me (this is the true meaning of crió),
it had left me to starve to death.   This can hardly be taken
as the expression of a cosmic view of life.

"The Status of Lechery," Anon. rev., Times Literary Supplement (February 25, 1965), 149.
The anonymous reviewer of Cohen's translation of LC
--which he calls "fairly adequate"--takes Cohen to task for
appropriating in his introduction the thesis that Melibea is a
conversa.   There is nothing in the text to support this speculation.   The text shows Melibea to be superior in status to
Calisto.   Nor is Calisto an exploiter; Rojas maintains a firm
moral balance of wickedness between the two lovers.

Vecchio, Frank, "El 'antifeminismo' de Sempronio," Proceedings of the Pacific Northwest Conference on Foreign Lan-
guages, XVI (1965), 115-118.
Vecchio believes that Sempronio's diatribe loses all
its importance as an antifeminist document once we see it
within the context of the whole work, and once we examine
the motives of Sempronio himself.   Moreover, Sempronio's
attachment to Elicia clearly indicates that his misogynist attitude is simply a tool in his hands to protect his master.

Therefore, in Act I, we are not faced with an anti-
feminist digression, but rather with a feminist debate between
Calisto and Sempronio, with the former expressing the atti-

tude of the courtly lover. Their debate is in no way related
to the virulent attacks of the misogynists of the fifteenth century. The feminist debate in LC is mitigated by irony and
soon disappears to give way to larger themes: Love, Life,
Death.

1966

Gilman, Stephen, "Mollejas el ortelano," Estudios dedicados
a James Homer Herriott. Madison, 1966, pp. 103-107.
        To illustrate the aliveness and unique existence of
each character, Gilman shows how pervasive the past is in
the lives of the personages. "Fragments of past experience
often come to the surface and participate in each speaker's
stream of self-revelation."
        On psychological complexity: Pármeno and Sempronio
are frightened in Act XII and reveal their cowardice to each
other. Yet "they are ashamed, so deeply ashamed that it
becomes a motive for murder."

Hesse, Everett H., "La función simbólica de La Celestina,"
Boletín de la Biblioteca de Menéndez Pelayo, XLII (1966),
87-95.
        Symbolically, Celestina functions as la Gran Madre,
la Vieja Sabia, la Madre Naturaleza, la Curandera, and la
hipócrita. Hesse shows how she functions as a human being within all these symbolic states. Her weaknesses bridge
the symbolic to the human and increase her universality.

Lida de Malkiel, María Rosa, "El ambiente concreto en La
Celestina," Estudios dedicados a James Homer Herriott.
        In this essay, probably written around 1954, Mrs.
Malkiel points out that we obtain a concrete picture of
clothes, homes, and the entire city without minute descrip-
tions and without a halt in the action. Rojas uses "el arte
de insinuar, más bien que de describir." Everything is
suggested by means of a few significant details.

Rüegg, August, "Rationalismus und Romantik in der Celestina," Zeitschrift für Romanische Philologie," LXXXII
(1966), 9-21.
        Rüegg contends that Bataillon [1961] undervalues the
romantic aspect of LC and overrates its intellectual and moral character. LC is a mixed and imperfect work, but it is
full of riches and contrasts: the beauty and ugliness of life,
human tenderness and human barbarity, all are represented
in this many-sided work. Rojas is not simply preaching a

moral lesson.   He creates sympathy and even pity for the
lovers.   Rüegg doubts that Rojas wrote with "the social and
moral health of Spain" in mind.

Another failure of Bataillon's is that he does not sense,
in LC, "the demonic power of Eros." It will not do, Rüegg
argues, to dismiss Calisto as an "insensé" and Melibea as
"fragile."

Ruggiero, Michael J., The Evolution of the Go-Between in
Spanish Literature through the Sixteenth Century.   Berkeley,
1966.

According to Ruggiero, Celestina is both a sorceress
and a witch.   It is the element of witchcraft which lends
originality to Rojas' characterization.

Ruggiero traces the evolution of the literary figure of
the go-between in Spain, beginning with the Libro de los
engaños, translated in 1253.   In literary tradition, the go-
between is a composite figure whose functions reflect the
folklore, mythology, and superstitions of the times.   But Rojas gave his character the awareness of being a witch.   The
alcahueta and the witch are interested in seducing the young.
The fact that Celestina herself believes that she is a witch
with supernatural powers is important only as a piece of
characterization.

Ruggiero opposes the idea that witchcraft is mere
decoration in LC.   The conjuring is important because it
shows Celestina's belief in it and in her powers to control
the devil for her own ends.   While Act I presents both the
possibilities of sorcery and witchcraft, Rojas chooses the
latter and conceives Celestina as a witch.   She combines in
her person and personality two traditions which had fused in
the mind of fifteenth-century man: Venus, considered as an
evil, procuring demon; and Satan, conceived in the same way.
Both of them eventually fuse in the figure of the procuress-
witch, producing a mixture of the evil demon and the degraded goddess of love who is both a prostitute and a bawd.

Celestina consciously uses the powers of magic to
further her profession.   Whereas Rauhut [1932] turns the
demonic into an abstract irrational force and separates it
from witchcraft, Ruggiero maintains that Celestina is demonic insofar as she is a witch.   Rauhut converts her into a
symbol, but Ruggiero sees her as a concrete situation.   The
demonic element does not exist as an abstract, irrational
force; it exists as a function of procuring.

The evolution of the literary type is the evolution from
Trotaconventos to Celestina.   But whoever comes after Celestina is still Celestina.   The portrayal of the go-between ap-

peared before 1499 in Western and Oriental literature, but it
was in LC that this dispersed and folkoric tradition took on
new life. Rojas uses magic and witchcraft not as a deus ex
machina but as a new element of character portrayal that
makes his personage bristle with individuality. Yet Celestina
is hardly demonic; she is deeply human. Her pact with the
devil is made only to earn her more money.

Rumeau, A., "Introduction à la Célestine. ... "una cosa
bien escusada ..." Les Langues Néolatines, LX (1966), 1-26.
        Rumeau reviews the positions scholars have taken with
respect to the opening scene of LC. All the interpretations
are concerned with the problem of connecting the action of
Scene I to that of the following scenes within a realistic time
sequence.
        Rumeau, on the other hand, seeks the solution to the
problem in the text of the individual arguments. But first
he turns for a clue to the Prologue of 1502, wherein the author disavows the individual arguments, attributing them to
the initiative of the editors. The author considers them "una
cosa bien escusada según lo que los antiguos scriptores usa-
ron." Therefore we may conclude that the individual arguments are the work of a well-meaning scribe or editor. The
latter, however, desirous of furnishing indications of time
and place, committed a few errors in summarizing the text.
        Rumeau points to specific instances in the different
arguments where the editor misinterprets the text and sometimes even contradicts it. Thus our conficence is shaken
with respect to details found in the arguments. Moreover,
we discover that the editor made the most significant error
in the argument of Act I. The editor rendered the opening
scene more perplexing to posterity by lifting the first phrase
of the argument directly from Act II, Scene II. The illustrations of the early editions unfortunately sought inspiration
in the "huerta" and falcon of the first sentence, and thus
perpetuated the error. In addition, the editor borrowed the
phrase "fue preso en el amor de Melibea" from the general
argument.
        The amalgamation of the two texts has caused the gen-
eral argument to be neglected, in spite of its containing information that leads to the opening scene, namely that Calisto has been in love with Melibea for some time. The author
of the general argument has prepared his readers according
to the conventions of his time, that if we go from the general argument to the beginning of the play, with the information we found in the former, but skipping the individual argument, we note that a continuity exists between the two.

Then the opening scene no longer seems abrupt. The author
clearly intended us to go from the general argument to the
play itself, to wit its last phrase, "para comienço de lo
cual," a typical formula found in other contemporary works
used as a means of transition between the prologue and the
work itself. In conclusion, the argument of Act I, "una
cosa bien escusada," is responsible for leading us astray.

Whereas it was customary for works to begin with a
general argument, the presence of the individual arguments
in LC represents an isolated instance, which explains why
the author disavowed them in the Prologue of 1502.

Once misled, critics have been unable to explain the
"huerto" and the "neblí" which ought to set the scene for the
beginning of the play.

The question remains how to dispose of the "huerta"
which appears once in the argument of Act I and is repeated
twice in the argument of Act XIV of the Comedia (in Act
XIV the reading is "huerto" but the editor of the Tragicomedia corrects it to "huerta"). How do we explain the
"huerta"? It is both anterior and exterior to the action and
it probably indicates the place of the first encounter.

Rumeau has dexterously woven the arguments for his
hypothesis. And he proceeds to a further hypothesis: that
the author of the first argument did not realize that when
Pármeno spoke of the meeting of "el otro día" he could not
possibly have been referring to the meeting in the opening
scene. The opening meeting represents a subsequent meeting and Pármeno had no knowledge of it. Rumeau thus proposes a new interpretation of Pármeno's exposition in Act II,
"Señor, porque perderse el otra día el neblí fue causa de tu
entrada en la huerta de Melibea a le buscar ..." Pármeno
here is referring to the circumstances of Calisto's chance
encounter with Melibea, but he still has no knowledge of the
ensuing meeting, that of the opening scene. Therefore it is
an error to think that Pármeno is providing the setting for
the opening scene, and that the author is thereby emending
the text.

The great error of the argument of Act I is that it
attributes to the opening scene an action and a setting which
take us back to the antecedents of the play, to how "empezó
el proceso amoroso." Rumeau deftly distinguishes the first
encounter from the first scene. The "lugar oportuno" of the
general argument, which in Calisto's words becomes a "tan
conveniente lugar" may have been a church or a religious
ceremony.

Rumeau succeeds in discrediting before our very eyes
the interpolated arguments, especially that of Act I. He

urges us to return to the text as the author had conceived it, with its unique and precious argument and with its invitation to pass directly to the text. This represents a further step in the direction taken by Bataillon [1961].

1967

Baldwin, Spurgeon W., Jr., "En tan pocas palabras," Romance Notes, IX (1967), 120-125.
　　　Reviewing the phrase in Act IV which has been emended to "por tales" in several editions, Baldwin attempts to make a case for the original reading. According to Baldwin, a correct understanding of the context of Melibea's speech and also of the true meaning of the verb expresar which she uses enables us to make good sense of the phrase "en tan pocas." Expresar must be understood as a demand for a clear, explicit request on the part of Celestina.

Bataillon, Marcel, "Défense et Illustration du sens littéral," Modern Humanities Research Association [Presidential Address]. London, 1967.
　　　Bataillon sets out to prove that the literal meaning of works often escapes us, in spite of the fact that we have access to many tools of research. Especially in a work entrenched in reality, it is difficult for us to reinterpret its literal meaning and to identify the living realities to which the authors refer, and, furthermore, to understand the particular meaning that this reality had for the audience of the author. The oddities or ambiguities which we discover in a work of art often ought to be attributed more to our lack of precise knowledge of a word or phrase than to the author's lapse from reality. In some instances, whole fields of knowledge are brought to bear on a particular word or phrase to eliminate false ambiguities which detract from the literal meaning.
　　　A case in point is LC. Even Mrs. Malkiel's monumental work [1962] did not suffice to demolish some of its ambiguities. The year 1966, however, marks a turning point in the history of the editions of LC. An exhaustive examination by Norton of the typographical production of that period revealed that all six editions of the Tragicomedia believed to have been published in 1502, were actually published between 1510 and 1520. Moreover, the 1507 Zaragoza edition, believed lost, made its reappearance at the Real Academia de la Historia in Madrid. A typographical examination reconfirmed its 1507 date, giving us the oldest extant edition of the Tragicomedia. It so happens that the 1507 Zara-

goza edition is of particular importance in the interpretation
of the literal meaning of Act I, Scene I.

It has long been disputed at what point of the action
Act I opens. The view that the initial scene represents the
very first encounter of the future lovers has become a commonplace. In 1966, Rumeau eloquently demonstrated not only
that the initial scene is a subsequent meeting, but that this
meeting does not correspond to the chance meeting Pármeno
describes in Act II. Rumeau is able to isolate the source
for the erroneous interpretation, namely the argument of Act
I and the often reproduced woodcut showing Calisto and Melibea in a garden, and nearby a falcon perched on a tree.

The argument of Act I describes the lovers' chance
meeting as taking place in Melibea's garden. The author of
this interpolated argument mistakes the "tan conveniente lugar" of the general argument for the "huerta" mentioned in
Act II, when these two are not one and the same. The opening of the drama implies a scene taking place earlier in time
in the "huerta" or estate of Melibea. The reader who is
not misled by the argument of Act I would easily connect the
"conveniente lugar" with a place of worship or its vicinity.
It is because of the earlier chance meetings on the grounds
of Melibea's estate that Calisto seeks the encounter with
which the play opens. In addition, it is important not to con-
fuse the "huerta" where it all begins, with the "huerto"
where love is brought to fruition, the latter safely protected
by high walls. The estate, probably located on the outskirts
of town, extended to the river.

Basing himself chiefly on the discrepancies found in
the arguments, and aided by the evidence of the 1507 Zaragoza edition, Rumeau, affirms Bataillon, deals a mortal
blow to one of the paradoxes [1947, Frank] of LC and gives
us a solid interpretation of Scene I.

The 1507 Zaragoza edition offers two distinctive
traits: it contains neither the illustrations nor the arguments
contained in the other extant editions. We can safely assume, therefore, that some editions of 1502 did not contain
the arguments, and that the editor in 1507 used one of the
editions where the arguments had been omitted.

Once a sequence of events is established, and a concatenation of characters and places is located within the realistic framework of LC, we need no longer seek explanations
outside the contours of reality, and turn to arbitrary conclusions. All incongruities swept away, realism once again reasserts its firm hold of LC.

Gerday, Jacqueline, "Le caractère des rameras dans La

Célestine, de la Comédie à la Tragicomédie." Revue des
langues vivantes, XXXIII (1967), 185-204.
    Miss Gerday seeks to refute Malkiel's contention
[1962] that the author of the Tragicomedia reversed the psychology of Elicia and Areusa as we find it in the Comedia.
The mochachas, according to Miss Gerday, continue in perfect conformity with the traits they exhibited in the text of
1499.

Hawking, Jane, "Madre Celestina," Annali dell'Istituto Uni-
versitario Orientale di Napoli, Sezione Romanza, IX (1967),
177-190.
    Miss Hawking defends a critic's right to apply the
terms of modern criticism to a work like LC. Thus in her
relation to Pármeno, Celestina becomes a mother-substitute,
a role which she creates in Pármeno's mind and then ex-
ploits for her own benefit. True, Pármeno is not blinded to
her real character, and he does try to maintain his independence. He even experiences a conflict of loyalties in his position between Calisto and Celestina. Finally Celestina over-
reaches herself. In the final struggle she rejects him as her
son, his love turns to hatred, and he kills her, unable to obtain the mother-love he needed but which she was incapable
of giving him.

                            1968

Bell, A. Robert, "Folklore and Mythology in La Celestina,"
Medieval Epic to the "Epic" Theater of Brecht, ed. R. P.
Armato and J. M. Spalek. Los Angeles, 1968.
    Using Stith Thompson's six-volume Motif-Index of
Folk Literature, Bell finds that the deceptively simply narrative of LC can be subsumed under a great number of folk
motifs. In this way Rojas achieves an effect of intense reality: "the plot becomes a nearly lifelike representation when
he draws from so many well-known common sources."
    What about Celestine as a witch? "By an abundant and
skilful employment of the literary, folkloristic trappings of
witchcraft in portraying her, the author spreads his own
doubts of the efficacity of her powers and the actuality of her
Goetic life."
    Rojas' characters all exceed a single and simple folk-
loric or romantic formula. They go beyond cliché: hence
their reality. Folkloric wisdom shows up in the endless maxims which the characters spout, but which their reality far
transcends.
    Almost all the folkoric sayings act in three ways: to

amplify the arguments presented by the characters; to serve as foreshadowing of later events; and to give Rojas' warning against the "wiles" and "lies" which have invaded the truly moral life.

All the characters are caught in these lies of old, useless folkloric or literary saws. They become real insofar as they "recover" from folkloric clichés.

LC is an anti-romance "because its form rejects the common use of any 'standard' element, process, or characterization common to the genre." Rojas objects to the courtly-love theme with its approval of illicit sexual relationships.

"Human understanding, Rojas says, which is based on the 'common sense' platitudes and mores, has failed to prepare men and women for the real-life experiences which they must face on any social level." Pleberio, for instance, will find no consolation in all the world's literature upon which he draws.

For Bell, in short, the great moral lesson of LC is that "life is far too complex to be rendered down to fit the maxims of folkloric law and morality."

Bell makes two incidental points: the first, that a certain amount of courting between Calisto and Melibea seems to have taken place before the episode of Act I; the second, that Calisto falls to his death by being struck with the armor which Melibea threw at him from the garden.

Clarke, Dorothy Clotelle, Allegory, Decalogue, and Deadly Sins in 'La Celestina'. Berkeley, 1968.

Miss Clarke's thesis is that the author of LC made use of lists of sins and moral transgressions--"sin allegories of the seven deadly sins and the ten Commandments"--to portray moral and allegorical types. We see Commendments broken, as when Calisto sets Melibea above God, "Melibeo soy e a Melibea adoro," thus shattering the First Commandment. Some of the deadly sins are worked in, like Melibea's pride, Celestina's gluttony and the envy of Pármeno, Elicia, and Areusa. Lust and sloth play a major role in LC, and the most blameworthy character is the lust- and sloth-ridden Calisto. Calisto is the antithesis of the traditional lover, for instead of spending his time in the service of his lady he slothfully leaves his wooing for others to do.

Sin vocabulary is woven in throughout the work. Miss Clarke traces this vocabulary in the dialogue and notes its high frequency. She also traces words or expressions reflecting the Commandments, and states that "the undertone-overtone of sin by way of vocabulary is a thematic constant in LC, worked with such artistry that the reader is not conscious of the collective power of these hundreds of miniscule tributaries."

LC is for Miss Clarke "the consummation of medieval allegory--in part momo, in part poetic debate and moral and love allegory, in part enxiemplo, didactic prose tale devised to illustrate a proverb, to conceal a precept, or to concretize an abstraction such as the concept of virtue or sin." The allegory is so well defined that the characterization could be presented in pantomime without loss of meaning. She notes a visual portrayal of the personification of sin. Sometimes a specific sin can be abstracted from the dialogue although it is not specifically mentioned.

Miss Clarke points to the strategic placing of sin vocabulary in the dialogue for special psychological effect on the reader. Moreover, "the sin motif serves as a sort of running commentary on the action and the circumstances and seems almost extraneous to them."

Rojas' artistic innovation consists in the reduction of the usual number of characters in the sin allegory. He achieves this by the use of interplay and coalescence of sins within the individual character and the interaction of sins within the group of characters. Rojas has embedded in each of his main characters two or three vices, and the minor characters reflect the varying degrees of the sins operative in the main characters. Sins are not paired off against virtues but mingle with each other. "The constant interplay of references touching upon the whole spectrum of sins indicates a more comprehensive aim than that specifically stated," namely "en reprensión de los locos enamorados." But Rojas does not simply deliver a sermon, the reader must infer his moral aim and the consequences of sin.

The series of events in the Comedia derives from traditional literary themes. But what Rojas achieves is the transposition of the lover and the messenger, with the messenger usurping the power and gaining control of the destinies of others, thereby becoming no longer the tool but the wielder. Rojas has fused the love allegory and moral allegory found in fifteenth-century Spanish literature. But his use of allegory is far more complex than in any other medieval Spanish work.

Much of the Comedia's dialogue is built on the principle of the poetic debate, though technically and stylistically far removed from it.

It is difficult to say which of the sins is considered the most abhorrent in the Comedia. Ire and pride are the most spectacular of the sins. They were therefore chosen for the most dramatic character: Melibea. Ire and pride are in conflict in the feminine characters. Melibea's pride

is humbled by her submission; but Calisto's ire is subdued
by his sloth. Avarice is the dominant trait of the insatiable
Celestina. But in her we also find greed-avarice combined
with pride-ire and moribund lust.

The author artfully links sin with sin both literally and
figuratively in a vicious circle: Calisto's gold chain is a
symbol of his slothful prodigality in allowing the messenger
to conquer Melibea for him. His chain also breeds covetous-
ness, anger, and lust. Prodigality, states Miss Clarke, constitutes the dramatic peak of the work, though it is not explicitly mentioned.

Miss Clarke stresses that the influence of both love
allegory and strictly moral allegory is prominent in the Comedia. Rojas' aim was to dramatize ideas and to create
characters who are in effect allegorical moral figures. However, he becomes absorbed in his characters and has to re-
mind himself periodically that the sins must be accounted
for. On these occasions, a placard is inserted in the text
as a warning to the reader. These placards referring to the
general moral conduct of man are expressed on almost every
page in didactic statements. Rojas touches upon the whole
spectrum of sins. Miss Clarke defines LC as a work of sin
personification where God's Commandments are broken through
the deadly sins. The author does not sermonize, he offers
us a poetical or literary catechism.

Gerday, Jacqueline, "Le remaniement formel des actes primitifs dans La Célestine de 1502," Annali dell'Istituto Orientale
di Napoli, Sezione Romanza, X (1968), 175-182.

A systematic examination of the changes made by the
author of the 1502 text could provide an insight into his preoccupations and contribute to the solution of the problem of
authorship.

In modifying the text, Rojas presented new psychological elements and developed traits he had only sketched out
before. He eliminated discordant and awkward traits. His
phrasing is often lighter and clearer. The dialogue is enriched by scenic directions. All this shows great artistic
care and craftsmanship. "The author of the emendations of
1502 is as much on a level with Rojas as Rojas could ever
be with himself," Miss Gerday concludes.

Himelbau, Jack, "A Further Contribution to the Ironic Vision in the Tragicomedia," Romance Notes, IX, 310-313.

As an addition to Mrs. Malkiel's analysis [1962] of
irony in LC, Himelbau points to the following areas:
1. Characters recite lines applicable neither to their na-

      ture nor to their station in life.
2. Multiple contradictory judgments are passed on Celes-
    tina and Calisto by those who know them.
3. Ironic differences occur between events which are pre-
    dicted and events which actually occur.

Rodríguez Puértolas, Julio, "El linaje de Calisto," Hispanófila, XII, No. 33 (1968), 1-6.
      For Rodríguez Puértolas' view of Calisto's failure to
consider marriage, see Chapter 7.

Vecchio, Frank B., "Sempronio y el debate feminista del
siglo XV," Romance Notes, IX (1968), 320-324.
      Vecchio rejects the idea, advanced by Ornstein (1941)
that LC can be placed in the category of anti-feminist literature. In particular, the debate between Calisto and Sempronio proves nothing, for Sempronio's words are belied by his
own ability to fall madly in love with Elicia. This places
his anti-feminist remarks in an ironical light.
      For the rest, the female characters of LC are pre-
sented from a very human point of view, neither better nor
worse than the men.

1969

Herriott, Homer J., "Notes on Selectivity of Language in the
Celestina," Hispanic Review, XXXVII (1969), 77-101.
      In this article, Herriott concentrates primarily on the
usage in LC of common, popular, or archaic words and their
synonyms. Some of these appear only in Act I, others in
Act I and the additions, still others throughout the whole
work. This is an effort to discover to what extent to attribute archaisms, both orthographical and textual, to the author, and to what extent they may be attributed to the Burgos
edition or earlier editions.
      An examination of the initial h- and f- and of person-
al pronouns reveals that the author of LC, unlike most of
his contemporaries, preferred consistently the modern forms,
thus showing a degree of selectivity on his part. According
to Herriott, good taste and selectivity dictated to Rojas some
of the forms examined.
      With respect to archaisms, Herriott examines those
which appear dispersed throughout LC and those appearing only
in Act I. Herriott observes that when Rojas selects a word
or phrase, he often repeats it within a brief time. The frequency of refranes suggests that the author was strongly attracted to them.

The sampling offers ample evidence that the same
method of selectivity prevails in all parts of LC. The author
always selects phrases as needed for the purpose of creating
a character. Herriott's illustrations allow us a glimpse into
the creative process of the author as well as into the character of the author himself. The chief conclusion to be derived
from this study is that the author used no models to which
he remained faithful--his process is one of transforming
phrases and expressions into something vital. Moreover, Herriott reaffirms that "we are not convinced that Fernando de
Rojas was not the author of Act I."

Zárate, Armando, "La poesía y el ojo en La Celestina,"
Cuadernos Americanos, CLXIV, No. 3 (1969), 119-136.
        Zárate sees a connection between the visual imagery
in LC and the process of sexual surrender. The visual experience becomes the determining factor for the surrender of
the protagonists. The process moves from the contemplation of the loved one to admiration, and finally to sexual surrender. The author takes us through the process which goes
from a beatified love to clandestine desire. Punishment follows from the enjoyment of the prohibited fruit.
        When Calisto declares, "En esto veo Melibea, la
grandeza de Dios," he is clearly attributing to Melibea the
function of the lumen gloria. Rojas is applying here the love
concept developed by Dante. The tragedy in LC is based, in
part, on Calisto's faulty perception. Blinded by his love he
confuses divine essence with human "beatitude."
        Zárate notes throughout the work the frequency of the
verb "to see," and the connection between the visual experience and the awakening of love. Zárate outlines the forms
of visual pleasure which lead to the catastrophe:
    1. Calisto contempla a Melibea.
    2. Calisto se contempla a sí mismo.
    3. Calisto es contemplado por Melibea.
The sight of the loved one leads to the development of love;
however, a distinction should be made between "ver bien"
and "ver mal." The former presupposes a development of
spiritual life, whereas the latter causes spiritual blindness,
leading to a fall, and inevitably to retribution.

1970

Ayllón, Cándido, "La ironía de La Celestina," Romanische
Forschungen, LXXXII (1970), 37-55.
        According to Ayllón, the function of irony in LC has
not yet been given wide enough attention, considering that a

reading of the work reveals that there is neither episode nor
character where the presence of irony is not felt.

Examples drawn from the text amply illustrate the all-
pervasive use of irony: verbal irony, irony of characters,
irony of deeds or situations, dramatic and tragic irony.
Irony also surges from the discrepancy between what the character says and the facts we know about his life.

Ayllón notes that irony functions throughout as part of
the structure of the work, it justifies the development of the
plot and supports the motivation of the characters.   A chief
example is the irony of Celestin'a death: Celestina, always
able to understand the psychological make-up of others, fails
to grasp the situation, and therefore fails in her art of per-
suasion.

By his constant use of irony, Rojas is able to under-
score his own bitter vision of the world.

Barbera, Raymond E. , "Medieval Iconography in La Celestina," Romanic Review, LXI (1970), 5-13.

According to Barbera, medieval iconography offers
sufficient evidence to support the contention that Rojas' work
held symbolic meaning for its contemporary reader.   Barbera discusses the symbolism of the hawk, of Melibea's garden and the wall around it, of Calisto's horse and the ladder
from which he falls.

Lorenzo-Rivero, Luis, "La celestinesca como creación de
Castilla la Nueva," Duquesne Hispanic Review, VII (1970), 1-
4.

Lorenzo-Rivero elaborates Criado de Val's line of
argumentation [Chapter 7, 1960] that the celestinesque theme
found in Greek, Latin or Arabic sources does not constitute
a literary antecedent of the theme as found in Spanish works.
The former are influences which are condensed but not imitated.   Homosexual love predominated in these, whereas in
Spanish celestinesque literature, feminine beauty is unequiv-
ocally the only objective.   The Arcipreste de Hita and Rojas
are the first Spanish writers to introduce in literature a
lover.who desires an unmarried woman, and who is driven
by a love whose force is stronger than the belief in God.
They are also the first to represent a woman inwardly rav-
aged by the power of love but who, nevertheless, outwardly
is able to maintain her social decorum.   This outer reserve
necessitates the aid of an intermediary.

Chapter 6

ETHICAL VALUES

1899

Menéndez Pelayo, Marcelino, ed. <u>La Celestina</u> (E. Krapf).
2 vols. Vigo, 1899-1900.
    For Menéndez Pelayo, LC is a poem of love, a drama
similar to that of Romeo and Juliet and an example of moral
expiation. The fatal events in it intervene to interrupt the
free reign of human passion, thus making manifest the rule
of a superior law.

1904

Desdevises du Dezert, M. G., "La comédie de Caliste et
Melibée," <u>Revue des Cours et Conférences,</u> XII (1904), 739-
756.
    For Desdevises du Dezert, love does not play a great
role in the Tragicomedia but passion does. Passion has to
be satiated and only then will its fury be abated. Therefore,
the author is expressing neither Christian nor Jewish values,
but a pagan concept of life.

1910

Menéndez Pelayo, Marcelino, <u>Orígenes de la novela,</u> Vol.
III. Madrid, 1905-1910.
    According to Menéndez Pelayo, Rojas' concept of love
is that of an evil influence which poisons and corrupts human
life. It is a force that seeks revenge in the children for the
sins of their fathers. The author's morality consists in an
epicurean pessimism and a transcendental and bitter irony.
But the people of his world are Christians, living within a
Christian society, though there seems to exist a confusion
between human and divine values. Menéndez Pelayo attributes
this ambiguity more to the anarchy of ideas and customs
which existed in Castille during the reign of Enrique IV than
to the religious skepticism which can be attributed to a <u>con-
verso.</u>

1912

Reynier, Gustave, "La Célestine," Les origines du roman réaliste. Paris, 1912.
Reynier sees the ostensible moral values as merely affixed to the work in an effort to disguise its actual moral laxity.

1913

Echalar, Bernardo de, "Fernando de Rojas: La Celestina," Estudios Franciscanos, XIII (1913), 96-109.
For Echalar, LC is not a work of moral edification but a compendium of material love, pagan in tone. A strong atmosphere of paganism, which he attributes to the influx of Renaissance concepts from Italy, pervades the entire work. Man is dedicated to a pagan cult of material goods and of the flesh. LC lacks an ethical aspect because the authors have sought artistic effects rather than those of edification.

1914

Azorín (Martínez Ruiz, José), "La Celestina," Valores literarios. Obras Completas, Vol. II. Madrid, 1959.
Azorín attacks the interpretations which have emphasized the moral wisdom of LC. He also rejects any notion of a demonic element. For him all the motivations are strictly human. He allows only the inexorability of fate as a superior force. The theme of the work is the inexorability of destiny and the sense of fatality resulting from the awareness of the brevity of material joys. Finally, fate, not the perversity of Celestina, is the ruling force of the action of LC.

1915

Cejador y Frauca, Julio, "La Celestina," Historia de la lengua y literatura castellana desde los orígenes hasta Carlos V. Madrid, 1915, pp. 425-442.
Cejador sees in the ending of Pleberio's lament, "¡Bienaventurados los que no conociste o de los que no te curaste!" the basis of Schopenhauer's philosophy, his pessimism concerning life and death, which in LC is equivalent to the ananke or fate expressed in Greek tragedy.

1925

Maeztu, Ramiro de, Don Quijote, Don Juan y La Celestina.
Madrid, 1925.
    See Chapter 7.

1930

Spitzer, Leo, "Zur Celestina," Zeitschrift für Romanische
Philologie, L (1930), 237-240.
    Spitzer states that LC exhibits an autonomous and hu-
man conception of life. But he emphasizes that the motifs
in it belong to the spirit of the Middle Ages. He quotes
from medieval French texts and the poetry of the Minne-
sänger to substantiate his point.

1932

Küchler, Walther, "Die erste bekannte Ausgabe der Comedia
de Calisto y Melibea," Romanistiches Jahrbuch, VI (1956),
315-323. (This article was actually written in 1932 and later
found among Küchler's papers.)
    Pleberio's lament expresses the senselessness of life.
Everything in the work is shown as meaningless except the
act of defiance of Melibea's suicide in the face of her overwhelming inconsolability.
    God has disappeared from LC. There is no medieval
renunciation of God in Calisto. Melibea is his God. Melibea begins with a more Christian attitude but quickly loses it.
The lower characters think only of pleasures of the flesh.
Nature motivates them, not God. Everyone is destroyed
through his subjugation to a life of the senses, and the work
ends with a desperate question--Why?--characteristic of the
waning of the Middle Ages when man experiences loss of
certainty and yet cannot joyfully accept a world without God.
It is a condition of restlessness which was strongly experienced by Petrarch, who felt that the only solution could be
found in stoical equanimity. The humanists wanted to put
man on the throne of life, and yet they were unable to separate themselves from the Christian tradition of distrust of
life. Life on earth without God did not appear to them as
something to be trusted, because this life is blind, purposeless, and senselessly destroys whatever is beautiful. The
Tragicomedia points to man's anxiety and helplessness. It is
the modern anxiety of a humanity without God, face to face
with a purposeless and senseless life.

Rauhut, Franz, "Das Dämonische in der Celestina," Festgabe
zum 60. Geburtstag Karl Vosslers. Munich, 1932, pp. 117-
148.
     According to Rauhut, Fate hangs over the love of Ca-
listo and Melibea from the very beginning. The death of Calisto, which is unacceptable as a realistic event, becomes
perfectly logical if seen as part of this demonic atmosphere
where doom has been present from the beginning. This is
part of the demonic frightfulness of the whole work. Calisto's
death has no cause in the rational sense because it is the expression of irrational fate. Rojas views the world as a terrifying abyss of irrationality where love and death are involved with each other. It is Pleberio with his full vision of
the irrationality of the world who has the last word. Order
does not rule our world; it is a desert where grief reigns.
     Love is seen as the demonic divinity which kills and
which invites or tempts all humanity into its dance of death.
Man cannot protect himself from this demonic power. There
is no Christian consolation here.
     The comic element and the moral of the story, to be-
ware of go-betweens, do not offer a sufficient positive note
to make the rule of the demonic power bearable. The only
consolation is to be found in the strong, fearless voice of the
poet, in his own tranquility in the face of this reality.

1939

Croce, Benedetto, "La Celestina," La Critica, XXXVII
(1939), 81-91.
     Croce does not want to place the work within a me-
dieval or Renaissance context because he believes that a poetic work, which is a work of humanity, overcomes all historical distinctions. Furthermore, the question whether LC
is a moral tale does not apply to a poetic or artistic work.
Neither does Croce consider valid the question of the characters' motivation because they are all sunk in the abyss of
the senses, incapable of pulling themselves out, indeed determined not to pull themselves out. No moral catharsis
takes place at the conclusion of the drama. The deaths of
the protagonists and of the servants are due to chance.
They have no human or divine meaning nor do they suggest
punishment.

1940

Ricard, Robert, "Sobre la moralidad de La Celestina,"
Abside, IV (1940), 15-18.

Ricard sees LC as a poetic world where characters
are totally unconcerned with the value and consequence of
their actions. Furthermore, the actions of the characters
imply a negation of free will. It is apparent, therefore, that
Rojas achieves the opposite of his proclaimed didactic purpose.

1943

Giusti, Roberto F. , "Fernando de Rojas. Su obra de humanidad española y de arte renancentista," Boletín de la Academia Argentina de Letras, XII (1943), 121-142.
          LC is "el Pánfilo vuelto a lo trágico." In the work
we find Love as a source of grief and the cause of death.
Fate is irrevocably cruel and the world offers no consolation
to the desperate Pleberio.

1946

García Bacca, Juan David, "Sobre el sentido de 'conciencia'
en La Celestina," Revista de Guatemala, VI (1946), 52-66.
          García Bacca seeks to draw an existential metaphysi-
cal value from Celestina's phrase, "así goce de mí." Since
being precedes essence, Rojas selects the experiences which
give us an awareness of being. He selects gozar as the experience which "nos hace ser más reales" and which "nos
hace notarnos más reales." "Gozarse uno de sí" is the
"manera más potenciadamente real que puede adquirir la conciencia."

1954

McPheeters, D. W. , "The Element of Fatality in the Tragicomedia de Calisto y Melibea," Symposium, VIII (1954), 331-
335.
          McPheeters interprets the manner of Calisto's death
in terms of the moral attitudes of the period, namely the medieval concept still prevalent in the fifteenth century that such
unexpected violent deaths were fitting punishment for those
who had transgressed moral laws.

1956

Gilman, Stephen, The Art of 'La Celestina'. Madison, 1956.
          For Gilman, the encounter of the tú and yo which con-
stitutes a life of mutual awareness interwoven through successive situations, brings about the undefined but inherent

theme of struggle, expressed in the Prologue. Beside the
theme of struggle, LC presents panoramic views of social
disorder and decay. Through his dialogue of consciousness,
Rojas unfolds a new circumstance of self-understanding--
"from man's conscious acceptance of destiny in terms of
salvation to the conscious rebellion of life against its condi-
tioning--a consciousness of total and final perdition."

1957

Anderson Imbert, E. , "La Celestina," Los grandes libros de
Occidente. Mexico City, 1957, 30-44.
    Anderson reviews all the arguments surrounding LC.
He stresses the individualism of the characters. Calisto and
Melibea's individualism lies in the fact that they do not even
consider marriage.
    Celestina is neither a satanic figure nor a simple go-
between; she is "una vida rebosante." In no way does the
author intend to punish his characters. No moral is necessary because there is neither God nor Satan in the work.
What the work glorifies is the flesh and what fails is also
the flesh. There is no notion of sin nor of repentance. The
power of the flesh acts as an equalizer of men. Both masters and servants fall prey to carnal love.
    The death of Calisto and Melibea is not retribution for
sin but an allegory of life, fleeting and deceiving, which
seeks its own pleasure but which destroys us once we are
possessed by love. Pleberio does not reproach his daughter
for her love; he bemoans love's tragic nature. Retribution
for sin implies a spiritual order, whereas the death of Calisto and Melibea is proof of chaos.

Garrido Pallardó, Fernando, Los problemas de Calisto y
Melibea y el conflicto de su autor. Figueras, 1957.
    Garrido Pallardó states that the characters in LC ex-
hibit traits of Hebraic morality. For example, had Pleberio
been a Christian, he would have tried to avenge his honor.
As for Melibea, she has the Christian concept of sin, but
not that of forgiveness. She continues to accept the Hebraic
"animam pro anima."

1958

Webber, Edwin J. , "The Celestina as an Arte de Amores,"
Modern Philology, LV (1958), 145-153.
    Webber affirms that Rojas composed a plot which
would dramatically epitomize the tragic consequences of rep-

rehensible actions. In the 16-act version, Rojas heightens
the effect of the tragic fall by introducing it suddenly into
the midst of the lovers' obliviousness. He thus provides the
contrast to drive home his professed moral aim.

1960

Prieto, Adolfo, "El sentimiento de la muerte a través de la
literatura española," Revista de Literaturas Modernas, II
(1960), 115-170.
    According to Prieto, death had lost for the author of
LC the meaning given to it by the Christian Middle Ages and
even that which had influenced the religious thought of his an-
cestors. Rojas was not able to exchange these religious concepts, which emphasized an ascetic acceptance of death, for
any other. Thus the reading of the Tragicomedia leaves an
impression of sadness and pessimism.

1961

Bataillon, Marcel, 'La Célestine' selon Fernando de Rojas.
Paris, 1961.
    For an interpretation of LC, Bataillon turns to Gaspar
Barth (1587-1658), who sees the work as a precious manual
of practical morality. Bataillon defends Barth against Menéndez Pelayo's allegations of extravagance and mental alienation [Chapter 4, 1910]. Barth demonstrated how the moral
meaning of LC surges from the whole structure of the work.
    Bataillon's thesis is that LC was originally conceived
and later continued as a moralizing work [Chapter 5], written "en reprensión de los locos enamorados, etc." Bataillon
states that the drama of the original first act is the seduction of Pármeno by the arguments of Celestina. Our attention is centered on the moral defeat of Pármeno. Rojas continues in the same vein and establishes a hierarchy of values
between the two servants, Sempronio-Pármeno, one diligent,
executing both good and evil; the other, addressing himself
to his master's conscience. This hypothesis is strengthened
by the second set of servants chosen by Calisto, creating a
parallel situation between the pair Sosia-Tristán and Sempronio-Pármeno.
    Bataillon rejects the modern skepticism with regard
to a moral interpretation of LC. He sees the work as a
moralité in which the dramatic techniques are inseparable
from its edifying aim. Bataillon examines to what extent the
formal structural devices are necessary for the work to
achieve its didactic intention. As was noted in Chapter 5,

Bataillon finds in the structure of the imitations confirmation
of his interpretation, since most of the imitations retain the
basic elements of LC. German Romanticism was responsible
for transforming the meaning of LC, because it was in the
Romantic character to exalt the passion which Rojas had intended to condemn. Only in the twentieth century is Calisto
seen in his true light, as "un obsédé ridicule."

The additions of 1502 do not break the moral significance of the whole. LC is a moral tragicomedy conforming
to the moral conceptions of its period, which acclaimed it as
such. The delay in Calisto's death illustrates the classic
theme of the delays of divine justice. It shows that sooner
or later, by means of secondary causes, divine will punishes
certain men in the same world in which they have sinned--
by a fall in the night if they have sinned in the night. The
subject of the whole play is Calisto's dishonor and misfortune. Bataillon does not see in Calisto's moral disorder and
his death any relation to Rojas' condition as a converso, nor
any relation to a world where feudal values have been reversed.

The moral and social theme of LC is the degradation
of a nobleman and of his love by his own unworthy servants,
who are connected through Celestina with the world of prostitution. Rojas is attacking a social and moral problem in his
presentation of this world. He accentuates the contrast between the baseness of the servants and the ridiculous trust
Calisto puts in them. The reason LC was neither banned nor
expurgated is that its redeeming social value was recognized
by Rojas' contemporaries. Even the satire on the clergy
cannot be considered audacious, except by those who lack historical and literary knowledge about the times of the Reyes
Católicos. Bataillon inveighs against the critics who apply
the criteria of their own time to LC. By applying Romantic,
bourgeois, or existential standards, we cannot arrive at the
ethical values which Rojas is trying to preserve.

As far as the question of marriage is concerned, it
should not be raised at all, since the Calisto-Melibea couple
did not interest either the first author or Rojas.

For Bataillon, the 1502 additions accentuate the moral
meaning of the 16 original acts, focusing on the comic blindness of the parents and especially on Melibea's fall. She is
overpowered by her own "frénésie amoureuse," worthy of
Calisto's madness. In the Comedia, Melibea dies right after
her surrender to Calisto, before she has an opportunity to
weigh her illicit love against marriage, obedience to her
parents, and society. But in the 1502 version, Melibea's
ruin takes on the character of a conscious and resolute ac-

tion both in her unwavering consent to Calisto and in her suicide. The fact that Melibea's sexual surrender has a witness, Lucrecia, helps to degrade her pleasure both in the
eyes of Rojas and of his careful readers. More than ever,
therefore, Rojas remains faithful to the initial purpose of the
Comedia, which was conceived by its first author as a moralité. For Bataillon, Melibea's moral fall was not explicit
enough in the 16-act version, where she could be considered
a victim of circumstances. The Tragicomedia clarifies her
behavior and her family's blindness. The sexual surrender
was prolonged in order to be judged more effectively, not in
order to be glorified.

Deyermond, A. D. , The Petrarchan Sources of 'La Celestina'.
Oxford, 1961.
        Deyermond points out how successfully Rojas was able
to incorporate the borrowed didactic material into his dialogue. Rojas' stylistic techniques allowed him to use the
Petrarchan material for his own creative purposes, as Gilman [1956] has so perceptively stated.
        Though Rojas drew heavily on Petrarch for the out-
look of his work, the point of view of LC differs from that
of its source. The difference between the two is apparent in
their concern over death, particularly in the element of consolation. Rojas makes Pleberio deliberately reject Petrarchan doctrine in favor of profound pessimism. In Pleberio's
speech, the Stoic attitude toward death is explicitly rejected,
while the Christian attitude is not considered at all. For
Petrarch, friendship was a basis for confidence, while Rojas,
who borrows seven sententiae on friendship, place it on the
same plane as passionate love or avarice--it leads straight
to disaster. The result is an even deeper pessimism.
Writers before Rojas borrowed and incorporated sententiae
in their work, but only Rojas was able to assimilate his
knowledge of Petrarch into both the dialogue and the outlook
of LC. Yet Rojas is driven by his own tragic and despairing vision of life to transform Petrarch's message in a way
that would have horrified its author.

Lida de Malkiel, María Rosa, Two Spanish Masterpieces:
The Book of Good Love and La Celestina. Urbana, 1961.
        See Note, Chapter 1, Lida de Malkiel, 1961.

Moreno, Báez, E. , "La obra y el autor," Nosotros y nuestros clásicos. Madrid, 1961, pp. 140-150.
        According to Moreno Báez, Rojas wanted to set an
example against concupiscence, for it is sensual desire that

leads the lovers to their death. Rojas' own pessimism leads
him to depict passions against which there is no protection.
Moreno Báez is convinced that Rojas' pessimism is "una
consecuencia de su pérdida de fe en la justicia alcanzada por
medio del cumplimiento de la Antigua Ley, sin haber llegado
nunca a creer en la lograda por los méritos de Cristo."

1962

Aguirre, J. M., Calisto y Melibea, amantes cortesanos.
Zaragoza, 1962.
    For Aguirre's interpretation of the moral attitude in
LC see Chapter 5.

Castro, Américo, 'La Celestina' como contienda literaria.
Madrid, 1962.
    Castro is interested in defining the creative tension
that made possible the creation of LC. For Castro, LC is
born out of a rupture with both the literary tradition of medieval Europe and that of the Graeco-Roman world. LC cannot therefore be classified either as medieval or as Renaissance. The authors' intention was not to continue or develop
earlier themes and forms, but to attack and destroy them.
That is why we find elements in LC which are not traceable
to any sources.
    Behind the destructiveness of LC lies the catástrophic
event of 1492, the expulsion of the Jews. Now Rojas' aim
is no longer to criticize the social or religious order, but to
turn it upside down; we find therefore in LC "la perversión
y el trastorno de las jerarquías de valoración vigentes, de
los ideales poéticos y caballerescos." Rojas pits value
against countervalue: heaven against earth, nature against
conscience--but all without redemptive hope, all values de-
voured in the consuming fire of life. Thus, for example, in
Calisto the old chivalric ideal is broken down. The roles of
Elicia and Melibea are reversed--the first is a lady, the
second has lustful desires. There is no allusion to a possible marriage between Calisto and Melibea because the harmony of marriage is outside the destructive vision of LC.
From this chaos--which is formal as well as thematic--only
Elicia and her likes emerge as able to control their destinies. "Con estos materiales caóticos u otros análogos,"
Castro writes, "construyó Rojas una construcción en la cual
caos de visión quieta se convirtió en caos litigioso y pluri-
dimensional." We have seen in Chapter 5 how Rojas' art
reflects this vision of chaos.

Correa, Gustavo, "Naturaleza, Religión y Honra en La
Celestina," PMLA, LXXVII (1962), 8-17.
            The opposition God-Nature is found in the Tragico-
media as a means of subverting the established traditional
values, both social and religious, in favor of the natural
world.   This reversal of values constitutes one of the structural characteristics of LC.
            Calisto's praise of Melibea is part of the celestial
glorification usually intended for angels and saints, but which
can also be applied to an earthly creature.   Thus all things
created by God can become an object of veneration in themselves.   Calisto's declaration, "en esto veo, Melibea, la
grandeza de Dios," reflects a scale of values in the lover's
mind and it implies a blasphemous transposition of the traditional religious values which are exclusively directed to the
supreme deity.
            The world of magic and witchcraft to which Celestina
belongs connects her with the world of the mysterious and
of the unknown in Nature.   She performs as a priestess of a
cult whose object is the veneration of the primary forces of
the earth, personified in the god Pluto.   Celestina's religiosity goes from the doctrine and veneration of God to that of
natural forces belonging to the realm of the diabolic.
            The same reversal of values is operated on the insti-
tution of honor.   By virtue of their social position Calisto
and Melibea belong to the category of "honra horizontal,"
which is maintained and protected by the institution of marriage.   Virginity is necessary to horizontal honor.   The love
of Calisto and Melibea is a catastrophic example of honor,
in which several characters are brought to their destruction
and ruin.   Celestina's sphere of existence bases its honor on
the destruction of honor itself.   Her actions reveal a "dia-
bolismo consustancial" which seeks a reversal of the traditional values of honor and implies a rebelliousness against
human and divine laws.
            Calisto's initial words proclaim a cult and a religious
doctrine which he fully realizes when he gains possession of
his god.   The delight and glory this possession affords him
is the final and supreme justification of his doctrine.   Melibea has fallen from the height of her honor but she has found
a new measure of glorification within the sphere of immediate satisfaction.   Celestina, on the other hand, has achieved
the greatest honor of her life with the conquest and destruction of Melibea.   Nature thus experiences its greatest triumph.
            For Correa, "el triunfo y exaltación de esta esfera de
valores está dominado, sin embargo, por criterios de re-

versibilidad y perversión paródica y disolvente de índole dia-
bólica." Celestina, allied to the anarchical forces of fecund
nature, becomes a demoniacal power which subverts the social order and the traditional categories which dignify man:
honor and religion. Melibea, spurred on by the demonic
powers of Celestina, abandons her rightful place in the social
ladder and betrays her own family. This subversion and reversal of values give a degree of triumph to the primary and
anarchical forces which lead man to an inexorable destiny of
destruction and death.

Lida de Malkiel, María Rosa, La originalidad artística de
'La Celestina'. Buenos Aires, 1962.
        For Mrs. Malkiel, Bataillon [1961] exaggerated the role
of the moral lesson in LC. His suggestion that morality is
a unique key to the conception and execution of the work actually diminishes the importance of the moral message. She
finds him guilty of didactic apriority. The idea of a strict
adherence to a didactic purpose minimizes the artistic
achievement of LC.
        Mrs. Malkiel maintains that the text, far from limit-
in itself to the exemplification of the frequently mentioned
subtitle, suggests and infinitely more grandiose and less orthodox teaching: "una visión de desgarramiento y conflicto den-
tro y fuera del hombre." The Comedia externalized the moral consequences of this vision at the end of the drama through
Pleberio's lament. But the Tragicomedia, with greater artistic exigency, pointed to it within the drama itself, showing
the lovers' death not as a purely casual consequence of their
abandonment to pleasure. As for the characters, they are
neither moral abstractions nor social categories; they are individuals with human faces. What LC does is to take a very
simple occurrence from reality and to develop it "sin cansarse
de contemplar su infinita complejidad." Rather than an abstract conflict of abstract categories, we get individual beings
entangled in an Herculean struggle of egoisms. As for the
overall amoral religiosity of LC, it is part of the work's
artistic vision, just as the amorality of the lovers, the alcahueta and the servants bitterly reflect Rojas' contemporary
reality.

Oostendorp, H. Th., El conflicto entre el honor y el amor
en la literatura española hasta el siglo XVII. The Hague,
1962.
        Oostendorp maintains that both Rojas and his predeces-
sor are moralists whose main purpose is to warn against the
dangers of loco amor, the intervention of an alcahueta and

deceitful servants.   If we want to capture the meaning of the
Tragicomedia, we must discard once and for all the idea that
the authors are in sympathy with the attitude of the lovers.
Oostendrop corroborates Bataillon's interpretation [1961] that
LC does not present the drama of young love, but the consequences of unrestrained passion.   Moreover, the original author pays little attention to the lovers.   He concentrates on
Calisto's folly, which is an easy target for Sempronio's and
Celestina's avarice.   Miss McDonald [1954] also pointed out
that both Rojas and his predecessor emphasized the weak and
unsympathetic aspect of Calisto's character.

There is no doubt that Calisto's death is intended as
just punishment for his moral weaknesses, whereas Celestina's death is the result of unrestrained avarice.   Melibea's
own death comes as the final consequence of the total blindness caused by loco amor.

Calisto is dependent on the intervention of an alcahueta
because Melibea's wealth stands between them.   Melibea's
father represents the insurmountable obstacle to the lovers'
legal union.   By their actions, the lovers contemptuously disregard the established social order and family obligations.
What Rojas condemns is their revolt against the existing social norms.   Rojas continues Act I in order to inculcate in
his readers a repugnance for all infringements of the established order, by pointing out that annihilation awaits all those
who have collaborated in the destruction of this order.   There
is no evidence to indicate that the original author had en-
visaged the same ending for his characters.   It is more likely that he would have given his work the happy ending of humanistic comedies.

Celestina is the worst adversary of the established social order.   Her relations with Satan confirm this.   Melibea's
seduction is brought on by the devil's intervention.   Rojas
shows how Celestina, aided by the devil, is able to incite
Melibea's rebellion against the social and moral order by cor-
rupting her virtue.   As for Calisto, his willingness to employ the depraved bawd underscores his moral weakness.   He
is ready to sacrifice everything, including his honor.

Oostendorp does not see LC as the work of a converso
or as containing Jewish values.   Though Pleberio's lament has
been generally interpreted as an expression of the despair of
a converso, for Oostendorp it functions as an epilogue to
warn the readers against the temptations of the world and of
love.   Pleberio laments the loss of his daughter who suc-
cumbed to the temptations of loco amor, the enemy of divine
and social order.   LC is not a naturalist drama but an ethical and moralizing work.   We cannot therefore accept the

notion that Pleberio was literally a shipbuilder or that this profession would make him a <u>converso</u>. Rojas is writing in the tradition of humanistic comedy, and all critical allusions to the existence of a <u>converso</u> are arbitrary. Pleberio's lament expresses a Christian attitude toward fleeting earthly. pleasures.

Melibea's suicide does not reveal the attitude of a <u>conversa</u> in an act of defiance against the Christian God. Rojas conceived Melibea's suicide and her eternal damnation as an inevitable consequence of sinful love. Furthermore, Rojas' aim was to instill in his readers a revulsion against <u>loco amor</u>. The scene of Melibea's death has therefore a profound ethical meaning. Melibea, although fully aware of her enslavement to passion, cannot free herself from its yoke. Pleberio is a witness to the ravages caused by love and cannot remain impassive to them.

Calisto's death, though an accident, is not devoid of ethical meaning. While Gilman [1955] sees a relationship between Calisto's fall and the turn of the wheel of Fortune-- a frequent theme in medieval works--he does not ascribe a symbolic meaning to Calisto's fall. Oostendorp, on the other hand, siding with Rauhut [1932] and Miss McDonald [1954], sees a punitive intent in it. Rojas conceives the accidental death as a means of punishment to prevent Calisto from repenting. Rojas thus warns lovers to restrain their passions and not to incur the risk of sudden death without confession.

Pleberio and his wealth stand as an obstacle to the lovers' legitimate union. This is supported by the textual indication that the lovers and their servants foresee Pleberio's vengeance as a possible danger.

The ethical meaning of LC was not understood by nineteenth-century critics, who sympathized with the lovers and their sense of independence from social order and moral laws. Rojas instead preaches complete submission to parental authority. He belongs to the conservative wing which at the beginning of the twelfth century fought against rampant individualism, whose chief demand was for freedom in contracting marriage. Rojas and his predecessor do not approve of freely choosing the marital partner. Hence they consider secret love as a rebellion against the social norm which deserves severe punishment. Even if there had been a secret marriage between Calisto and Melibea, Rojas would have disapproved of their independent action.

1963

Ayllón, Cándido, "Negativism and Dramatic Structure in <u>La</u>

Celestina," Hispania, XLVI (1963), 290-295.
                "All roads in the Tragicomedia lead to tragedy and
destruction:" such is Ayllón's theme in this article. Citing
characteristic speeches of every character in LC, including
Pleberio's final lament, Ayllón brings out the tone of pessimism, loneliness and disillusionment which again and again
surges to the fore.

Ayllón, Cándido, "Petrarch and Fernando de Rojas," Romanic
Review, LIV (1963), 81-94.
                Ayllón examines the borrowings from Petrarch with a
view to determining whether these endow the Tragicomedia
with psychological depth. Ayllón shows that they sustain
Rojas' pessimism [Chapter 5]. Rojas did not utilize Petrarch's optimistic stoicism nor his Christian hope but rather
his melancholy, his medieval Christian pessimism and his
skepticism.

Heugas, Pierre, ed. La Célestine. Paris, 1963.
                Heugas, like Bataillon [1961], sees LC as a vast ex-
emplum concerning distrust of the flesh, a theme announced
in the subtitle. Courtly love exalted heroism and gentleness
in the lover. Woman guided man on the road to virtue. But
the road Calisto takes is one of degradation, ending with just
punishment. However, the moral nihilism and pessimism of
LC is attenuated by its exaltation of love and life as an ir-
repressible force. Still, the systematic destruction of all
moral standards betrays the nihilism of the conversos which
we find from Rojas to Mateo Alemán.

                                   1964

Gilman, Stephen, "Fernando de Rojas as Author," Romanische Forschungen, LXXVI (1964), 255-290.
                Gilman attempts to deal directly with Rojas' intentions
in creating LC and the manner in which he proceeded. The
unknown first author "must have been at least partially aware
that his attention had turned from predefined virtue and vice
to an exploration of how human minds operate in changing
situations." Furthermore, "we may even go on to surmise
that it was this innovation that fascinated Rojas and incited
him to embark upon the continuation."
                Gilman does not deny that for Rojas LC was both in-
itially and ultimately a moral work. In Pleberio's desperate
soliloquy, Rojas made his essential revelation about the meaning of life explicit. Rojas converted the initial didactic moral, the warning by exemplum against blasphemy and the de-

ceit of servants, into a Stoic contemplation of human condition. The only moral error of father and daughter is to have
overlooked fundamental Stoic precepts on evaluation. The
forthright stoicism of the conclusion cannot be divorced from
Rojas' use of Petrarchian commonplaces to communicate an
ironical understanding of speaker, speech, and thought. The
onflowing of consciousness is always juxtaposed ironically
with the static recipes the individual pretends to live by.
"LC is a work in which the Stoic moral, although never denied, is always betrayed by life and which ends by inflicting
the most suffering on the character who is least responsible."
        Pleberio's lament contains an explicit denial of order.
The very disorder of the universe suggests the familiar literary pattern of the Dance of Death. Rojas looks back on
LC as a "Dance of Love," a dance as fatal, frightful and
carelessly ordered as its predecessor. The Dance of Death
theme translates the ultimately desperate alienation of the
solitary Spanish converso.

Green, Otis H. , Spain and the Western Tradition, Vols. 2-4.
Madison, 1963-1964.
        Green argues against the view held by Castro and
others that LC is a tragedy and that Rojas is a "despairing
genius." For example, the reference to the Heraclitean
struggle of the elements in the Prologue must not be taken
in a cosmic sense. Rojas is merely alluding to the other
men of letters who are sure to attack him and his work.
The words he chooses--suginelo, milanos, and so forth--do
not lend themselves to a tragic interpretation.
        What of Calisto's remark that he sees in Melibea the
greatness of God? This is not, as Castro affirms, unchristian nature-philosophy. Rojas is in the medieval tradition
of natura naturans: Melibea's beauty is a manifestation of
the greatness of God. Nature continues God's work. Rojas
is not deviating into heresy.
        LC is a highly moral work, but it is not a tragedy.
For that matter, it is an error to ascribe an attitude of despair to conversos in general, beginning with Rojas. "The
lovers come to a disastrous end because the author has
willed that by their personal disaster they shall show the inevitable wages of sin." Thus, Rojas "offers his play as a
service, both to his patron and to his country." He is writing in reproof of crazed lovers. To drive his lesson home,
he allows his lovers to die without Christian consolation.
Such is the punishment he metes out to those who yield to
"wild unreason." In this light, Pleberio appears as "shallow-
minded" in his lament. His values are worldly. "There is

no devotion, no respect to a Higher Harmony." Not tragedy, then, but a sense of disillusion, meant for the young man to whom the author dedicated his book.

Maravall, José Antonio, El mundo social de 'La Celestina'. Madrid, 1964.

According to Maravall, Rojas followed the literary tradition of the exemplum and adapted it to the spirit of the Renaissance. The traditional idea of unity and harmony as the governing law of the universe is supplanted by a concordantia oppositorum.

The new leisure class is responsible for the social conflict and is the cause of what Bataillon [1961] has called "un dérèglement des critères moraux." The social environment of LC is a product of the urban civilization which developed in the Renaissance. It marks the development of a new urban leisure class, for which the idea of conspicuous consumption is of primary importance. It is to this new class that the characters of LC belong. The resentment of the plebeian characters represents a social protest against their inferior social and economic position as salaried servants. Traditional servant loyalty is now replaced by self-interest. For example, Centurio's role cannot be compared to that of the miles gloriosus because his social situation differs from that of the Latin character. Sentiments of loyalty no longer unite master and servant; only an economical arrangement exists between them. These new social conditions allowed Rojas artistic freedom in the characterization of his servants. The Renaissance cult of the individual is apparent in his characterization: the servants want to be free. Their actions betray a desire for economic and social autonomy. They seek the freedom not to serve, hence their egotism.

The new socio-historical conditions are also responsible for the renewed interest in the role of Fortune. Man can control the arbitrariness of Fortune by a rational and calculated personal intervention. Interest in magic power is another expression of the age's desire to control hidden natural forces. The practice of witchcraft coincides with the moral and social problems that the characters are experiencing.

Hedonism effaces the traditional concept of pleasure. Pleasure is the ultimate goal. Love is experienced as an irresistible force. It causes moral disorder because under its influence the will does not obey reason; love annihilates individual will. The only escape from its power is through death. And this is the moral to be drawn from LC. Love

assumes the role of a new sport for the affluent leisure class
of the fifteenth century.   Calisto's socio-economic position
holds the key to the understanding of LC.   For this new urban society, the dangerous practice of love is a substitute for
action on the battlefield.

Maravall states that Rojas' own position as a converso
is not responsible for the moral imbalance of his characters.
Rather, his attitude reveals the moral state of his society
and the individual's break with traditional values.   Rojas is
addressing himself to the affluent and lower classes, both of
which have lost sight of the after-life and seek fulfillment in
pleasure and in the accumulation of wealth.   Rojas' thought
is conditioned by a particular historical moment and not by
personal agnosticism.   For he himself remains attached to
traditional moral values.

Rojas' work is a warning to the rich bourgeoisie that
social decorum is essential to a sound way of life and that
the external practice of religion is an element of that decorum.   The glorification of pleasure and of life causes the sudden destruction of life itself.   This is the moral meaning of
LC.   Rojas secularizes the work to render the evils more
poignant to the secular, pragmatic, egotistical society in
which he lived.

Moore, John A., "Ambivalence of Will in La Celestina,"
Hispania, XLVII (1964), 251-255.
Fate in LC is a blind impersonal force which is, however, more likely to strike down the rash than the prudent.
Rojas gives all his characters the chance to avoid destruction.   In no case is there an overwhelming tragic destiny set
from the outside.   Tragic fate triumphs only because of the
ambivalent will in each character.   The character is given
due warning, he often has an urge to act prudently, but the
seed of evil is in all men, and finally they choose the rash
course of action which leads to their undoing.

Wardropper, Bruce W., "Pleberio's Lament for Melibea and
the Medieval Elegiac Tradition," Modern Language Notes,
LXXIX (1964), 140-152.
Wardropper maintains that Pleberio's lament is an
elegiac peroration that summarizes the entire meaning of
LC [Chapter 5].

1965

Ayllón, Cándido, La visión pesimista de 'La Celestina'.
Mexico City, 1965.

Rojas has conferred two major characteristics on his work: bitter irony and pessimism. His epicurean pessimism is accentuated by the fact that the characters of LC live in a Christian world but behave like gentiles [1910, Menéndez Pelayo]. The final impression of the work is one of deep sadness and pessimism. Rojas' is the vision of a somber and painful world. The conflict in this world is heightened by the egotism and cynicism of some of the characters.

Rojas was influenced both by the pessimistic trends of his age and his own conflicts as a cristiano nuevo. Disillusionment and bitterness are prevalent in the works of conversos.

LC moves on two planes: one structural where all is cause and effect, and the other conceptual where fatalism and fortune govern.

Ayllón notes that Petrarch's maxims express Rojas' own pessimism both in the Prologue and in the original 16 acts [1963, Ayllón]. Rojas uses passages which reflect Petrarch's melancholy, medieval Christian pessimism and skepticism in order to reinforce his own pessimistic view of the world. But he gives them a new vigor and vitality, and imbues his sources with his own mordant irony.

Pleberio's invective against fortune expresses the conflict between man and this elusive cosmic force which defeats man at every turn. There is a close relationship between the concept of the fall and the pessimism prevalent in Rojas' time and work. Gilman [1956] has already underscored the close relationship between the fall, the fortune, and the pessimism of the Tragicomedia, where all pleasure becomes grief and where all the characters fall to their death.

All elements are in conflict. Even love ends in destruction. The theme of love is the focus of the action in the Tragicomedia. Love is related to many other themes but is always a destructive and annihilating force.

The preoccupation with time reveals the characters' awareness of the brevity of life.

The struggle between man and the forces of the universe, as expressed in the Prologue, is essential to an understanding of the world of LC. Rojas presents conflict as the essential reality of the world. There is struggle between youth and old age, between man and woman. Forces such as love, fear, envy, and avarice keep placing man in a state of conflict with other men. Avarice leads to violent action and is a motivation for struggle in the world of LC. But all struggle ends with destruction.

Barrick, Mac E. , "Erna Ruth Berndt, Amor, Muerte y For-

tuna en 'La Celestina' " (rev. art.), <u>Hispanic Review,</u>
<u>XXXIII (1965), 401-406.</u>
Taking issue with Berndt, Barrick reads LC as a
moralizing work in which unChristian behavior is duly pun-
ished.   The love affair between Calisto and Melibea is in the
courtly tradition.   We are shown what happens when "locos
enamorados" follow the tenets of courtly love.
As for the theme of death, Barrick suggest that the
constant presence of death causes the characters to seek joy
in life and to live as intensely as possible.

Foster David William, "Some Attitudes Towards Love in the
Celestina," <u>Hispania,</u> XLVIII (1965), 484-492.
While love is the unifying force in LC [Chapter 5],
Pleberio's lament shows that Rojas entertains no hopeful il-
lusions about this emotion.   All human emotions--love or any
other--are treacherous, for Fate puts man at an intrinsic
disadvantage.

Green, Otis H., "The Artistic Originality of <u>La Celestina</u>"
(rev. art.), <u>Hispanic Review,</u> XXXIII (1965), 15-31.
This is a review article of Mrs. Malkiel's work
[1962].   In it, Green reiterates some of his own views.   He
differs with Mrs. Malkiel's view of Rojas as a thoroughgoing
pessimist, and once again places emphasis on Rojas' moral
intentions, as defined in his Prologue of 1502.
The term "mundo" in LC is to be taken as the world
of here-and-now and as the "enemigo de Dios."   It is the
world of fools and sinners.   Pleberio's lament is addressed
to this world, in which he has placed his trust and which has
betrayed him.   We get therefore a tacit condemnation of the
worldly view of life.
LC is an eminently moral work.   It deals out punishment for transgression.   Gilman [1956] is wrong in his ap-
plication of existentialist concepts to LC.   Bataillon [1961],
on the other hand, is right in stressing the work's moral
character, though he goes too far in his view of LC as exclusively a Morality.

1966

Fraker, Charles F., "The Importance of Pleberio's Soliloquy," <u>Romanische Forschungen,</u> LXXVIII (1966), 515-529.
Taking issue with Green and Bataillon, Fraker asserts
that Pleberio's soliloquy is of central importance in LC.
Pleberio's pessimism, his complaint that Providence does
not rule human affairs, his view that love is a destructive

force--all this is thoroughly borne out by the text of LC.
Pleberio clearly speaks for Rojas.

At the same time, Fraker argues that this pessimistic
world-view was well within the range of an informal orthodoxy, and he cites other works of the period with similar
tendencies. LC is a morality, an exemplum of the kind popular in the fifteenth century. That its orthodoxy was acceptable is shown by the fact that the Inquisition left it alone for
many years, and thereafter required only minor suppres-
sions.

In Rojas' world-view, irregular love exposes a man
to the onslaught of Fortune. Calisto's fall is a chance event,
but it is a chance event to which concupiscence exposes him.
Calisto tempts fate. His fall, and the tragic end of the other characters, are then commented upon by Pleberio in his
lament.

Rojas appears to Fraker as a highly original writer
who was able to bend the comic character of the first act to
his own pessimistic purpose.

Ricard, Robert, "La Celestina vista otra vez," Cuadernos
Hispano-americanos, LXVI, No. 198 (1966), 469-480.

According to Ricard, the plot of LC "se desarolla en
un mundo irreal y según modalidades irreales, rasgos que
confieran a la obra una extraña poesía."

Thus LC appears as a non-Christian work in a Christian society. It is, as Castro has put it, "una obra láica
si las hay." The characters live without any consciousness
of sin or remorse in a secularized society that bears no resemblance to the Spain of Rojas' time. Calisto fails to ask
Melibea in marriage because solutions of a religious sort do
not enter into anyone's mind.

The fact that a work like LC could be written and
printed indicates that Spanish society under the Reyes Católicos had not yet achieved full homogeneity. At the same
time, however, Ricard points out that LC has no Jewish or
Moslem flavor either. Its ideology is entirely its own.
Hence the "irritante fascinación" which it keeps exerting.

1967

Brault, Gérard J. "Interpretations of the Celestina, Old and
New." Bulletin of the Pennsylvania State Modern Language
Association, XLVI, Nos. 1 and 2 (1967-8), 3-8.

Brault contrasts some recent interpretations of LC
with the earliest views available to us, beginning with that
of Alfonso Ordóñez in 1506. The early commentators of LC

stressed the moralistic purpose of the author to the exclu-
sion of anything else.

Rojas' contemporaries discussed LC in moral terms.
And the work, according to Brault, went out of vogue because of a change in the attitude of the public, which became
weary of moralistic works. Mabbe's translation (1631) is
proof of this change.

Critics like Blanco White [1824] continued to exhibit
the critical attitudes of their time. Only recently has proper
attention been given to the thematic unity of LC, with particular attention to the theme of Fortune, Love, Death.
Many source studies have also appeared.

Bataillon [1961] takes up again the question of moral
purpose and urges us to interpret Rojas' work in this light.

Today we are still endeavoring to grasp the full meaning of LC, confronted by the dilemma offered by any work of
art: Should we give Rojas' play a literal interpretation, allowing the author's own words and those of his contemporaries to guide us: or should we allow ourselves to react
to this masterpiece in the light of our own personal experience and familiarity with the vast possibilities of literature?
Both approaches are good and necessary, states Brault, but
we must distinguish between the two.

Kulin, Katalin, "La Célestine et la période de transition,"
Acta literaria Academiae Scientiarum Hungaricae, IX (1967),
63-85.

In this essay, the social and philosophical values implicit in LC are attributed to the historical period of transition in which the authors found themselves. LC constitutes
an implacable sounding of contemporary society. As far as
religion is concerned, it was without meaning to the authors.
Yet the contradiction between the words and the actions of
the characters reveals that the old values had not completely disappeared. As a result, LC exhibits the indecisions
and anxieties and pessimism characteristic of a transitional
epoch.

In this world of unresolved contradictions, free-will,
the fundamental condition of human dignity, can only be fully
realized in suicide.

1968

Bell, A. Robert, "Folklore and Mythology in La Celestina,"
Medieval Epic to the "Epic" Theater of Brecht, ed. R. P.
Armato and J. M. Spalek. Los Angeles, 1968.
See Chapter 5.

Casa, Frank P., "Pleberio's Lament for Melibea," Zeit-schrift für Romanische Philologie, LXXXIV (1968), 19-29.
           Casa calls for a more thorough interpretation of Ple-berio's lament. According to him, an analysis of Pleberio's lament must take into consideration Petrarch's influence and, at certain points in LC, reactions against Petrarchan con-cepts.
           Casa sees Pleberio as a particular man faced with a particular problem. The elements which point to an indi-vidualization of his character have been generally ignored by critics, whereas those which form part of a tradition have been seen as personal traits. The series of questions, ¿Para quién edifiqué torres? ¿Para quién fabriqué navíos?, is generally seen as proof of a particular social background. Casa, on the contrary, holds that the source of these is Petrarch's De remediis utriusque fortunae, Book I. These remarks denote Pleberio's disillusion. He had believed in the existence of order and in the logical succession of events. But now he finds that life has no order, no logic, no reason. As a man disabused of his error, Pleberio reacts with a vehemence that only those who feel deeply betrayed experi-ence.
           We cannot view the work from the point of view of Christian morality. For Rojas is employing rhetorical de-vices formulated by Petrarch, and therefore his characters turn to a non-Christian set of values. Casa refuses to judge Pleberio's lament on the basis of omissions. To judge the actions according to purely Spanish Christian values consti-tute a distortion of the work. Casa views the lament exclu-sively within its humanistic tradition. And yet, Pleberio cannot find comfort in the classical examples because they are irrelevant to his situation. Thus Rojas creates an indi-vidual response while working with traditional elements.
           Casa finds in the work an underlying conception of love as an external force that dominates men.
           And finally, Pleberio's lament is directed toward a consideration of three seemingly abstract entities: Death, Love, and the World. These are powerful forces that shape the very existence of humanity. Casa sees the lament as a reflection on the human problem conducted on two levels, the personal and the generic. On the first level, we see Ple-berio's personal reaction to the death of his daughter, and his personal disillusionment. On the second, we obtain a view of the relationship between man and the forces of life, and Man constantly faced by the dual threat of Love and For-tune.
           Rather than a moral lesson, Rojas is giving us a

tragic message.   The tragedy lies in man's very existence,
in his eternal struggle against superior powers.   Social
values, concludes Casa, pale into significance compared to
the transcendental problems that confront man.

Clarke, Dorothy Clotelle, Allegory, Decalogue, and Deadly
Sins in 'La Celestina'.   Los Angeles, 1968.
          See Chapter 5.

Groult, Pierre, "Une source méconnue de La Celestina,"
Les Lettres Romanes, XXII (1968), 207-227.
          Groult examines the points of contact between LC and
the "Exemplum de canicula lacrimante" in the twelfth-century
Disciplina Clericalis by Pedro Alonso.   He also discusses
the relationship of later versions of the Exemplum to LC
[Chapter 3].
          Once having established the common ground between
LC and this neglected source, Groult concentrates his discussion on the most significant elements which separate Rojas' work from the different versions of the exempla, namely the death of the protagonists and of Celestina.   This final
punishment in LC underscores the moral lesson which the
authors of the exempla did not succeed in giving to us.   In
the catastrophe, Rojas punishes the three principal characters and those who have been of aid in the illicit love affair.
The dénouement constitutes Rojas' most important contribution to his source.   Rojas alone, states Groult, was unable
to lift to a moral as well as to a dramatic plane all the cele-
tinesque tradition which originated with the Sendebar.   He
alone obliterated the moral ambiguity which persisted in all
the adaptations before him.
          Rojas' work offers us a long and dramatic exemplum,
whose principal aim is "en represión de los locos enamorados que vencidos en su desordenado apetito, a sus amigas
llaman y dicen ser su Dios."   He warns against the "engaños
de las alcahuetas."   And, finally, he fulfills his third promise to caution us against the "malos y lisonjeros sirvientes."
Rojas has skilfully enriched the elements found in the exemplum.

1969

Rodríquez-Puértolas, Julio, "Nueva aproximación a La
Celestina," Estudios Filológicos, No. 5 (1969), 71-90.
          See Chapter 7.

Weiner, Jack, "Adam and Eve Imagery in La Celestina,"

Papers on Language and Literature, V, No. 4 (1969), 389-396.

LC contains two basic didactic themes: obedience to God's laws, and the concatenated effect of each man's responsibilities and actions toward his fellow man. To develop these themes, Rojas utilized as a literary device elements from the Genesis story of Adam's Fall because it is an exemplum par excellence on these two themes.

An examination of the force which moves the plot and motivates the characters reveals all the elements which led to the Fall of man: Temptation, desire, seduction, gratification, and punishment. Weiner points out, moreover, that the Adam and Eve theme appears with frequency in Spanish literature.

Rojas also uses another literary tradition, the disputa or debate, in which the vices and virtues of man were weighed, usually to woman's discredit. The dialogue between Calisto and Sempronio in Act I is such a disputa, and serves as an introduction to the seductions and misfortunes which are to follow. Weiner lists the many allusions to the Adam and Eve story in this disputa. The disputa serves both as an artistic prologue and to create the image of woman as causing man's Fall. Calisto is here warned against eating the forbidden fruit. The scene is thus set for the arrival of the serpent: Celestina. Celestina carries out the author's didactic purpose and the theme of seduction, for virtually every character in the work is in some way seduced by Celestina.

Rojas' imagery combines the Biblical with the mythological, the legendary with the historical, often in the same speech.

Weiner suggests that Celestina's death is drawn from a careful balance of Biblical lessons with those of classical mythology. The death of the lovers is also an artful blending of Greek and Biblical sources. Calisto's fall from Melibea's garden concludes the allegorical parallels to the Garden of Eden. Calisto eats of the forbidden fruit and falls to his death.

Weiner conjectures that Rojas was consciously utilizing elements from the Adam and Eve story, thus making it necessary for Calisto to seek the aid of a procuress. Without the element of seduction there is no way for Calisto to gratify his appetite; without the forbidden fruit there would be no fall. His death is the symbolic death of mankind.

All the principal characters die through a chain of events touched off by Calisto's love for Melibea.

1970

Ruggiero, Michael J. , "La Celestina: Didacticism Once
More," Romanische Forschungen, LXXXII (1970), 56-64.
        Ruggiero examines the comments found in La Celes-
tina comentada, a sixteenth-century manuscript [1954, Pen-
ney], in order to determine whether or not a reader of Rojas' time saw in LC the didactic intent that scholars [1961,
Bataillon] have attributed to it.   He notes that the commen-
tator of this manuscript lists the literary source for many
of the ideas expressed in the speeches or draws compari-
sons between LC and other works.
        By concentrating on the same details of LC which are
often cited as offering proof of Rojas' didactic intent, Ruggiero concludes that the only sixteenth-century commentary
does not support a didactic reading of LC.   Ruggiero, therefore, sides with the scholars who maintain that Rojas' intention was not a didactic one.

Chapter 7

THE HISTORIC MOMENT OF 'LA CELESTINA'

1824

Blanco White, José María, "Revisión de obras: Celestina, Tragicomedia de Calisto y Melibea," Variedades o Mensajero de Londres, I (April 1, 1824), 224-246.
    Blanco White is the first modern scholar to deal with the question of which Spanish city Rojas uses as background for the action of LC. Because of a reference in the text to a navigable river bordered by tenerías, he concludes that Sevilla was the city intended.

1902

Foulché-Delbosc, R., "Observations sur La Célestine," Revue Hispanique, IX (1902), 171-199.
    Foulché-Delbosc feels certain that the action of LC takes place in Toledo. But he does admit that there is no trace of the Calle de Arcediano in that city.

Serrano y Sanz, M., "Noticias biográficas de Fernando de Rojas, autor de La Celestina y del impresor Juan de Lucena," Revista de Archivos, Bibliotecas y Museos, VI (1902), 245-299.
    Serrano y Sanz states that the action of the Tragicomedia takes place in Salamanca, * and that the author is taking poetic license in making the Tormes navigable.
    Serrano y Sanz reproduces the Inquisitorial documents concerning Juan de Lucena and his family and Rojas' father-in-law, Alvaro de Montalbán. The charges made by the Inquisitors give an insight into what was considered heretical behavior. The defendant was considered to be judaizante or a heretic if witnesses testified that he was known to eat unleavened bread, light candles on Friday, cook Saturday's meals on Friday and utter certain prayers.
    *[The earliest mention of Salamanca as Rojas' locale is found in Bernardo Gómez de Bobadilla's Ninfas y pastores de Henares (Alcalá de Henares, 1587).]

La Celestina Studies

205

1908

Jorge, Ricardo, "La Celestina en Amato Lusitano. Contribución al estudio de la famosa Comedia," Nuestro Tiempo,
VIII (1908), 191-199.
    Jorge finds a reference to Celestina's house in Ama-
to's Dioscorides, Bk. II. Since Amato studied in Salamanca,
the fact that he mentions the existence of Celestina's house in
that city is further evidence for considering Salamanca the
setting for LC.

1910

Menéndez Pelayo, Marcelino, Orígenes de la novela, Vol.
III. Madrid, 1905-1910.
    For Menéndez Pelayo, Salamanca is the most unlikely
candidate since there is no mention of university life in the
work, though Calisto and Sempronio do think and speak like
students. He believes instead that Rojas extracted different
elements from several Spanish cities and used these to create an ideal city for his characters.
    Menéndez Pelayo points out that in spite of the reli-
gious skepticism expressed in the Tragicomedia, the work
was first expurgated in a Madrid edition of 1632. It was only in 1793 that the book was prohibited by the Santo Oficio.

1923

Esténega y Echevarría, Narciso de, "Sobre el bachiller Fernando de Rojas y otros varones toledanos del mismo apellido," Boletín de la Real Academia de Bellas Artes y Ciencias de Toledo, IV (1923), 78-91.
    Esténaga was the first to report on the 1616 "expedi-
ente de limpieza" of Juan Francisco Palavesín y Rojas, who
sought an appointment as canon of the cathedral of Toledo
[1966, Gilman and Gonzálvez].
    In this article, Esténaga sums up the information con-
cerning Fernando de Rojas and his family that is provided by
the documents in the Fondo de Expedientes de Limpieza de
Sangre in the Archives of the Cathedral of Toledo. He also
gives an account of his investigations in Talavera de la Reina
[Chapter 1, 1938, Careaga]. Esténga states that Rojas' authorship of LC was considered common knowledge at the time.

1925

Maeztu, Ramiro de, Don Quijote, Don Juan y La Celestina.

Madrid, 1925.

Maeztu offers the suggestion that Rojas wrote LC to express the feelings that led him and others to abandon the Jewish faith. His is the skepticism of a judío. Rojas is no longer Jewish but neither is he a Christian. He expresses the despair of a man who has nothing to hold on to and who has experienced a reversal of values.

Maeztu further suggests that Rojas did not write another work because of the suspicions about him.

Rojas, who saw his people persecuted after the Inquisition was established in 1480, became painfully aware that God had not come to the help of his chosen people. The belief in the omnipotence of a Hebraic God is thus shaken. There is also a disbelief in the Hebraic doctrine on the damnable nature of sensual love. As a result Rojas sees no value in any form of moral activity and stoically accepts his despair. Justice will not prevail. For Maeztu LC is one of the first books where the Spanish people learned the possibility of living without ideals.

1926

Espinosa Maeso, Ricardo, "Dos notas para La Celestina," Boletín de la Academia Española, XII (1926), 178-185.

Espinosa Maeso chooses Salamanca as the setting for LC because this is where the best imitation of the work, La Tragicomedia de Lisandro y Roselia by Alonso Gómez de Muñón, takes place. He was able to locate in Salamanca a street which might have been called Calle del Arcediano in Rojas' time.

1938

Macaya Lahmann, Enrique, "La evocación local española en La Celestina," Estudios Hispánicos (Costa Rica), II (1938), 29-59.

Macaya finds a textual basis for Sevilla as the setting for LC. He refers to Pleberio's, "¿Para quién planté yo árboles?, ¿Para quién fabriqué navíos?," which leads him to believe that Pleberio was a shipbuilder. But in spite of the above reference, Macaya does not totally discard the idea that Rojas did not have a specific city in mind. It is obvious to him that Rojas wanted to suppress all realistic details in order not to localize the action. Although there are a few concrete references to streets and churches, it is apparent that Rojas did not want to give to his work a definite folkloric or urban environment. Macaya notes that a similar

topographical vagueness pervades the other Celestinas. He
considers this a premeditated vagueness since the morality
of the characters would not have pleased the citizens of any
city in Spain. He concludes that LC evokes life in Italy during the Renaissance.

1943

Giusti, Roberto F., "Fernando de Rojas. Su obra de human-
idad española y de arte renacentista," Boletín de la Academia
Argentina de Letras, XII (1943), 121-142.
      Giusti suggests that the action of LC takes place in
Toledo.

1947

Frank, Rachel, "Four Paradoxes in the Celestina," Romanic
Review, XLVIII (1940), 53-68.
      LC reflects the disintegration of the set social molds
typical of the Middle Ages. Rojas allows the most common
members of society to act, feel, think, and talk as though
they were members of the aristocracy. Rojas tried to per-
suade his readers that the servants were as good as their
masters and thus raises them to the level of the rich in a
process of equalization.

Green, Otis H., "The Celestina and the Inquisition," Hispanic Review, XV (1947), 211-216.
      Green maintains that Rojas had no cause to fear the
Inquisition as he composed his work, or fear punishment by
it after the work was published. In support of his argument,
he states that the Tragicomedia was first mentioned in the
Index of 1640 makes its excisions of the text without comment, deleting passages which imply a degree of rebellion
against church doctrine. Few expurgations are ordered in
the Index of 1667 and the whole book was not forbidden until
1793.

Green, Otis H., "Fernando de Rojas, Converso and Hidalgo,"
Hispanic Review, XV (1947), 384-387.
      Green pursues his argument that Rojas was not sus-
pect by the Inquisition and had no cause to conceal his authorship for fear of reprisal by the murmuradores. Rojas
was a converso, but he was born a Christian. Furthermore,
Rojas' family was regarded as belonging to the hidalguía.
Fernando de Rojas and his family lived like cristianos viejos
in spite of his marriage to the daughter of a converso.

We may assume that when Alvaro de Montalbán appeared before the Inquisition in 1525, he was attempting to bolster his case by showing that his daughter was married to a converso in good standing. Green maintains that the court's refusal to accept Rojas' testimony is simply a case where the court would not allow the son-in-law to represent his father-in-law, for Rojas' testimony was perfectly acceptable in the case of another converso, Diego of Oropesa.

1948

Green, Otis H., "Additional Note on the Celestina and the Inquisition," Hispanic Review, XVI (1948), 70-71.
Inquisitorial documents found by J. E. Gillet reveal that some deletions from the text of LC were made by zealous individuals without official responsibility and were filed by the Holy Office. It is not known whether Sotomayor's expurgator had any knowledge of these.

1950

Morales, Rafael, "Otro escenario más para La Celestina," Cuadernos de Literatura, VII (1950), 221-231.
According to Morales, Talvera de la Reina should be included among the cities which probably served as background for LC. He finds certain similarities between the topographical indications of the text and the city of Talavera, but only the discovery of a document identifying the Calle del Vicario Gordo would offer a solution to the problem.
Morales suggests that Rojas did not dare reveal the name of his city for fear of reactions to his mordant description of the clergy, and also because of Rojas' status as a converso. But he insists that Talavera de la Reina seems the most likely place, if only because Rojas lived and worked and held office there.

1952

Bataillon, Marcel, "¿Melancolia renacentista o melancolía judía?," Homenaje a Archer M. Huntington. Wellesley, 1952, pp. 39-50.
For Bataillon the intensely melancholic notes of peninsular literature differ from the European norm because of an exceptional absorption of Jeremiac sensitivities. This particular romantic melancholy, if not created by the conversos themselves, certainly appealed to them and found greater expression in their works.

1954

Ugualde, Louis, "The Celestina of 1502," Boston Public Library Quarterly, VI (1954), 206-222.
          Ugualde suggests that the locale of LC represents the synthesis of many Spanish cities, for Rojas may not have wanted to set the action against the background of any particular city.

1955

Gilman, Stephen, "Fortune and Space in La Celestina," Romanische Forschungen, LXVI (1955), 342-360.
          Gilman reviews the present status of the problem of the locale of LC. At this point, Sevilla and Salamanca are the leading candidates for the framework of the action. Salamanca is preferred because of certain humanistic or academic aspects of the work and because biographical evidence indicates that Fernando de Rojas was a student there. However, the scholars favoring Salamanca are faced with one formidable obstacle--the "vista de los navíos" from the rooftop of Melibea's house. This has raised the question whether or not the Tormes could have floated anything resembling navíos. Since the answer is in the negative, Sevilla with its navigable Guadalquivir has been favored as the background for the action.
          Gilman finds the question trivial. He is more interested in determining the artistic function of space than in identifying a specific geographical place. For to consider the problem in any other way would involve us in a dangerously naive equation of literature and life.

1956

Figueroa de Amaral, Esperanza, "Conflicto racial en La Celestina," Revista Bimestre Cubana, LXXI (1956), 20-68.
          Miss Figueroa sees LC as a vehicle of protest against religious intolerance. She relates Rojas' Jewishness to that of the characters in LC. The details of their lives express the living conditions of Rojas' time. All the enigmas of the Tragicomedia would disappear if we accepted Melibea as a conversa and if we saw the characters in the light of the historical moment in which they lived.
          Love in LC is not condemned because it is love but rather because it represents a threat to social order, as suggested by the mixture of two religions, both struggling for survival. Calisto's cry, "Melibeo soy," is the cry of a

Christian who wants to act independently of social pressures.
As for Melibea, the heroic center of the work, she is the
victim of that social order and of the destiny of her own
people.

For Miss Figueroa, the key to Melibea's race lies in
the reference made to the navíos. She assumes that the action of LC takes place in Sevilla: first, because of the reference to maritime commerce; second, because Sevilla is
the place where Jews sought refuge. She asserts that maritime commerce was a Jewish occupation. As for Melibea's
nobility, it is obvious to her that Rojas as a converso was
referring to Melibea's purer and more ancient blood. No
mention is made of Christian nobility. In this connection, we
are aware of the small number of servants in Pleberio's
house when compared to the "fastuosa servidumbre" around
Calisto. (There is no question of a disparity in wealth,
since it was the wealth of the Jews which attracted the anger
of the pueblo.) The answer is that Jews were not allowed to
have Christian servants. We are to suppose that Lucrecia
was also a conversa.

The actions of the characters are necessitated by the
historical tension. Calisto's actions show that it is simpler
to be a tonto and an involuntary victim than to be a hero.
Pleberio's lament, on the other hand, expresses the profound
despair of a converso in a hostile world. As for Celestina,
she is a caricature of the "vida popular cristiana."

Martí-Ibáñez, Félix, "The medico-pharmaceutical Arts of
La Celestina. A Study of a Fifteenth-Century Spanish Sorceress and 'Dealer in Love'." International Record of Medicine and General Practice Clinics, CLXIX (1956), 233-249.
The study of Celestina's impressive array of herbs
and concoctions should afford us a good idea of the state of
physiotherapy in that period.

In all her activities, we recognize in Celestina a
clever woman who knows how to exploit to the full the rich
vein of popular superstition. The bits and scraps of animals
she stores serve to show the magical value which at that
period was set on such relics. She practices a kind of ani-
mal therapy common in the Middle Ages and later known as
"garbage pharmacy."

Celestina's power as a healer stems from her self-
confidence and the trust she inspires in her patients. A
healer or quack was well aware that he had to resort to
"theatrical braggartism." Celestina does not rely fully on
her drugs or incantations; she has full confidence in her power of suggestion. She is as much a psychologist as a quack.

According to Martí-Ibáñez, Celestina is the offspring
of a period of sexual repression in which aphrodisiacs and
love potions were the mainstays of libidinous dealings.

1957

Baader, Horst, "¿Melibea conversa?," Romanistiches Jahrbuch, VIII (1957), 287-289.

For Baader, the fact that Melibea does not call for
confession before her death or invoke Mary does not offer
evidence in support of the conversa hypothesis, but rather
points to the excesses of loco amor, against which Rojas is
warning us. But even if she were Jewish, Lea and Green
have shown that marriages between conversos and Christians
were common. As for Pleberio's commercial occupation,
Richard Konetzke, in his Entrepreneurial Activities of Spanish and Portuguese Noblemen in Medieval Times (Explora-
tions in Entrepreneurial History, Vol. 6, No. 2, 1953-1954)
shows that noblemen often engaged in shipbuilding and commerce.

Garrido Pallardó, Fernando, Los problemas de Calisto y
Melibea y el conflicto de su autor. Figueras, 1957.

Garrido Pallardó begins his work with the premise
that nothing of significance has been written on LC except for
the works of Menéndez Pelayo and Julio Cejador. His own
principal aim is to underline the social and historical significance of LC. Noting that LC was written after the expulsion of the Jews, he feels that it reveals the attitude of
Cardinal Cisneros toward the conversos.

The chief problem of the work is why there is no
mention of marriage, a question first asked by Alberto Lista
(Lecciones de literatura española. Madrid, 1836) and later
by Juan Valera (El superhombre y otras novedades, Madrid,
1898). Garrido Pallardó states that there is a basic hidden
structure in LC, the understanding of which would help solve
this and other problems. This hidden structure can be discovered by examining the imitation of LC by Sancho de Muñón printed in 1542, and by giving relevance to the parts
where Muñón's work deviates from the original. He concludes from the dramatic discrepancies between the two works
that all the unresolved problems in LC can be explained by
the fact that Melibea belongs to a family of conversos.

Garrido Pallardó states that there are 15 problems
unresolved in LC, beginning with the question as to why there
is no mention of marriage between Calisto and Melibea.
Melibea shows a strange humility and an illogical passiveness

The Historic Moment

before the excesses of Calisto. Calisto, on the other hand, does not fear that a caballero belonging to Melibea's family would seek to avenge his honor. Furthermore, the fact that Melibea's family had lived near Celestina proves that they do not belong to the aristocracy. On the contrary, it proves that Melibea and her family still lived in the judería, which would explain their acquaintance with Celestina, who is also a convert. As for Pleberio and his wife, they are probably still practicing their own religion. And Alisa may have allowed Celestina to frequent her house for fear that the latter might denounce them to the Santo Oficio in retaliation.

Garrido Pallardó goes so far as to state that Rojas wrote about an event which actually took place in Toledo. But in his work, Rojas combines characteristics of both Toledo and Salamanca to hide his own identity in view of the climate of insecurity and fear in which he lived.

Orozco Díaz, Emilio, "La Celestina. Hipótesis para una interpretación," Insula, XII, No. 124 (1957), 1, 10.
Here again we find expressed the idea that Rojas' Jewishness is responsible for LC. In spite of its literary elements, LC is inseparable from the ideologic and religious problems typical of fifteenth-century Spain. LC was born in the atmosphere of hatred between conversos and cristianos viejos which prevailed at the time of the Inquisition. Thus, in order to understand the psychological and cultural complexity of LC, it is necessary to be familiar with the structure of medieval Spanish society.

Tragedy stems from the difficulty of uniting in marriage a Christian nobleman with the daughter of a powerful converso. Melibea's first reaction is to reject Calisto because she knows that between them only an illicit love can exist. That is why the question of marriage does not arise, and why the services of Celestina are needed.

Pleberio in his lament reveals the source of his wealth, when he says, "¿Para quién planté yo árboles?, ¿Para quién fabriqué navíos?" This clearly points to the kinds of commercial activity open to converts. Pleberio despairs not only in the face of his daughter's death, but also before the incompatibility of conversos and cristianos viejos. Pleberio's despair, however, also reflects Rojas' need to express his personal anguish before "la inquietud del ambiente creado al implantarse la Inquisición."

Russell, P. E., "The Art of Fernando de Rojas," Bulletin of Hispanic Studies, XXXIV (1957), 160-167.
In Russell's opinion, Rojas makes no attempt to estab-

lish the place and time of his action in geographical or historical terms. Rojas is simply interested in his characters as men and women, not as members of any particular racial or political group.

1958

Custodio, Alvaro, "Sobre el secreto de Melibea," Cuadernos Americanos, CI (1958), 209-213.
          Custodio discusses the socio-religious interpretation of LC offered by Orozco [1958] and by Segundo Serrano Poncela [1958], both of whom attribute the intervention of Celestina to the fact that Pleberio was a judío converso and Calisto a cristiano viejo.
          Custodio feels that their interpretation is arbitrary. The alcahuetería was one of the most natural means of communication open to lovers in Spain at the time of "encerramiento y de invencibles prejuicios religiosos y sociales." Therefore Celestina's intervention does not need to be explained through racial or religious impediments. Melibea's abrupt rejection left no course of action open to Calisto than to seek Celestina's help. Melibea kills herself at the end simply because she has lost both her honor and her man.

Laza Palacios, Modesto, El laboratorio de Celestina. Malaga, 1958.
          Although Laza Palacios reviews the questions which have engaged LC scholars, his book consists chiefly of a glossary of medical ingredients found in parts of the Corbacho, Diálogo entre el amor y un viejo and LC. The common denominator of these cosmetics, unguents and drugs is that they belong to the repertory of Christians, Moors and Jews. It becomes apparent from the definitions, descriptions, and references found under each entry of this glossary that the ingredients used by Celestina and her predecessors are not mere artistic inventions but rather part of Spanish life.

Maldonado de Guevara, F., "La casa de Celestina," Anales Cervantinos, VII (1958), 287-289.
          Maldonado states that the reference to Celestina's house in Salamanca by Rojas' contemporaries, notably the Portuguese Amato Lusitano, establishes that Rojas had Salamanca in mind when he wrote LC.
          Maldonado attempts to prove that Melibea's house was within the walls of the Alcázar. He points to the engravings of the 1502 Sevilla edition where he identifies the wall of the Alcázar in Salamanca and Melibea's garden by the wall of

the Alcázar.

1959

Bravo-Villasante, Carmen, "Otra interpretación de La Celestina," Insula, XIV, No. 149 (1959), 1-2.
        While Orozco [1957] sees Melibea's Jewishness as the
obstacle to a lawful union with Calisto, Miss Bravo-Villasante
replies that it is Calisto who is unworthy of her. As Herrero García [1923] pointed out, not until Act II is Calisto's
nobility mentioned. Since Calisto is in an inferior position,
he has no other choice than to turn to Celestina. Miss Villasante maintains that it is inconceivable that a converted Jew
would not consent to give his daughter in marriage to a cristiano viejo.
        As for Pleberio's lament, "¿Para quién planté yo ár-
boles?," etc., Miss Villasante maintains that this does not
point to Pleberio's occupation, but rather that he is here
enumerating all the things he did to give pleasure to his only
daughter. These phrases do not reveal the origin of his
wealth, but the use he made of it.
        In conclusion, Miss Villasante states that had there
been a socio-religious conflict in the work, Rojas' contemporaries would have been the first to recognize it.

Deyermond, A. D., "Celestina," Times Literary Supplement
(July 17, 1959), 423.
        For Deyermond, Garrido Pallardó's thesis [1957] fails
the test of logic. It seems improbable to him that a document of social protest would pass unnoticed as such for 450
years.

Mallo, Jerónimo, "¿Hay un problema racial en el fondo de
La Celestina?," Cuadernos del Congreso por la libertad de
la Cultura, XXXVII (1959), 51-57.
        Though Orozco's hypothesis [1957] was affirmed by
Garrido Pallardó [1957] and presented anew by Serrano Poncela [1958], Mallo feels that LC reflects Rojas' own beliefs.
        Undoubtedly, Pleberio's lament reflects a Hebraic con-
cept of religion and life, but this does not imply that Pleberio
was intended to be portrayed as a converted Jew. Rather it
expresses the agnosticism of the conversos who, like Rojas
himself, had ceased to believe in the Jewish religion but had
not totally assimilated the Christian faith. None of Rojas'
characters are truly Christian, not even Calisto, and yet Rojas imagined them all to be Christians.
        Mallo finds no indications in the text that support the

thesis of Melibea's Jewishness. Furthermore, as there is
no indication of a racial problem in the imitations of LC, we
can conclude that Rojas' contemporaries did not find a Seph-
ardic note in the work. There is no reason to suppose that
Rojas based LC on questions of religious intolerance. As
for Pleberio's commerce, Claudio Sánchez-Alborñoz in España: Un enigma histórico offers abundant documentation to
show that Spaniards were not so inept at commercial activities as has been supposed heretofore, and that men in high
social positions engaged successfully in commerce and indus-
try.

　　　　Since the intention of the author is made clear by the
subtitle, Mallo sees no reason to invent artificial explanations.

Romero y Saráchaga, Federico, Salamanca, teatro de 'La
Celestina'. Madrid, 1959.
　　　　Romero favors Salamanca as the locale for the action
of LC. He bases his argument on Amato Lusitano's reference to Celestina's house in that city, and on the fact that
Cervantes' La tía fingida, which is based on LC, takes place
in Salamanca. As for the text itself, the best proof is offered by the reference to Celestina as "la que solía morar a
las tenerías, cabe el río," since it is well known that tenerías flourished by the Tormes. Moreover, Romero is able
to locate the church of San Miguel and that of the Magdalena
in Salamanca, as well as the much disputed Calle del Arcediano. But the reference to an unnamed main square in the
work is the principal basis for the Salamanca hypothesis,
since the main square of Salamanca is the center of all activity, including public executions. It will be remembered
that Sempronio and Pármeno "quedan descabeçados en la
plaça como públicos malhechores." As for Melibea's tower,
he notes that the nobles of Salamanca in the fifteenth century
considered the building of towers essential to their protection from rival factions. Romero thus concludes that a rival-
ry between two noble families precludes the marriage of Calisto and Melibea.

"Star-Crossed Lovers," Anon. rev., Times Literary Supplement (June 19, 1959), 368.
　　　　The reviewer agrees with the socio-religious interpretations presented by Orozco [1957] and Garrido Pallardó
[1957]. Once the Tragicomedia is seen against its true social background, it becomes both more explicable and more
moving. An understanding of the "untouchability" of the converted Jewish middle-class from the point of view of the

aristocratic old Christian suffices to answer Valera's question
as to why the lovers did not seek a legal union.

Wilson, Edward T., "Celestina," Times Literary Supplement,
(July 3, 1959), 399.
    Wilson disagrees with Garrido Pallardó's interpreta-
tion of LC as a work of religious intolerance. He sees the
novel as a work about a mad lover who worships a woman
instead of God, and seeks to satisfy his lust instead of asking her in marriage. His selfishness brings death and disgrace.

1960

Criado de Val, Manuel, "La celestinesca," Teoría de Castilla la Nueva. Madrid, 1960, pp. 308-330.
    An historical perspective of life in the Toledo region
of the fifteenth-century is necessary to understand the development of the celestinesque genre. The Tragicomedia, a
point of departure for this genre, portrays faithfully the internal problems of the region of New Castille. The genre
could not possibly have enjoyed its extraordinary popularity
for more than two centuries had it not been closely connected
to a vital problem of the society to which it belonged.
    Love in the celestinesque manner, first portrayed in
the Libro de buen amor, has its root in Spanish society of
the Middle Ages and is not derived from the classical or
Arabic world. Celestinesque literature underscores the conflict between an immoral picaresque world and the severely
moral society in which strict paternal vigilance is exercised
over provincial young ladies. In a work like Rojas' tragedy
arises from a break in the traditional social structure and
the consequent intermingling of the two worlds. The dangerous rapprochement and ultimate clash between these contrasting social milieus is "celestinesque love," i.e., love requir-
ing the services of a go-between for its development.

Prieto, Adolfo, "El sentimiento de la muerte a través de la
literatura española," Revista de Literaturas Modernas, II
(1960), 11-170.
    According to Prieto, only through a knowledge of
Spanish history is it possible to understand LC, for it reveals the spiritual crisis of a converso, an attitude first
found in Sem Tob and Juan de Mena, "cuyo más acusado
rasgo se resuelve en la dramática pugna de dos tendencias:
afirmación de la vida y voluntad expresa de negarla."

1961

Bataillon, Marcel, 'La Célestine' selon Fernando de Rojas.
Paris, 1961.
     Bataillon sees no connection between Rojas' background
as a converso and the world he depicts in LC.   The hypothesis of a religious impediment to a marriage between Calisto
and Melibea has no foundation in the text.   Furthermore,
such an interpretation was never suggested by any Spaniard of
the sixteenth or the seventeenth century--and these were the
times when Spain was obsessed with the idea of purity of
blood.
     The hypothesis which deems the clandestine love nec-
essary because of insurmountable racial obstacles does not
have any basis in the reality of the fifteenth century, when
most noble families allied themselves freely with conversos.
The latter profited from these unions because they were able
to enter the society of hidalgos and caballeros.   Moreover,
even if the obstacle of impure blood had existed, it would not
have required the intervention of Celestina and her world.
     All the partisans of the racial hypothesis maintain that
Pleberio is a cristiano nuevo because he laments, "¿Para
quién edifiqué torres?, ¿Para quién fabriqué navíos?" But
for Bataillon, this statement simply indicates the noble life
Pleberio and his family led.   Melibea is seen as a noble-
woman and not simply a rich heiress.   For that matter, the
boats may be pleasure boats.

Deyermond, A. D., The Petrarchan Sources of 'La Celestina'. Oxford, 1961.
     Deyermond sees Rojas' intense pessimism as resulting
from the morbid atmosphere of the end of the fifteenth century, as Huizinga* defined it.   Undeniably, however, Rojas'
background as a converso had its effects too.
     *[J. Huizinga, The Waning of the Middle Ages, trans.
by F. Hopman, London, 1924.]

Lida de Malkiel, María Rosa, Two Spanish Masterpieces:
The Book of Good Love and La Celestina.   Urbana, 1961.
     See Note, Chapter 1, Lida de Malkiel, 1961.

Russell, P. E., "La magía como tema integral de la Tragicomedia de Calisto y Melibea," Homenaje a Dámaso Alonso.
Madrid, 1961, pp. 337-354.
     Russell discusses the widespread interest in witch-
craft in Europe during the Middle Ages and how it kept gaining momentum even in the Renaissance.   Russell reports that

the practice of witchcraft was not relegated to one particular
religious group. He concludes that Rojas' Jewish background
has no connection with Celestina's summoning of supernatural
powers.

1962

Castro, Américo, 'La Celestina' como contienda literaria.
Madrid, 1962.
    According to Castro, the tension between the three
castas which form the basis of Spanish society made possible
some of the great works of Spanish literature. Castro thus
establishes a relationship between the work of art and the social and historical reality of Spain, which for him lies in the
"convivencia de las tres castas"--Moors, Jews, and Christians.
    Rojas, living in an environment of fear in which any
new Christian was suspect, claimed that he was completing
a work started by another writer simply because he was
afraid of his public. His letter to a friend is his defense
against a public whose presence we feel in the texture of a
literary work for the first time in the history of Spanish letters.
    Rojas allowed someone else to reveal the name of the
first author. Castro believes that Rojas not only knew the
name of the original author but also his cultural background,
otherwise he would not have been able to enmesh the subsequent acts so perfectly.
    Rojas turns the "caos litigioso" of his society into an
expression of Petrarch's eternal chaos. His intention is to
destroy all harmony. This destructive passion is born out of
his personal and historical circumstances, his being a cristiano nuevo in fifteenth-century Spain.

Lida de Malkiel, María Rosa, La originalidad artística de
'La Celestina'. Buenos Aires, 1962.
    It is difficult to establish the locale of LC because its
authors have purposely eliminated all the elements that would
have helped define it. The authors aspire to a concrete artistic portrayal but not to a specific geographic area. In LC,
we find characteristics which are common to most Spanish
cities but not peculiar to any.
    Mrs. Malkiel notes that Pleberio's attitude vis-à-vis
the loss of his honor does not conform to the accepted social Castilian convention. Neither do the professional activities of Pleberio coincide with those of a Castilian lord.
    During Rojas' time, obsession with family honor af-

fected parental attitudes.   But the figures of the parents in
LC are utterly free of this obsession.   Mrs. Malkiel attributes the portrayal of intensely human parents to Rojas' Jewish background, for they display a striking similarity to Biblical parents.

Martín-Aragón Adrada, Félix Julián, "La medicina en La
Celestina," Boletín de la Sociedad española de historia de la
medicina, II, No. 3 (1962), n. p.
   From textual references, we learn that Rojas was
well versed in the art of medicine and in all types of remedies.   In the field of remedies, Rojas was the faithful inter-
preter of Arabic tradition.

1963

Criado de Val, Manuel, "Siguiendo a La Celestina," Campo
literario de Castilla la Nueva.   Madrid, 1963.
   Criado de Val establishes Toledo as the locale for the
action of LC.   He states that in Toledo we can still find the
churches of Magdalena and San Miguel.

Gilman, Stephen, "The Case of Alvaro de Montalbán, Modern
Language Notes, LXXVIII (1963), 113-125.
   Gilman maintains that without an understanding of the
extreme tension and instability which existed during Rojas'
lifetime in Spain and the potential explosiveness of converso
existence, it is difficult to appreciate the uniqueness of LC
as a human expression.   The immediate human and social
situation gave LC its important characteristics: "its mordant
irony, its implicit attack on God, its almost epic destruction
of meaning and value."
   An understanding of the circumstances of Alvaro de
Montalbán's arrest--due to a verbal expression of agnosti-
cism--and of converso existence in general is essential to
our grasp of Rojas' own effacement.   Rojas tried to achieve
collective anonymity and did so by "refining himself out of
existence" in a work of art made of uninterrupted dialogue.
It is only in the final verses, "Concluye el autor," that Rojas fully adopts the point of view of the watchers around him.
His "falsos judíos" help to effect his own disappearance.

1964

Gilman, Stephen, "Fernando de Rojas as Author," Romanische
Forschungen, LXXVI (1964), 255-290.
   Marriages between conversos and Christians were still

quite possible during Rojas' time.   Furthermore, only in the
twentieth century have critics seen Calisto's failure to pro-
pose marriage to Melibea as evidence of a racial conflict.

Maravall, José Antonio, El mundo social de 'La Celestina'.
Madrid, 1964.
      See Chapter 6.

                              1966

Gilman, Stephen, and Ramón Gonzálvez, "The Family of
Fernando de Rojas," Romanische Forschungen, LXXVIII (1966),
1-26.
      Gilman and Gonzálvez examine the original 1616 "ex-
pediente de limpieza" of one don Juan Francsco Palavesín y
Rojas, aspiring to the position of canon of the cathedral of
Toledo [1923, Esténaga y Echevarría].   Since there was a
strong opposition to this candidate's appointment, the investi-
gators sought and examined information concerning the several families by the name of Rojas, among which was the family of the Bachiller Fernando de Rojas.   The records of the
investigation that even a remote relationship to the author of
LC was a grave matter in sixteenth- and seventeenth-century
Spain.   The mere fact of having associated with the Bachiller's family occasioned a great deal of suspicion.
      During the investigation of Palavesín, Rojas' descend-
ants tried to deceive the inquisitors by substituting another
person for their maternal grandfather, Alvaro de Montalbán,
who had been condemned by the Holy Office.   Gilman's ex-
acting documentation of inquisitorial and genealogical investigations reveals the atmosphere of suspicion and torment that
enveloped the Bachiller.
      The documented genealogical tree "supports Castro's
portrayal of Rojas as a resentful outsider, a marginal man,
who observed the society around him from an ironical distance.   The pages of LC testify to the world of tension, intrigue, passion and irrationality, in which he lived."
      From the examination of these documents, Gilman and
Gonzálvez show that it was common to juggle with the genealogical tree to escape persecution.   And they go on to suppose that the Bachiller was not the son of the Asturian Garci
González de Rojas but rather of Hernando de Rojas, who had
been condemned as a judaizante in 1488.   Gilman and Gonzálvez reconstruct Rojas' biography as follows.   When his
father was condemned, Fernando de Rojas, probably twelve
years old, was given shelter by a relative, Garci Ponce,
who had fled to Puebla.   It was the grandchildren who in-

vented the Asturian camouflage to claim limpieza de sangre. Thus it would seem that Rojas was born in Toledo and not in Puebla. The acrostic verses of LC would then constitute the family's first step in deception.

Ruggiero, Michael J., The Evolution of the Go-Between in Spanish Literature through the Sixteenth Century. Berkeley, 1966.

According to Ruggiero, utilization of witchcraft was possible only from the fifteenth century onward because the witch mania was strictly limited in time from about 1450 to 1750. The fact that Celestina is a witch reflects the critical period in the Church's history when belief in sorcerers threatened to damage its position. The type developed according to the peculiar religious and secular situation that led to the Inquisition's actual creation of witchcraft.

1967

Kulin, Katalin, "La Célestine et la période de transition," Acta literaria Academiae Scientiarum Hungaricae, IX (1967), 63-85.

See Chapter 6.

Macías de Cartaya, Graziella, "La infrahistoria de La Celestina," Horizontes (Puerto Rico), XI (1967), 5-33.

The author here draws from the text an abundant catalogue of details of daily life which constitute the infrahistoria of LC.

Miss Macías finds enough concrete references in LC pertaining to houses, furniture, manner of dress of men and women, cosmetics, types of amusement, musical instruments, formulas of courtesy, superficial aspects of religion, types of punishment, hints at the juridical systems, and capital punishment, to affirm that the work constitutes a costumbrista document.

The mode of living plus some concepts, such as honor, reputation, and, of course, the function of the alcahueta, offer us an insight into the life surrounding Fernando de Rojas.

Ruiz, Higinio and Carmen Bravo-Villasante, "Talavera de la Reyna (1478-1498), ¿lugar de acción de La Celestina?," Actas del II Congreso Internacional de Hispanistas. Nijmegen, 1967, pp. 529-541.

The authors availing themselves of the historical documentation offered by the Crónica de los Reyes Católicos

and upon close examination of all concrete details in LC,
find enough similarity in the circumstances described in both
texts to determine that the city in which Calisto and Melibea
lived is none other than Talavera de la Reyna.

The point of departure for their painstaking historical
and geographical research is Pármeno's retelling of an event
which occurred 20 years before:

> Hazía con esto maravillas, que cuando vino por
> aquí el embaxador francés, tres vezes vendió por
> vírgen una criada que tenía.

The authors argue that the Ambassador came between
1476 and 1481, which would bring the date of the action of
LC to about 1496.   A French delegation headed by the Bishop
of Lumbierns came to the court of the Catholic Kings in
1479.   But even assuming that the delegation mentioned in
LC is an imaginary one, a number of details in the work coincide with the characteristics of Talavera.

1968

Barbera, Raymond A. , "Fernando de Rojas, converso,"
Hispania, LI (1968), 140-144.
        Barbera's article is a response to Green's downplay-
ing of the supposedly precarious life of the converso [1947].
Barbera tries to show that, quite on the contrary, the converso's life was painful and terrifying.   Rojas must have
been deeply affected by this constant insecurity.   For Barbera, this anxiety is directly mirrored in Pleberio's lament
and in Rojas' rejection of Petrarchan doctrine in favor of a
profound and unchristian pessimism.

Parker, Alexander A. , "Recent Scholarship in Spanish Literature," Renaissance Quarterly, XXI (1968), 118-124.
        Parker deals with Castro's view [1962] that the pessi-
mism of LC reflects the tragedy which befell the Jews of
Spain in 1492, and comments on Castro's urge to find converso influence in the tone of much of Spanish literature.
The fact is, says Parker, that if it had not been known that
Rojas was a converso, LC would have been quite adequately
explained in terms of contemporary condemnations of the literary excesses perpetrated under the religion of Love.

Rodríguez-Puértolas, Julio, "El linaje de Calisto," Hispanófila, XII, No. 33 (1968), 1-6.
        Far from Melibea being a conversa, the truth, as the

text repeatedly shows, is that the obstacle between the two lovers consists in a deficiency in Calisto's "linaje." The words of Sempronio--to his master and alone with his friends --as well as Calisto's own reference to himself and to his father all tend to prove that something significant is lacking in his ancestry. He has to rely on his own talents and possessions; he has no ancient blood to support him. It is Calisto, in short, who belongs to a family of Jewish origins, according to the hints spread throughout the work. Rodríguez Puértolas thus rejects Mrs. Malkiel's contention [1962] that the failure to mention marriage is simply due to the literary tradition of courtly love.

1969

Rodríguez-Puértolas, Julio, "Nueva aproximación a La Celestina," Estudios Filológicos, No. 5 (1969), 71-90.
It seems now unquestionable that Rojas was deeply affected by his situation as a converso, and that his work portrays faithfully the social tensions of this time. Rodríguez-Puértolas suggests that we approach LC with the idea that it reveals the problems of the life of a converso in a ubiquitous and varied manner.
The author proposes that we accept Rojas' own words that he found Act I. Moreover, one of the major differences between Rojas' work and the original Act I resides in the bourgeois realism and the melancholy pessimism which Rojas injected into his work. In other words, the work became a pretext for Rojas to express his personal views. Accordingly, we note a change of style and intention beginning with Act II: everything is leading, inevitably, toward tragedy.
Rojas writes of a particular social situation: the lonely individual hopelessly struggling against obscure powers in an alien world, and longing for some form of community. Darkness marks a significant difference between Calisto and the other inhabitants, and it underscores his social isolation. His nocturnal imaginative escapism becomes a way of life and a solution for his personal problems. Calisto has devised for himself a way of life and created a refuge in an ephemeral and artificial paradise, and in a God all his own-- a God and a paradise which are not Christian. Briefly, Calisto is a converso. He has to "hacerse por sí mismo" and "a contracorriente." In his isolation, we see the tragic history of many influential Jewish families that fell into disgrace and social contempt. With his work, Rojas invented a marvelous vehicle of social satire interwoven with reality.
Rojas presents a complete social picture of a symbol-

ic Spanish city. His is an urban, bourgeois society, including the lower classes which form an integral part of that city. Rojas exhibits an attitude of destructive irony towards this society. Rodríguez-Puértolas observes in LC a conscious determination to destroy by means of irony, not only a literary world as noted by Castro [1962], but a whole system of human life based on religious, economic and social injustice. This corrosive determination indicates a second-class citizen, a man alienated from the society in which he lives, not unlike Calisto, who is alienated from his own city.

It is on the basis of Rojas' historic moment that we must seek the reason for Calisto's isolation and loneliness, and for his desire to submerge himself in the enveloping shadows of Melibea's garden. Only then can we understand the alienation of the man in love and also his tragic, inevitable end. A social problem and a converso problem, both intimately connected in LC, faithfully mirroring a concrete and well-defined historical situation, are here preceding something much more modern: the conflict between individual and society.

In the unequal struggle with society, the individual comes out the loser. This is the final idea of the work and Rojas' own view, hence his tragic pessimism. Time has a particular function in the work. It serves as a demarcation of man's limitations and obliges him to seek a way of communicating with other human beings. Calisto's death represents the total defeat of a human being incurred by alienation and by his failure to communicate. Calisto is not alone in this; other characters express the need to communicate their feelings. With Pleberio, however, human drama reaches its most anguished moment, that of loneliness.

Pessimism in LC springs from the pre-established idea that the world is governed by an inexorable concatenation of cause and effect in which men--those belonging to the celestinesque city--are pawns, conscious of this law, over which they can exercise no control.

Rodríguez-Puértolas stresses that Rojas has gone from a particular historical situation to the universal problem of existence: man's existential loneliness in a hostile universe. The struggle for existence dominates everything. And human grief is the equalizer.

Finally, the whole ideology of LC can be summed up by Pleberio's existentially tragic statement, "¿Por qué me dexaste triste e solo in hac lachrymarum valle?"

1970

Lorenzo-Rivero, Luis, "La celestinesca como creación de Castilla la Nueva," Duquesne Hispanic Review, VII (1970), 1-4.

    Celestinesque literature, states Lorenzo-Rivero, grew out of a social need in a circumscribed geographical area, namely Castilla la Nueva. Love carried out in the celestinesque manner, that is with the help of an intermediary is necessitated by the severe parental supervision to which young women were subjected. The environment in Toledo and in the rest of New Castille, where a woman's chastity was a supreme virtue, rendered a love relationship virtually impossible. Celestinesque literature offers a glimpse into the social tensions of life in Toledo in the fifteenth century [1960, Criado de Val].

    The theme of celestinesque love is first found in the Arcipreste de Hita and later refined by Rojas. Since social decorum required that all love encounters be secret, the intermediary was needed to facilitate the relationship between the lovers.

BIBLIOGRAPHY

Abbreviations

AION-SR	Annali Istituto Universitario Orientale, Naples, Sezione Romanza
ALitASH	Acta Litteraria Academiae Scientiarum Hungaricae
Approdo	L'Approdo Letterario
Archiv	Archiv für das Studium der Neueren Sprachen und Literaturen
AUC	Anales de la Universidad de Chile
BAAL	Boletín de la Academia Argentina de Letras
BBMP	Boletín de la Biblioteca Menéndez Pelayo
BH	Bulletin Hispanique
BHA	Boletín de Historia y Antigüedades
BHS	Bulletin of Hispanic Studies
BPLQ	Boston Public Library Quarterly
BRAE	Boletín de la Real Academia Española
CA	Cuadernos Americanos
CCLC	Cuadernos del Congreso por la Libertad de Cultura
CEr	Cervantes
CHA	Cuadernos Hispano-Americanos
CL	Comparative Literature
CL	Cuadernos de Literatura
CNRS	Centre National de Recherche Scientifique
DA	Dissertation Abstracts
DD	Doctoral Dissertation
EL	La Estafeta Literaria
EMod	La España Moderna
EMP	Estudios dedicados a Menéndez Pidal
FdL	Forum der Letteeren
FiMod	Filología Moderna
FK	Filológiai Közlöny
FR	Filologia Romanza

GSLI   Giornale Storico della Letteratura Italiana

Hispano   Hispanófila
HPR   Horizontes (Puerto Rico)
HR   Hispanic Review

IRMGPC   International Record of Medicine and General
              Practice Clinics

JDShakG   Jahrbuch der Deutschen Shakespeare-Gesellschaft

LGRP   Literaturblatt für Germanische und Romanische
              Philologie
LNL   Les Langues Neolatines
LR   Les Lettres Romanes

MF   Mercure de France
MLN   Modern Language Notes
MP   Modern Philology

Neophil   Neophilologus
NRF   Nouvelle Revue Française
NRFH   Nueva Revista de Filología Hispánica
NS   Die Neueren Sprachen
NT   Nuestro Tiempo
NTg   Die Nieuwe Taalgids

PhQ   Philological Quarterly
PMLA   Publications of the Modern Language Association
PPNCFL   Proceedings of the Pacific Northwest Conference
              on Foreign Languages
PSA   Papeles de Son Armadans

RABM   Revista de Archivos, Bibliotecas y Museos
RCHA   Revista Crítica Hispano-Americana
RenQ   Renaissance Quarterly
RF   Romanische Forschungen
RFE   Revista de Filología Española
RFH   Revista de Filología Hispánica
RFHC   Revista de la Facultad de Humanidades y Ciencias
RFi   Revista de Filología
RH   Revue Hispanique
RHM   Revista Hispánica Moderna
RJ   Romanistisches Jahrbuch
RL   Revista de Literatura
RLC   Revue de Littérature Comparée
RLiM   Revista de Literaturas Modernas

RLV	Revue des Langues Vivantes
RNC	Revista Nacional de Cultura
RomN	Romance Notes
RPh	Romance Philology
RR	Romanic Review
RRAL	Rendiconti della Reggia Accademia dei Lincei

SFR	Studi di Filologia Romanza
ShQ	Shakespeare Quarterly
SP	Studies in Philology
SRo	Studi Romanzi

| TLS | Times Literary Supplement (London) |

| UCPMPh | University of California Publications in Modern Philology |

| ZRP | Zeitschrift für Romanische Philologie |

Bibliography

The numbers in brackets following most items refer to the chapters in the Survey in which the contribution is abstracted.

Items I have not been able to examine are preceded by an asterisk.

The absence of both asterisk and bracketed numbers indicates that I have examined the contribution without abstracting it in the Survey. Some of these items are omitted because the material in them reappears in another contribution by the same author.

Adinolfi, Giulia. "La Celestina e la sua unità di composizione," FR, I (1954), 12-60. [1, 5]

_____. "Diálogo y estilo en La Celestina," NRFH, VIII (1953), 461-469.

Aguilera, E. M., ed. La Celestina. Barcelona, 1958.

Aguirre, J. M. Calisto y Melibea, amantes cortesanos. Zaragoza, 1962. [5]

*Alborg, Juan Luis. Historia de la literatura española. Madrid, 1970.

Allen, H. Warner, ed. La Celestina, trans. by James
    Mabbe. London, 1923. [1, 4, 5]

Alonso, Amado. "Sobre antecedentes de La Celestina,"
    RFH, IV (1942), 265-268. [3]

_____. La lengua poética de Góngora. Madrid, 1935.

Alvarez, Guzmán. El amor en la novela picaresca española.
    The Hague, 1958. [5]

Amador de los Ríos, José. Historia crítica de la literatura
    española, Vol. VII. Madrid, 1865.

Amarita, León, ed. La Celestina. Madrid, 1822.

Anderson, Imbert E. "La Celestina," Los grandes libros
    de Occidente. Mexico City, 1957, pp. 30-44. [6]

*   _____. "Comedia de Calisto y Melibea," Realidad, III
    (1949), 301-308.

*André, Marius. "M. Martinenche et La Célestine," His-
    pania (Paris) III (1920), 289-294.

Anzoátegui, Ignacio B. Tres ensayos españoles: Mendoza o
    el héroe; Góngora o el poeta; Calixto o el amante.
    Buenos Aires, 1938 (also in Hispania, VIII (1938), 55-
    59.)

Arciniega, Rosa. "La Celestina, antelación del Don Juan,"
    Revista de las Indias, VI (1939), 258-277. [5]

Aribau, Buenaventura Carlo. "La Celestina. Discurso pre-
    liminar sobre la primitiva novela española," Biblioteca
    de autores españoles, Vol. III. Madrid, 1846.

Asensio, Manuel J. "El tiempo en La Celestina," HR, XX
    (1952), 28-43. [5]

_____. "El tiempo y el género literario en La Celestina,"
    RFH, VII (1945), 147-159.

_____. "A Rejoinder," HR, XXI (1953), 45-50. [5]

Asín, Jaime Oliver. "Más reminiscencias de La Celestina en
    el teatro de Lope de Vega," RFE, XV (1928), 67-74. [4]

Ayllón, Cándido. "Death in La Celestina," Hispania, XLI (1958), 160-164. [5]

_____ . "La ironía de La Celestina," RF LXXXII (1970), 37-55. [5]

_____ . "Negativism and Dramatic Structure in La Celestina," Hispania, XLVI (1963), 290-295. [6]

_____ . "Pessimism in the Celestina," DA, XVI, 2454 (Wisconsin), 1956.

_____ . "Petrarch and Fernando de Rojas," RR, LIV (1963), 81-94. [3, 5, 6]

_____ . La visión pesimista de 'La Celestina'. Mexico City, 1963. [6]

Aznar, Manuel. "Las fuentes petrarquianas de La Celestina," ABC (November 10, 1961), s. p.

_____ . "Petrarca, Fernando de Rojas y La Celestina," ABC (November 9, 1961), s. p.

Azorín (Martínez Ruiz, José). "La Celestina," Valores Literarios. Obras completas, Vol. II. Madrid, 1959, pp. 994-1011. [1, 5, 6]

_____ . "Comentarios a un suceso," El oasis de los clásicos. Madrid, 1952.

_____ . "Las nubes," Castilla, 2nd ed. Madrid, 1943.

_____ . "Tragedia en Toledo," Dicho y hecho. Barcelona, 1957.

Baader, Horst. "¿Melibea conversa? Randbemerkungen zu einem neunen Interpretationsversuch der Celestina," RJ, VIII (1857), 287-289. [7]

Baldelli, Ignacio. "Girolamo Clarizio editore della Celestina," GSLI, CXVII (1950), 111-116. [2]

Baldinger, Kurt. "Célestine: A Critical Edition of the First French Translation (1527)" (rev. art.), ZRP, LXXXII (1966), 241-250.

Baldwin, Spurgeon W., Jr. " 'En tan pocas palabras' (La
    Celestina, Auto IV)," RomN, IX (1967), 120-125. [5]

Barbera, Raymond E. "Calisto: The Paradoxical Hero,"
    Hispania, XLVII (1964), 256-257. [5]

_____. "Fernando de Rojas, converso," Hispania, LI
    (1968), 140-144. [7]

_____. "A Harlot, a Heroine," Hispania, XLVIII (1965),
    790-799. [5]

_____. "Medieval Iconography in La Celestina," RR,
    LXI (1970), 5-13. [5]

_____. "Sempronio," Hispania, XLV (1962), 441-442.
    [5]

Barrick, MacE. "Erna Ruth Berndt: Amor, Muerte y For-
    tuna en 'La Celestina' " (rev. art.), HR, XXXIII
    (1965), 401-408. [6]

_____. "A New Adaptation of the Celestina," Hispania,
    XLIV (1961), 445-447.

Basdekis, Demetrius. "Romantic Elements in La Celestina,"
    Hispania, XLIV (1961), 52-54. [5]

Bataillon, Marcel. "La Célestine primitive," Studia Phil-
    ologica et litteraria in honorem L. Spitzer. Bern,
    1958, pp. 39-55.

*_____. "La Célestine: Réalisme et poésie au théâtre,"
    CNRS (1960), 11-22.

_____. 'La Célestine' selon Fernando de Rojas. Paris,
    1961. [1, 2, 4, 5, 6, 7]

_____. "Défense et illustration du sens littéral," Modern
    Humanities Research Association [Presidential Address].
    London, 1967. [5]

_____. "Gaspar von Barth, interprète de La Célestine,"
    RLC, XXXI (1957), 321-340.

_____. "Langue et littérature de la péninsule ibérique
    et de l'Amérique latine," Annuaire du College de

France, LXIV (1964), 479-488.

_____ . "¿Melancolía renacentista o melancolía judía?,"
Homenaje a Archer M. Huntington. Wellesley, 1952,
pp. 29-50. [7]

_____ . "L'originalité de La Célestine d'après un ouvrage
récent" (rev. art.), RLC, XXXIX (1965), 109-123.

_____ . "Pour une histoire exigeante des formes: Le cas
de La Célestine," Proceedings of the Congress of International Comparative Literature Association, ed. W. P.
Friedrich. Chapel Hill, 1959, pp. 35-44. [4]

Bayo, Marcial José. "Nota sobre La Celestina," Clavileño,
No. 5 (1950), 48-53. [3]

Bell, A. Robert. "Folklore and Mythology in La Celestina,"
Medieval Epic to the "Epic" Theater of Brecht, ed. R.
P. Armato and J. M. Spalek. Los Angeles, 1968.
[3, 5]

*Bergamín, José. "Rojas, mensajero del infierno. Releyendo
La Celestina," RFHC (Montevideo), VI, No. 9 (1952),
61-74.

Berndt, Erna Ruth. Amor, Muerte y Fortuna en 'La Celestina," Madrid, 1963. [3, 5]

_____ . "Tratamiento de algunos temas humanísticos en
'La Celestina," DA, XX, 2275 (Wisconsin), 1960.

Berzunza, Julius. "Notes on Witchcraft and Alcahuetería,"
RR, XIX (1928), 141-150.

Bihler, Heinrich. "Zur 'Originalidad artística' der Celestina" (rev. art.), RJ, XVII (1966), 258-273.

Blanco White, José María. "Revisión de obras: La Celestina, Tragicomedia de Calisto y Melibea," Variedades
o Mensajero de Londres, I (April 1, 1824), 224-246.
[1, 7]

Bohigas, Pedro. "De la Comedia a la Tragicomedia de Calisto y Melibea," Estudios dedicados a R. Menéndez
Pidal, Vol. I. Madrid, 1957, pp. 153-175. [1]

Bonet, C. M.   "El estilo de la Celestina y su relación con
el plateresco," Criterio (Buenos Aires), XXV (1953),
942-944.

Bonilla y San Martín, Adolfo.   "Algunas consideraciones
acerca de la Tragicomedia de Calisto y Melibea y sus
autores," Anales de la Literatura Española, VII (1904),
7-24.   [1, 2]

_____.   "Antecedents del tipo celestinesco en la litera-
tura latina," RH, XV (1906), 372-386.   [3]

_____.   Las bacantes o del orígen del teatro.   Madrid,
1921.

Boughner, Daniel C.   The Braggart in Renaissance Comedy.
Minneapolis, 1954.   [4]

Brancaforte, Benito.   "La Celestina y la Mandragola: La razón
como medio de corrupción," BHS, XLVII (1970), 201-
209.

Brault, Gérard J., ed.   'Célestine': A Critical Edition of
the First French Translation (1527).   Detroit, 1963.
[2, 4]

_____.   "English Translations of La Celestina in the Six-
teenth Century," HR, XXXVIII (1960), 301-312.

_____.   "Interpretations of the Celestina, Old and New,"
Bull. of the Penn. State Mod. Lang. Assn., XLVI
(1967-1968), 3-8.   [6]

_____.   "Textual Filiation of the Early Editions of the
Celestina and the First French Translation (1527),"
HR, XXXVI (1968), 95-109.   [2]

Bravo-Villasante, Carmen.   "Otra interpretación de La
Celestina," Insula, XIV, No. 149 (1959), 1-2.   [7]

_____.   See Ruiz, Higinio.

Brelum C., Mauricio.   "Egoísmo y no amor en La Celestina," Lectura (Mexico), CLXXII (1968), 93-96.

Buceta, Erasmo.   "La opinión de Blanco White acerca del
autor de La Celestina," REF, VII (1920), 372-374.

*Camón Aznar, J. "La Celestina, tragedia social," El Na-
cional (Caracas), (April 17, 1958), suplemento literario.

Carayón, Marcel. "L'amour et la musique. Sur un passage
de La Célestine," RLC, III (1923), 419-421. [4]

Careaga, Luis. "Investigaciones referentes a Fernando de
Rojas en Talavera de la Reina," RHM, IV (1938), 193-
208. [1]

Casa, Frank P. "Pleberio's Lament for Melibea," ZRP,
LXXXIV (1968), 20-29. [6]

Casalduero, Joaquín. "La influencia de La Celestina," RFE
XIX (1932), 185-187. [4]

Casas Homs, José María. See Vallata, Juan de. [3]

Castanien, Donald G. "La segunda Celestina: Seventeenth
and Eighteenth Centuries," Hispania, XLIII (1960), 599-
564.

Castro, Américo. "Algunos temas de La Celestina," La
Nación (Buenos Aires), February 17 and 24, 1929.
(Reprinted in Santa Teresa y otros ensayos.) [5]

_____. 'La Celestina' como contienda literaria. Madrid,
1962. [3, 5, 6, 7]

_____. "La Celestina de Fernando de Rojas como repre-
sentación del concepto renacentista de la vida," Con-
ferencias, University of Santiago. Santiago, 1924.

_____. "El problema histórico de La Celestina," Santa
Teresa y otros ensayos. Santander, 1929. [5]

Castro Calvo, José María. Historia de la literatura española, Vol. I. Barcelona, 1964.

Castro Guisasola, F. "Notas sobre La Celestina--¿uno o
dos autores?" (see Vallejo, J., F. Castro Guisasola,
and M. Herrero García, 1924). [1]

_____. Observaciones sobre las fuentes literarias de
'La Celestina'. Madrid, 1924.

*Cassuto, J. D. "A Poem of Joseph Samuel ben Zarfati, the
    First Hebrew Comedy," Jewish Studies in Memory of
    George A. Kohut. New York, 1935, pp. 121-128.

Cejador y Frauca, Julio. "El Bachiller Hernando de Rojas
    verdadero autor de La Celestina," RCHA, II (1916),
    85-86. [1]

"Cejador y Frauca, ed. La Celestina." Anon. rev., RFE,
    II (1915), 1856.

Cejador y Frauca, Julio, ed. La Celestina. Madrid, 1913.
    [1, 2, 3, 5]

_____, ed. La Celestina. 2 vols. Madrid, 1962-1963.

_____. "La Celestina," Historia de la lengua y literatura
    castellana desde los orígenes hasta Carlos V. Madrid,
    1915, pp. 425-442. [3, 6]

*Cerro González, Rafael. "La Celestina y el arte médico,"
    Medicamenta, XXXIX, No. 389 (1963), 166.

Cirot, G. "La Célestine de Paul Achard" (rev. art.), BH,
    XLV (1943), 98-100. [5]

Clarke, Dorothy Clotelle. Allegory, Decalogue, and Deadly
    Sins in 'La Celestina'. Berkeley, 1968. [5]

Clemens, J. Th. W. "A Curious Celestina Edition," RLC,
    XXXIV (1960), 245-250. [2]

Cohen, J. M., trans. The Spanish Bawd. London, 1965.

Correa, Gustavo. "Naturaleza, religión y honra en La
    Celestina," PMLA, LXXVII (1962), 8-17. [6]

Cortabarría, P. "El cuento español: De La Celestina a
    nuestros días," Revista de las Antillas, II, No. 3
    (1914), 33-36.

Cotarelo, E. Controversias sobre la licitud del teatro.
    Madrid, 1904.

Crawford, J. P. W. The Spanish Drama before Lope de Vega.
    Philadelphia, 1922.

Creizenach, Wilhelm. Geschichte des Neuren Dramas, Vol. II. Halle, 1903, pp. 153-147.

Criado de Val, M. "Siguiendo a La Celestina," Campo literario de Castilla la Nueva. Madrid, 1963. [7]

_____. De la Edad Media al Siglo de Oro. Madrid, 1965.

_____. "Errores de lectura," RFE, XL (1956), 238-240.

_____. Indice verbal de 'La Celestina'. Madrid, 1955. [1]

_____. "Melibea y Calisto ante el juicio de Don Quijote," Anales Cervantinos, IV (1954), 187-196. [5]

_____. "La celestinesca," Teoría de Castilla la Nueva. Madrid, 1960, pp. 308-330. [7]

Criado de Val, M., and G. D. Trotter, ed. Tragicomedia de Calixto y Melibea, libro también llamado 'La Celestina'. Madrid, 1958. [2]

Croce, Benedetto. "La Celestina," La Critica, XXXVII (1939), 81-91. [5, 6]

_____. "La Celestina," Poesia antica e moderna. 3rd ed. Bari, 1950.

_____. Ricerche Ispano-Italiche. Napoli, 1896.

Custodio, Alvaro. "La Celestina y la literatura estatal del siglo de oro," CA, LXX (1953), 262-275. [4]

_____. "Sobre el secreto de Melibea," CA, CI (1958), 209-213. [7]

Dávalos, B. "Las dos elegías que engendraron La Celestina," Letras de México, II (1939), 7-8. [3]

Davis, Ruth. "New Data on the Authorship of Act I of the Comedia de Calisto y Melibea," University of Iowa Studies in Spanish Language and Literature. Iowa City, 1928. [1]

Delogu, F. M. "La Tragicomedia de Calisto y Melibea,"
Cervantes. Messina, 1938, pp. 223-289.

Delpy, G. "Les profanations du texte de La Célestine,"
BH, XLIX (1947), 261-275. [1]

Depta, M. V. "Die Celestina in ihrem Verhältnis zu den
novellistischen Komödien der Propaladia des Torres
Naharro." DD (Breslau), 1921.

Desdevises du Dezert, G. N. "La cómedie de Caliste et
Melibée," Revue des Cours et Conférences, XII (1904),
739-756. [1, 2, 5, 6]

Desportes, Philippe. Cartels et Masquerades, Epitaphes,
ed. V. E. Graham. Geneva, 1958.

Devoto, Daniel. "Un ingrediente de Celestina," Filología,
VIII (1962), 98-104. [5]

Deyermond, A. D. "Celestina," TLS (July 17, 1959), 423.
[7]

_____. "La crítica de La Celestina de Jacques de La-
vardin," Hispano, V, No. 13 (1961), 1-4. [4]

_____. "The Index to Petrarch's Latin Works as a
Source of La Celestina," BHS, XXXI (1954), 141-149.

_____. The Petrarchan Sources of 'La Celestina'. Ox-
ford, 1961. [1, 3, 5, 6, 7]

_____. "The Text-book Mishandled: Andreas Capellanus
and the Opening Scene of La Celestina," Neophil,
XLV (1961), 218-221. [3, 5]

Díaz-Plaja, G. "Pre-renacimiento y renacimiento," Historia
general de las literaturas hispánicas, Vol. II. Barcelona, 1951.

Dulsey, Bernard. "La Celestina, ¿versión larga o corta?,"
Hispano, IV, No. 11 (1961), 23-28. [5]

Earle, Peter G. "Four Stage Adaptations of La Celestina,"
Hispania, XXXVIII (1955), 46-51.

_____. "Love Concepts in La cárcel de amor and La
Celestina," Hispania, XXXIX (1956), 92-96. [5]

Eberwein, E. "Zur Bedeutung der erweiterten Celestina-
fassung," Zur Deutung mittelalterlicher Existenz.
Bonn and Cologne, 1933, pp. 54-79. [3]

Echalar, Padre Bernardo de. "Fernando de Rojas: La
Celestina," Estudios Franciscanos, XIII (1913), 19-31.
[5, 6]

Eggert, C. A. "Zur Frage der Urheberschaft der Celestina,"
ZRP, XXI (1897), 32-42. [1]

_____. "La Celestina: The Question of Authorship and
Position in Spanish Literature," PMLA, XI (1896), 63.

Espinosa Maeso, Ricardo. "Dos notas para La Celestina,"
BRAE, XIII (1926), 178-185. [1, 7]

Esquer Torres. "Salamanca, teatro de La Celestina" (rev.
art.), RL, XV (1959), 137-138.

Esténaga y Echevarría, Narciso de. "Sobre el bachiller
Fernando de Rojas y otros varones toledanos del mismo
apellido," Boletín de la Real Academia de Bellas Artes
y Ciencias Históricas de Toledo, IV (1923), 78-91.

Eyer, Cortland. "Juan Cirne and the Celestina," HR, V
(1937), 265-268. [4]

Farinelli, Arturo. "Note sulla fortuna del Boccaccio in
Spagna nell'Età Media," Archiv, CXIV (1905), 347-429;
CXV (1906), 368-388; CXVI (1906), 67-96; CXVII (1907),
114-141. [3]

_____. Sulla fortuna del Petrarca in Ispagna nel Quattro-
cento. Turin, 1904.

_____. "Wilhem Fehse: Cristof Wirsungs deutsche Celes-
tina übersetzungen," Deutsche Literaturzeitung, XXIII
(1902), 2786-2794. [4]

Fehse, Wilhelm. Cristof Wirsungs deutsche Celestina-über-
setzungen. Halle, 1902.

240   Bibliography

Fernández, Dominique. "Retour à la Célestine," NRF, X
    (1962), 518-521. [5]

Fernández, Sergio. Ensayos sobre la literatura española de
    los siglos XVI and XVII. Mexico City, 1961.

Ferreccio Podestá, Mario. "Una edición nueva de La Celes-
    tina," Boletín de Filología (Chile), XII (1960), 259-271.
    [2]

_____. "La formación del texto de La Celestina," AUC,
    CXXIII (1965), 89-122. [1, 2]

_____. "Hacia una edición crítica de La Celestina,"
    Anuario de Letras, V (1965), 47-76. [2]

Figueroa de Amaral, E. "Conflicto racial en La Celestina,"
    Revista Bimestre Cubana, LXXI (1956), 20-68. [7]

*Fink, J. H. "The Celestina and its Jewish Author," Jahadut
    Zorfat (Le judaïsme français). Paris, 1951, pp. 168-
    186.

*Fitzpatrick, Juan José. "La Celestina: el proceso de la
    creación literaria visto a través de una tragicomedia,"
    La Torre, III (1955), 139-152.

Flightner, James A. "Pleberio," Hispania, XLVII (1964),
    79-81. [5]

Foster, David W. "Some Attitudes towards Love in the
    Celestina," Hispania, XLVIII (1965), 484-492. [5, 6]

Fothergill-Payne, Louise. "La Celestina como esbozo de una
    lección maquivélica, RF, LXXXI (1969), 158-175.

Foulché-Delbosc, R. "L'édition princeps de la Tragicomedia,"
    RH, LXXVII (1930), 547-599.

_____. "Observations sur La Célestine," RH, VII (1900),
    28-80. [1, 2, 5]

_____. "Observations sur La Célestine," RH, IX (1902),
    171-199. [1, 3, 5, 7]

_____. "Observations sur La Célestine, III," RH,
    LXXVIII (1930), 544-599. [2]

_____, ed. La Comedia de Calisto y Melibea. Biblio-
teca Hispánica, Vol. XII. Madrid, 1900. [2]

_____. "Rojas alcalde mayor," RH, VII (1900), 510.

Fraker, Charles F. "The Importance of Pleberio's Soliloquy," RF, LXXVIII (1966), 515-529. [6]

Frank, Rachel. "Four Paradoxes in the Celestina," RR
XLVIII (1947), 53-68. [5, 7]

Frank, Waldo. "Father of Spanish Prose: Fernando de
Rojas," Menorah Journal, XI (1925), 152-158.

Fuentes de Aynat, J. M. "La botica de La Celestina,"
Medicamenta (edición para el farmacéutico), XLIV
(1951), 267-268.

Furgerson, M. "The Influence of La Celestina in Spanish
Drama through the Siglo de Oro." M.A. Thesis (Columbia), 1924.

*Gallardo, Bartolomé J. "Historia de Talavera y apuntes
biográficos del bachiller Fernando de Rojas, autor de
La Celestina." Ms. in the Biblioteca Nacional, Madrid, Vol. 187, fols. 256-257.

García Bacca, J. D. "Sobre el sentido de conciencia en La
Celestina," Revista de Guatemala, II (1946), 52-66.
[6]

García Gómez, E. "Celestinas en la España musulmana,"
CEr, I (1940-1941), 190-191.

Garrido Pallardó, Fernando. Los problemas de Calisto y
Melibea, y el conflicto de su autor. Figueras, 1957.
[1, 5, 6, 7]

_____. "Un secreto muy mal guardado," Canigó, LXXIV
(April, 1960), s. p.

Garro, J. E. "Ensayo psicológico sobre La Celestina, AUC,
XCII (1934), 5-16.

Gerday, Jacqueline. "Le caractère des rameras dans La
Celéstine, de la Comédie à la Tragicomédie," RLV,

XXXIII (1967), 185-204. [5]

_____ . "Le remaniement formel des actes primitifs dans La Célestine de 1502," AION-SR, X (1968), 175-182. [5]

Gillet, J. E. " 'Comedor de huevos'(?), (Celestina: Aucto I)," HR, XXIV (1956), 144-147.

_____ . 'Propaladia' and Other Works of Torres Naharro. Bryn Mawr, 1951.

Gilman, Stephen. "A propos of 'El tiempo en La Celestina' by Manuel J. Asensio" (rev. art.), HR, XXI (1953), 42-45. [5]

_____ . "The 'Argumentos' to La Celestina," RPh, VIII (1954), 71-81. [5]

_____ . The Art of 'La Celestina'. Madison, 1956. [1, 3, 4, 5, 6]

_____ . "Aspetti del retoricismo nella Celestina" (rev. art.), NRFH, X (1956), 73-80.

_____ . "The case of Alvaro de Montalbán," MLN, LXXVIII (1963), 113-125. [7]

_____ . "Diálogo y estilo en La Celestina," NRFH, VII (1953), 461-469. [5]

_____ . "The Fall of Fortune: from Allegory to Fiction," FR, IV (1957), 337-354. [5]

_____ . "Fernando de Rojas as Author," RF, LXXVI (1964), 255-290. [5, 6, 7]

_____ . "Fortune and Space in La Celestina," RF, LXVI (1955), 342-360. [5, 7]

_____ . "Mollejas el ortelano," Estudios dedicados a James Homer Herriott. Madison, 1966, pp. 103-107. [1, 5]

_____ . "Rebirth of a Classic: Celestina," Varieties of Literary Experience, ed. Stanley Burnshaw. New York, 1962, pp. 283-305.

———. "A Rejoinder to Leo Spitzer," HR, XXV (1956), 112-121.

———. "A Reply to Ulrich Leo," RF, LXXV (1963), 362-364.

———. See Severin, Dorothy S.

———. "The Spanish Writer, Fernando de Rojas," Yearbook of the American Philosophical Society. 1961, pp. 503-505. [1]

———. "El tiempo y el género literario en La Celestina," RFH, VII (1945), 147-159.

Gilman, Stephen, and Ramón Gonzálvez. "The Family of Fernando de Rojas," RF, LXXVIII (1966), 1-26. [7]

Gilman, Stephen, and Michael J. Ruggiero. "Rodrigo de Reinosa and La Celestina," RF, LXXIII (1961), 225-284. [3]

Giusti, Roberto F. "Fernando de Rojas. Su obra de humanidad española y de arte renacentista," BAAL, XII, No. 45 (1943), 121-142. [1, 5, 6, 7]

Givanel Mas, J. "Contribución al estudio bibliográfico de La Celestina," RCHA, V (1919), 77-121.

Goldman, P. B. "A New Interpretation of 'comedor de huevos asados'," RF, LXXVII (1965), 363-367. [5]

González Aguejas, L. "La Celestina," EMod, VI, No. 67 (1894), 78-103. [1, 5]

González, Ollé, Fernando. "El problema de la autoría de La Celestina," RFE, XLIII (1960), 439-445. [1]

Gorchs, Tomás, ed. La Celestina. Barcelona, 1841. [2]

Green, Otis H. "Additional Note on the Celestina and the Inquisition," HR, XVI (1948), 70-71. [7]

———. "The Artistic Originality of La Celestina" (rev. art.), HR, XXXIII (1965), 15-31. [5, 6]

———. "The Celestina and the Inquisition," HR, XV

(1947), 211-216. [7]

_____. "Celestina, Auto I: 'Minerua con el can',"
NRFH, VII (1953), 470-474. [5]

_____. "A Critical Survey of Scholarship in the Field of
Spanish Renaissance Literature," SP, XLIV (1947),
228-250.

_____. "Did the 'World' 'Create' Pleberio?," RF, LVII
(1965), 108-110. [5]

_____. "Fernando de Rojas, converso and hidalgo," HR,
XV (1947), 384-387. [7]

_____. "La furia de Melibea," Clavileño, IV (1953), 1-
3. [5]

_____. "Lo de tu abuela con el ximio (Celestina: Auto
I)," HR, XXIV (1956), 1-12. [5]

_____. "On Rojas' Description of Melibea," HR, XLV
(1946), 254-256. [5]

_____. Spain and the Western Tradition, Vols. 2-4.
Madison, 1963-1964. [6]

Grismer, Raymond L. The Influence of Plautus in Spain before Lope de Vega. New York, 1944. [3, 5]

_____. "Seneca in the Celestinesque Novel." (See
Heller, J. L., and R. L. Grismer.)

Groult, Pierre. "Une actualité d'autrefois et d'aujourd'hui:
La Célestine," LR, XVIII (1964). 329-241.

_____. "Une source méconnue de La Celestina," LR,
XXII (1968), 207-227. [1, 6]

Guerra, Conde. "Gil Vicente y La Celestina," EL, No. 343
(1966), 8, 9. [4]

Haebler, K. "Bemerkungen zur Celestina," RH, IX (1902),
139-170. [1, 2]

Hanrahan, Thomas, S. J. "Sin, La Celestina and Iñigo

López de Loyola," RomN, XI (1969), 385-391. [4]

Hawking, Jane. "Madre Celestina," AION-SR, IX (1967), 177-190. [5]

Heller, J. L. , and R. L. Grismer. "Seneca in the Celestinesque Novel," HR, XII (1944), 29-48. [1, 3]

Herrero García, M. , and J. Vallejo. See Vallejo, J. [1]

Herriott, James Homer. "The Authorship of Act I of La Celestina," HR, XXXI (1963), 153-159. [1]

_____ . "The 'Lost' Zaragoza 1507 Edition of the Celestina," Homenaje a Rodríguez-Moñino, Vol. I. Madrid. 1966, 253-260. [2]

_____ . "Notes on Selectivity of Language in the Celestina," HR, XXXVII (1969), 77-101. [5]

_____ . Toward a Critical Edition of the 'Celestina'. Madison, 1964. [2]

Hesse, Everett W. "La función simbólica de La Celestina," BBMP, XLII (1966), 87-95. [5]

Heugas, Pierre, ed. La Célestine. Paris, 1963. [3, 4, 5, 6]

_____ . "Variation sur un portrait: de Melibée à Dulcinée," BH, LXXI (1969), 5-30. [3]

Hillard, Ernest H. Kilgore. "Spanish Imitations of the Celestina," DA (Illinois), 1957.

Himelbau, Jack. "A Further Contribution to the Ironic Vision in the Tragicomedia," RomN, IX (1968), 310-313. [5]

Hodcroft, F. W. "La Celestina: errores de interpretación en el estudio de su sintaxis," FiMod, IV, No. 14 (1964), 154-156.

Horrent, Jules. "Cavilaciones bibliográficas sobre las primeras ediciones de La Celestina," AION-SR, V (1963), 301-309. [2]

Hors, E. , and A. Valbuena. "La biblioteca de Fernando de Rojas," RFE, XVII (1930), 183.

Houck, H. P. "Mabbe's Paganization of the Celestina," PMLA, LIV (1939), 422-431. [4, 5]

House, Ralph E. "The Present Status of the Problem of Authorship of the Celestina," PhQ, II (1923), 38-47. [1, 2, 5]

House, Ralph E. , Margaret Mulroney, and Ilse G. Probst. "Notes on the Authorship of the Celestina," PhQ, III (1924), 81-91. [1, 2]

Iventosch, Herman. "Renaissance Contaminatio: The Technique of an Imitation of La Celestina, La Seraphina (1517 ?)," Symposium, XVI (1962), 17-27.

Jaramillo, G. G. "Don Juan Rodríguez Freyle y La Celestina," BHA, XXVII (1940), 582-586. [4]

Jordan, L. "Reseña de 'Das Dämonische in der Celestina' por F. Rauhut" (rev. art.), ZRF, LIII (1933), 192-193.

Jorge, R. "La Celestina en Amato Lusitano. Contribución al estudio de la famosa comedia," NT, VIII (1908), 191-199. [7]

Klein, J. L. "Das spanische Drama," Geschichte des Dramas, Vol. I. Leipzig, 1871.

Krause, Anna. "Deciphering the Epistle-Preface to the Comedia de Calisto y Melibea," RR, XLIV (1953), 89-101. [1]

Kruse, Margot. "Stand und Aufgaben der Celestina-Forschung," RJ, VI (1956), 324-341. [1]

Küchler, Walther. "Die erste bekannte Ausgabe der Comedia de Calisto y Melibea," RJ, VI (1956), 315-323. [1, 2, 3, 5, 6]

Kulin, Katalin. "A Celestina és az átmenti kor," FK, XIII (1967), 23-40.

_____. "La Celestina et la période de transition," ALitA
IX (1967), 63-85. [6]

La Grone, G. C. "Salas Barbadillo and the Celestina," HR,
IX (1941), 440-458. [4]

Lapesa, Rafael. "La originalidad artística de La Celestina"
(rev. art.), RPh, XVII (1963), 55-74.

Lavigne, Germond de, ed. La Célestine. Paris, 1841.
[1, 5]

Laza Palacios, Modesto. El laboratorio de Celestina. Malaga, 1958. [7]

Leo, Ulrich. "Die literarische Gattung der Celestina: Eine
methodoligische Betrachtung," RF, LXXV (1963), 54-
80. [5]

Lida de Malkiel, María Rosa. "El ambiente concreto en
La Celestina," Estudios dedicados a James Homer Herriott. Madison, 1966, 145-164. [5]

_____. "De Centurio al Mariscal de Turena: Fortuna de
una frase de La Celestina," HR, XXVII (1959), 150-
166. [4]

_____. "El fanfarrón en el teatro del Renacimiento,"
RPh, XI (1958), 268-283.

_____. La originalidad artística de 'La Celestina'.
Buenos Aires, 1962. [1, 3, 4, 5, 6, 7]

_____. Two Spanish Masterpieces: 'The Book of Good
Love' and 'La Celestina.' Urbana, 1961. [1, 3, 4, 5]

Lievsay, John Leon. " 'La Celestina y Otelo, estudio de
literatura dramática comparada' by Margarita Quijano
Terán," ShQ, X (1959), 113-114.

Loehlin, Marian R. "Celestina of the Twenty Hands," Hispania, XLII (1959), 309-316. [5]

Llopis, A. "Un estudio sobre La Celestina de Rojas,"
[rev. art.] Destino (April 18, 1958), 39-40.

Lorenzo-Rivero, Luis. "La celestinesca como creación de
Castilla la Nueva," Duquesne Hispanic Review, VII
(1970), 1-14. [3, 5, 7]

MacDonald, Inez. "Some Observations on the Celestina,"
HR, XXII (1954), 264-281. [5]

McPheeters, D. W. "Alonso de Proaza, Representative Figure of the Spanish Renaissance." DD (Columbia), 1952.

_____ . "Cervantes' Verses on La Celestina," RomN, IV
(1963), 136-138. [4]

_____ . "The Corrector Alonso de Proaza and the Celestina," HR, XXIV (1956), 13-25. [1]

_____ . "The Element of Fatality in the Tragicomedia de
Calisto y Melibea," Symposium, VIII (1954), 331-335.
[5, 6]

_____ . El humanista español Alonso de Proaza. Valencia, 1961. [1]

_____ . "Newly Discovered Correspondence of Alonso de
Proaza, Editor of La Celestina," Symposium, XVII
(1963), 225-229. [1]

_____ . "The Present Status of Celestina Studies," Symposium, XII (1958), 196-205.

_____ . "Una traducción hebrea de La Celestina en el
siglo XVI," Homenaje a Rodríguez-Moñino, Vol. I.
Madrid, 1966. [4]

Macaya Lahmann, Enrique. Estudios hispánicos: Investigaciones literarias, Vol. II. San José (Costa Rica),
1938. [7]

Macías de Cartaya, Graziella. "La infrahistoria de La
Celestina." HPR, XI (1967), 5-33. [7]

Madariaga, Salvador de. "Discurso sobre Melibea," Sur,
LXXVI (1941), 38-69. [5]

Maeztu, Ramiro de. Don Quijote, Don Juan y La Celestina,
ensayos de simpatía. Madrid, 1925. [5, 7]

Maldonado de Guevara, Francisco. "La casa de Celestina," Anales Cervantinos, VII (1958), 287-289. [7]

Mallo, Gerónimo, "¿Hay un problema racial en el fondo de La Celestina?," CCLC, XXXVII (1959), 51-57. [7]

Maravall, José Antonio. El mundo social de 'La Celestina'. Madrid, 1964. [6]

*Márquina, R. Hervor de tragedia. Madrid, 1932, pp. 9-21.

Martí-Ibáñez, Féliz. "The Medico-pharmaceutical Arts of La Celestina. A Study of a Fifteenth-Century Spanish Sorceress and 'Dealer in Love'," IRMGPC, CLXIX (1956), 233-249. [7]

Martin, John W. "Some Uses of the Old Spanish Past Subjunctives (With Reference to the Authorship of La Celestina)," RPh, XII (1958), 52-67. [1]

Martín-Aragón Adrada, Félix Julián. "La medicina en La Celestina," Boletín de la Sociedad española de historia de la medicina, II, No. 3 (1962), n. p. [7]

Martinenche, E., ed. La Célestine. Paris, 1920.

_____. "Quelques notes sur La Célestine," BH, IV (1902), 95-103. [1, 2]

Martínez de la Rosa, F. Obras literarias, Vol. II. Paris, 1825, pp. 353-354. [5]

Martínez Lacalle, Guadalupe. "Manuscript Version of Mabbe's Celestina," RLC, XXXIX (1965), 78-91. [4]

Martín-Moreno, J. G. "Celestina, madre de pícaros," Santa Cruz (Valladolid), XVI (1956), 10-11.

Mazzei, P. "Per la fortuna di due opere spagnole in Italia: La Celestina e Pepita Jiménez," RFE, IX (1922), 384-386. [4]

Mazzoni, G. "Qualche accenno italiano alla Celestina," RRAL, VII (1931), 5-10. [4]

Mele, Eugenio. "Un 'villancico' della Celestina," GSLI, CVI (1935), 288-291.

250   Bibliography

Mendeloff, Henry. "On Translating La Celestina into French
    and Italian," Hispania, LI (1968), 111-115. [4]

_____ . "The Passive Voice in La Celestina (With a Par-
    tial Reappraisal of Criado de Val's Indice Verbal),"
    RPh, XVIII (1964), 41-46. [1]

Menéndez Pelayo, Marcelino, ed. La Celestina (E. Krapf).
    2 vols. Vigo, 1899-1900. [1, 3, 4, 5, 6]

_____ . "La Celestina," Estudios de crítica literaria.
    2nd series. Madrid, 1912, pp. 75-104.

_____ . Orígenes de la novela, Vol. III. Madrid, 1905-
    1910. [1, 2, 3, 4, 5, 6, 7]

Menéndez Pidal, Ramón. Antología de prosistas castellanos.
    Madrid, 1917.

_____ . "La lengua en tiempos de los Reyes Católicos,"
    CHA, XIII (1950), 9-24. [1, 3, 5]

_____ . "Una nota a La Celestina," RFE, IV (1917), 50-
    51.

_____ . "Romance de Calisto y Melibea, pliego suelto
    (1510?)," Romancero Hispánico, Vol. II. Madrid,
    1953.

Michaëlis de Vasconcellos, Carolina. "Foulché-Delbosc's
    'Observations sur La Célestine' " (rev. art.), LGRP,
    XXII (1901), 19-32. [1]

_____ . "Zwei Worte zur Celestina-Frage," ZRP, XXI
    (1897), 405-409. [1, 2]

Millares Carlo, Agustín. Literatura española hasta fines
    del siglo XV. Mexico City, 1950, pp. 300-324.

Millé y Giménez, J. "Acerca de la génesis de La Celestina,"
    RH, LXV (1925), 140-141. [3]

Miranda, Edelmira Esther. "Safo en La Celestina y en la
    'Imitación de diversos' de Fray Luis de León," BAAL
    VII (1939), 577-584. [3]

Montero Padilla, José. "Una edición, hasta ahora desconocida, de la Comedia de Calisto y Melibea," Arbor, LIV, No. 207 (1963), 104-107. [2]

Montesino Samperio, J. V. "Sobre la cuantificación del estilo literario: Una contribución al estudio de la unidad de autor en La Celestina de Fernando de Rojas," RNC (Caracas), LV (1946), 94-115; LVI (1946), 63-68. [1]

Montesinos, J. F. "Dos reminiscencias de La Celestina en las Comedias de Lope," RFE, XIII (1926), 60-62. Reprinted in Estudios sobre Lope de Vega. Mexico City, 1951, pp. 112-114. [4]

_____. "Notas sobre La Celestina--¿uno o dos autores?," RFE, XI (1924), 402-412.

Moore, John A. "Ambivalence of Will in La Celestina," CL, VII (1950), 221-231. [7]

Morales, Rafael. "Otro escenario más para La Celestina," CL, VII (1950), 221-231. [7]

Moratín, Leandro Fernández. "Orígenes del teatro español," Tesoro del teatro español, Vol. I. Paris, 1838. [1, 5]

Morby, Edwin S. "La Celestina viewed as a Morality Play" (rev. art.), RPh, XVI (1963), 323-331.

_____. "Some Observations on Tragedia and Tragicomedia in Lope," HR, XI (1943), 185-209.

Moreno Báez, E. "La obra y el autor," Nosotros y nuestros clásicos. Madrid, 1961, pp. 141-150. [1, 5, 6]

_____. "Meditaciones sobre La Celestina," Archivum, VIII (1958), 206-214. [1]

Morreale, Margherita. "Reseña de la traducción de La Celestina por M. H. Singleton" (rev. art.) HR, XXVII (1960), 368-372.

Nagy, Edward. Lope de Vega y la 'Celestina': Perspectiva pseudocelestinesca en comedias de Lope. (Cuadernos de la Facultad de Filosofia, Letras y Ciencias 39.) Mexico, 1968.

Norton, F. J.   Printing in Spain 1501-1520.   Cambridge,
England, 1966, pp. 141-156.

O'Kane, Eleanor.   "The Proverb: Rabelais and Cervantes,"
CL, II (1950), 360-369. [5]

Oliver, Asín J.   "Más reminiscencias de La Celestina en el
teatro de Lope," RFE, XV (1928), 67-74.

Olson, Paul.   "An Ovidian Conceit in Petrarch and Rojas,"
MLN, LXXXI (1966), 217-221.

Oostendorp, H. T.   El conflicto entre el honor y el amor en
la literatura española hasta el siglo XVII. The Hague,
1962. [4, 6]

*   . "De invloed van de Spaanse tragikomedie La
Celestina op enige Nederlandse toneelschrijvers," NTg,
LVII (1964), 353-364.

Orozco Díaz, Emilio.   "La Celestina. Hipótesis para una
interpretación," Insula, XII, No. 124 (1957), 1, 10.
[7]

            . "El huerto de Melibea," Arbor, XIX, Nos. 65-
68 (1951), 47-60. [5] (Reprinted in Paisaje en la
poesía española. Madrid, 1968, pp. 83-103.)

*Ortega, Teófilo.   El amor y el dolor en la 'Tragicomedia
de Calisto y Melibea'. Valladolid, 1927.

*   . Hervor de tragedia. Madrid, 1932.

Ortiz de Pinedo, J.   "Melibea," ABC (May 28, 1957), s. p.

Pabst, Walter.   " '¿Ay tal muger nascida en el mundo?.'
Zur göttlischen Abkunft der Celestina," Homenaje a
Dámaso Alonso, Vol. II. Madrid, 1961, pp. 557-576.
[3]

Palmer, Margaret E.   "An Interpretation of La Celestina,"
DA (Washington), 1955.

Parker, A. A.   "Recent Scholarship in Spanish Literature,"
RenQ, XXI (1968), 118-124. [7]

Peeters-Fontaines, J. F. "Une édition perdue de La Célestine, Anvers, 1558," Papyrus, I (1936), 28-30. [2]

Penney, Clara Louisa. The Book Called 'Celestina'. New
York, 1954. [1, 2]

Pérez, L. C. "Coplas desconocidas del tema celestinesco,"
Homenaje a Rodríguez-Moñino, Vol. II. Madrid, 1966,
pp. 51-57. [4]

Pérez Pastor, C. "Testamento de Constanza Núñez (cuñada
de Fernando de Rojas)," RABM, VI (1902), 295-299.

Petriconi, H. "Lo demoníaco en La Celestina," Boletín
del Colegio de Graduados de la Facultad de Filosofía
y Letras (Buenos Aires), XVIII (1936), 1-4.

_____. "Die Schuldfrage," Die verführte Unschuld. Ham-
burg, 1953. [5]

_____. "Trotaconventos, Celestina, Gerarda," NS,
XXXII (1924), 232-239. [4, 5]

Peña Prado, M. Cuatro ensayos de literatura castellana.
El Quijote, el Poema de Mío Cid, La Celestina, Fray
Luis de León. Lima, 1937, pp. 53-74.

Picoche, Louis. "Brault, Gérard J., ed. La Célestine"
(rev. art.), RPh, XVIII (1964), 251-252. [4]

Pollard, Alfred Wm. J. P. Morgan Catalogue, Vol. III.
London, 1907, pp. 157-159.

Poston, Lawrence. "The Celestina: A Novel in Dialogue"
(rev. art.), HR, XXVI (1958), 241-243.

_____. An Etymological Vocabulary to the 'Celestina',
A-E. New York, 1938. [5]

Poyán, Daniel, ed. Comedia de Calisto y Melibea. Zurich,
1961. [2]

*_____. "Literatura y Pirineos. La Celestina al gusto
francés." FiMod, VIII (1968), 229-251.

Praag, J. A. van. "De meesterlijke interpretatie van een
meesterwerk," FdL, IV (1963), 215-227.

Prieto, Adolfo. "El sentimiento de la muerte a través de
    la literatura española," RLiM, II (1960), 115-170. [6,
    7]

Prieto, Antonio, ed. La Celestina. Avila, 1967.

Purcell, H. D. "The Celestina and the Interlude of Calisto
    and Melibea," BHS, XLIV (1967), 1-5. [4]

Quijano Terán, Margarita. 'La Celestina' y 'Otelo': Estudio
    de literatura dramática comparada. Mexico City,
    1957. [5]

Ramos Jiménez, José. 'Algo más que tenerías' (Algunas
    notas en torno a la localización de 'La Celestina').
    Salamanca, 1950.

Rank, Jerry R. "An Edition of the Comedia de Calisto y
    Melibea: Seville, 1501; With Commentary on Variants
    and Filiation of Early Texts of the Celestina," DA
    (Wisconsin), 1968.

Rauhut, Franz. "Das Dämonische in der Celestina," Fest-
    gabe zum 60. Geburtstag Karl Vosslers, Vol. I.
    Munich, 1932, pp. 117-148. [1, 5, 6]

*Real de la Riva, César. "Notas a La Celestina," Acta
    Salmanticencia, XVI (1962), 383-392.

Redondo, Agustín. "Fernando de Rojas et l'Inquisition,"
    Mélanges de la Casa de Velázquez (Paris), I (1965),
    345-347.

Reischmann, Karl. Die stylistische Abwechslung in der
    spanischen Tragikömodie 'La Celestina'. Bonn, 1928.
    [1, 5]

Reynier, Gustave. "La Célestine," Les origines du roman
    réaliste. Paris, 1912. [3, 4, 5, 6]

Reynolds, J. J. " 'La moça que esperava al ministro'
    (Celestina: Auto III)," RomN, V (1964), 200-202. [5]

Ricard, Robert. "La Celestina vista otra vez," CHA, LXVI,
    No. 198 (1966), 469-480. [6]

_____ . "Sobre la moralidad de La Celestina," Abside,
    IV (1940), 15-18. [6]

Richthofen, Erich von. "El Corbacho: Las interpolaciones
    y la deuda de La Celestina," Homenaje a Rodríguez-
    Moñino, Vol. II. Madrid, 1966, pp. 115-120. [3]

Rico, Francisco. "María Rosa Lida de Malkiel sobre La
    Celestina," Insula, XVIII, No. 195 (1963), 3, 12.

Riquer, Martín de. "Fernando de Rojas y el primer acto de
    La Celestina," RFE, XLI (1957), 373-395. [1]

Rodríguez-Puértolas, Julio. "El linaje de Calisto," Hispano,
    XII, No. 33 (1968), 1-6. [5, 7]

_____ . "Nueva aproximación a La Celestina," Estudios
    Filológicos (Chile), No. 5 (1969), 71-90. [6, 7]

Romero, Leonardo. "Maravall, J. A.: El mundo social de
    'La Celestina'," RL, XXVI (1964), 208-209.

Romero y Sarāchaga, Federico. Salamanca, teatro de 'La
    Celestina'. Madrid, 1959. [7]

Roques, M. "Sobre Rojas: Comedia de Calisto y Melibea
    (único texto auténtico de La Celestina)," Romania, XXX
    (1901), 477.

Rosenbach, A. W. S. "The Influence of the Celestina in
    Early English Drama," JDShakG, XXXIX (1903), 43-61.
    [4]

Rösler, Margarete. "Beziehungen der Celestina zur Alexius-
    legende," ZRP, LXVIII (1938), 365-367. [3]

Ruano, Argimiro. "El ingenioso hidalgo don Quijote de la
    Mancha y La Celestina," Atenea, I (1965), 61-70.

Rubio García, Luis. "La Celestina," RABM, LXIX (1961),
    655-749.

Rüegg, August. "Rationalismus und Romantik in der Celes-
    tina," ZRP, LXXXII (1966), 9-21. [5]

Ruggiero, Michael J. "La Celestina: Didacticism Once
    More," RF, LXXXII (1970), 56-64. [6]

_____. The Evolution of the Go-Between in Spanish Literature through the Sixteenth Century. Berkeley, 1966.
[5, 7]

Ruiz, Higinio and Carmen Bravo-Villasante. "Talavera de la Reyna (1478-1498), ¿lugar de acción de La Celestina?," Actas del II Congreso Internacional de Hispanistas. Nijmegen, 1967, pp. 529-541. [7]

Rumeau, A. "Introduction a La Célestine. '... una cosa bien escusada...'," LNL, LX (1966), 1-26. [5]

Russell, P. E. "The Art of Fernando de Rojas," BHS, XXXIV (1957), 160-167. [5, 7]

_____. "Celestina," TLS (July 10, 1959), 411. [5]

_____. "Literary Tradition and Social Reality in La Celestina," BHS, XLI (1964), 230-237.

_____. "La magia como tema integral de la Tragicomedia de Calisto y Melibea," Homenaje a Dámaso Alonso. Madrid, 1961, pp. 337-354. [5, 7]

_____. "Notes: Ambiguity in La Celestina" (rev. art.), BHS, XL (1963), 35-40.

_____. "A Stuart Hispanist: James Mabbe," BHS, XXX (1953), 75-84.

Sáinz de Robles, F. C., ed. La Celestina. Madrid, 1944.

Saisset, Léon et Frédéric. "Un type de l'ancienne comédie, l'entremetteuse," MF (August 15, 1962), 116-129.

Samoná, Carmelo. Aspetti del retoricismo nella 'Celestina'. Rome, 1953. [1, 5]

Sánchez Castañer, Francisco. "Antecedentes celestinescos en las Cantigas de Santa María," Mediterráneo, I-IV 33-90. [3]

Satrústegui, José María. "La Celestina en la literatura popular vasca," RL, XVI (1959), 146-158. [4]

Schack, Adolphe Friedrich von. Geschichte der dramatischen

Literatur und Kunst in Spanien, Vol. I.   Berlin, 1854.

Schalk, Fritz, ed.   Celestina, trans. E. Hartmann and F.
R. Frier. Bremen, 1950.

Schevill, Rudolph.   "Celestina or the Tragicomedy of Calisto
and Melibea" (rev. art.), Hispania, VII (1924), 412-
414.   [4]

_____. Ovid and the Renascence in Spain.   Berkeley,
1913.

Schiel, Nicholas Edward.   "A Theological Interpretation of
La Celestina," DA (St. Louis), 1966.

Schiff, Mario.   "La Celestina," SFR, XXIV (1901), 172.
[2]

Schoeck, R. J.   "The Influence of La Celestina in England,"
BPLQ, VII (1955), 224-225.   [4]

Scoles, Emma.   "Note sulla prima traduzione italiana della
Celestina," SRo, XXXIII (1961), 155-217.   [2]

_____. "La prima traduzione italiana della Celestina:
repertorio bibliografico," Studi di letteratura spagnola.   Rome, 1964, pp. 209-230.   [4]

Segre, Cesare.   "L'originalità della Celestina," Approdo,
IX (1963), 137-144.

Serrano Poncela, Segundo.   "El secreto de Melibea," CA,
C, No. 17 (1957), 488-510.   Reprinted in El secreto
de Melibea y otros ensayos.   Madrid, 1959.

Serrano y Sanz, M.   "Documentos referentes a Catalina de
Rojas, hija de Fernando de Rojas," RABM, VI (1902),
245-299.   [1]

_____. "Noticias biográficas de Fernando de Rojas, autor
de La Celestina, y del impresor Juan de Lucena,"
RABM, VI (1902), 245-299.   [7]

Severin, Dorothy S. , ed.   La Celestina.   (Introduction by
Stephen Gilman.)   Madrid, 1969.

Simón Díaz, J.   Bibliografía de la literatura hispánica,

Vol. III.   Madrid, 1953.

Sisto, David T.   "The String in the Conjurations of La Celestina and Doña Bárbara," RomN, I (1959), 50-52. [4]

*Skwarcynska, S.   "Celestina w concepji Poetyckiej Rojasa,
Acharda i L. Schillera," Studia i Szkice Literackie.
Warsaw, 1953, pp. 187-188.

Soravilla, Javier.   La Celestina.   Madrid, 1895.   [1, 2, 5]

*   .   "Toledanos ilustres: el Bachiller Fernando de
Rojas," Toledo, VIII, No. 186 (1922), 427-430.

Spector, Norman B.   "The Procuress and Religious Hypocrisy," Italica, XXXIII (1956), 52-59. [5, 6]

Spitzer, Leo.   "New Book on the Art of the Celestina" (rev.
art.), HR, XXV (1957), 1-25.

              .   "Note sur La Célestine," RFE, XVI (1929), 59-
60. [1, 3]

              .   "Zur Celestina," ZRP, L (1930), 237-240. [3,
6]

"Star-Crossed Lovers."   Anon. rev. , TLS (June 19, 1959),
368. [5, 7]

"The Status of Lechery."   Anon. rev. , TLS (February 25,
1965), 149.

Terron, Carlo.   "Le ragioni d'un intervento," Sipario, CXC
(1962), 4-5, 23-24.

Thomas, Henry.   "Antonio (Martínez) de Salamanca, printer
of La Celestina, Rome, c. 1525," Library, VIII (1953),
45-50.

              .   Catalogue of Books Printed in Spain before 1601
in the British Museum.   London, 1921.

Ticknor, George.   History of Spanish Literature.   London,
1849, pp. 239-248. [1, 5]

Toro-Garland, Fernando de.   "La Celestina en Las mil y una

noches," RL, XXIX (1966), 5-33. [3]

———. "Celestina, hechicera, clásica y tradicional,"
CHA, LX (1964), 438-445. [5]

Torre, Guillermo de. "La Celestina según Bataillon" (rev.
art.), Insula, XVII, No. 182 (1962), 1, 5.

Trotter, G. D. "The Coplas de las comadres of Rodrigo de
Reynosa and La Celestina," Homenaje a Dámaso Alonso.
Madrid, 1961, pp. 527-537. [3]

———. "The Date of the Comedia Thebayada," MLR, LX
(1965), 386-390. [4]

———. "J. Homer Herriott, Towards a Critical Edition of the
'Celestina'," (rev. art.), BHS, XLIII (1966), 61-62. [2]

———. Sobre 'La furia de Melibea' de Otis H. Green"
(rev. art.), Clavileño, V (1954), 55-56. [5]

Ugualde, Louis. "The Celestina of 1502," BPLQ, VI (1954),
206-222. [1, 2, 4, 5, 7]

———. "A Reply (to Schoeck)," BPLQ, VII (1955), 226-227. [4]

Ureña, Pedro Henríquez. "La Celestina," Plenitud de España. Buenos Aires, 1940, pp. 139-143.

*Urquijo e Ibarra, Julio de. La tercera Celestina y el canto
de Lelo. Paris, 1911.

Val, Joaquin del, ed. La novela picaresca. Madrid, 1960.

Valbuena, A. "La biblioteca de Fernando de Rojas," (see
(see Hors, E., and A. Valbuena.)

Valbuena Prat, A. "La Celestina y los prosistas de los
Reyes Católicos," Historia de la literatura española,
Vol. I. Barcelona, 1960.

Valdés, Juan de. Diálogo de la lengua, ed. J. F. Montesinos. Madrid, 1928.

Valera, Juan. "Nueva edición de La Celestina," El superhombre y otras novedades. Madrid, 1903, pp. 223-235.

_____ . Obras completas, Vol. II. Madrid, 1942, pp.
1017-1018.

Valero Martín, Alberto. "El barrio de Calisto y Melibea,"
Castilla Madre. Madrid, 1916, pp. 193-203. [1]

Vallata, Juan de. Poliodorus, ed. José María Casas Homs.
Madrid, 1953. [3]

Valle Lersundi, Fernando del. "Documentos referentes a
Fernando de Rojas," RFE, XII (1925), 385-396; XVII
(1930), 183. [1]

_____ . "Testamento de Fernando de Rojas, autor de La
Celestina," RFE, XVI (1929), 366-388. [1]

Vallejo, J., F. Castro Guisasola, and M. Herrero García.
"Notas sobre La Celestina--¿Uno o dos autores?,"
RFE, XI (1924), 402-412. [1]

Vecchio, Frank. "El 'antifeminismo' de Sempronio,"
PPNCFL, XVI (1965), 115-118. [5]

_____ . "Sempronio y el debate feminista del siglo XV,"
RomN, IX (1968), 320-324. [5]

Verdevoye, Paul. "La Célestine et l'adaptation de Paul
Achard" (rev. art.), BH, XLV (1945), 198-201.

Vindel, Francisco. El arte tipográfico en Burgos y Guadala-
jara durante el siglo XV, Vol. VII. Madrid, 1951.
[2]

Wardropper, Bruce W. "Pleberio's Lament for Melibea and
the Medieval Elegiac Tradition," MLN, LXXIX (1964),
140-152. [3, 5, 6]

Webber, Edwin J. "The Celestina as an Arte de Amores,"
MP, LV (1958), 145-153. [3, 5, 6]

_____ . "Tragedy and Comedy in the Celestina," Hispania,
XXXV (1955), 318-320. [3]

Weiner, Jack. "Adam and Eve Imagery in La Celestina,"
Papers on Language and Literature, V, No. 4 (1969),
389-396. [6]

Whinnom, Keith. "The Relationship of the Early Editions of the Celestina," ZRP, LXXXII (1966), 22-40. [2]

_____. Spanish Literary Historiography: Three Forms of Distortion. Exeter, 1967. [1]

Wilson, Edward T. "Celestina," TLS (July 3, 1959), 399. [7]

Wolf, Ferdinand. "Sobre el drama español--La Celestina y sus traducciones," EMod, VII, No. 80 (1895), 99-123. [1, 4, 5]

Wright, Leavitt O. "The -ra Verb Form in Spain," UCPMPh, XV (1932), 2-159. [1]

Ynduráin, Francisco. "Una nota a La Celestina," XXXVIII (1954), 278-281. [3]

Zambrano, M. "Los sueños en la creación literaria: La Celestina," PSA, XIX (1963), 21-35.

Zárate, Armando. La poesia y el ojo en La Celestina," CA, CLXIV (1969), 119-136. [5]

Zelson, L. G. "The Celestina and its Jewish Authorship," The Jewish Forum, XII (1930), 459-466.

Zertuche, F. M. "La comedia o tragicomedia de Calisto y Melibea," Armas y Letras, III, No. 6 (June 30, 1946), 1, 5.

Date D